Islamism

Islamism

CONTESTED PERSPECTIVES ON POLITICAL ISLAM

Edited by Richard C. Martin and Abbas Barzegar

Stanford University Press
Stanford, California

Stanford University Press
Stanford, California

Printed in the United States of America on acid-free, archival-quality paper

Library of Congress Cataloging-in-Publication Data

Islamism : contested perspectives on political Islam / edited by Richard C. Martin and Abbas Barzegar.
     p. cm.
  Includes bibliographical references.
  ISBN 978-0-8047-6885-6 (cloth : alk. paper)—ISBN 978-0-8047-6886-3 (pbk. : alk. paper) 1. Islam and politics. I. Martin, Richard C. II. Barzegar, Abbas.
  BP173.7.I88 2009
  320.5'57—dc22

                                                 2009021882

Typeset by Westchester Book Group in 10/14 Minion

CONTENTS

PART 3 RECONSIDERING THE ARGUMENTS

PREFACE

IN 1991, James Davison Hunter published *Culture Wars*, a popular investigation of public skirmishes in America over such hotly debated issues as abortion, gun control, censorship, individual privacy, separation of church and state, and prayer in the public schools. The subtitle of Hunter's book, *The Struggle to Define America*, reminded readers that something of vital importance was at stake in these debates.[1] But 1991 was also a watershed year in other political developments that would weigh in on the definition of America. The same year saw the collapse of the Communist Soviet Empire and the first Gulf War led by the United States and its allies against Iraq for its military occupation of Kuwait. Almost seamlessly these two events signaled the rise of another contentious issue that would begin to divide public attitudes in the West, namely, activist Muslim religious and political movements. According to many commentators, militant Islam would soon replace Soviet Communism as America's most worrisome imagined national threat.[2] Indeed, a decade earlier, the Iranian Revolution and the taking of American hostages invited public concern about religious fundamentalism.[3] Thus, already for two decades preceding September 11, 2001, militant expressions of political Islam, or what some call *Islamism*, had increasingly become a dominant concern in Western public discourse.

This book is about the struggle in American public spaces, especially since September 11, 2001, to define and understand the rise and role of Islamic religious politics on the world stage. One term and concept in particular dominates this discussion: Islamism. References to Islamism and Islamists abound in the news media, on Capitol Hill, in think tanks, and in the American academy. Nonetheless, there seems to be little clarity, much less consensus, on the meaning or accuracy, of this widely deployed label. This glaring ambiguity has motivated the authors and editors of this volume to attempt to uncover the implications and clarify the parameters of the term Islamism in the format of a debate between scholars, activists, and policy makers.

Participants in this debate include Muslims, some of whom by nationality and self-identification are Americans. Also included are non-Muslims (and some Muslims) who regard Islamist groups and organizations as a serious threat to democracies and civil society. Indeed, among the sixteen scholars and intellectuals writing in this volume, no two advocate identical understandings of Islamism, although they tend to cluster around a number of general approaches. Philosopher John Rawls has famously argued that requisite for civil discourse are overlapping consensuses in the ideas articulated by those who join public debate. The reader must decide whether or not different groups of contributors to this volume have significant points of agreement that amount to at least a limited shared position. This, we propose, is the readers' share of responsibility in entering this debate; in other words, this volume does not seek to impose definitions of concepts such as Islamism, but rather invites readers to engage with the arguments presented in each essay. Indeed, it is the emphasis on debate that should serve as a warning to readers that they will not find easy answers or blanket generalizations in the essays and critical responses that follow. Readers are invited to grapple with the competing ideas expressed in the essays, to be challenged by them, and then perhaps to find voices that overlap with their own more focused thoughts, and thus establish a more informed and nuanced understanding of the debate about Islamism.

Richard C. Martin
Abbas Barzegar

ACKNOWLEDGMENTS

THE IDEA FOR A BOOK on Islamism came as a result of a discussion that took place at the annual meeting of the Middle East Studies Association (MESA) in San Francisco in 2004. The convener of the discussion was Dr. Daniel M. Varisco, professor of anthropology and specialist in Muslim societies at Hofstra University. Dan invited four other scholars, me included, to participate in the discussion with position papers on the usefulness of the term *Islamism* in academic and general public discourse. By November 2004, use of the term was growing rapidly in the media and in public policy statements. It was a lively conversation, and it quickly emerged that Varisco's critique of the term *Islamism* and the ad hominem implications it held for Muslims generally had drawn a carefully argued rejoinder from another colleague on the panel, Dr. Donald K. Emmerson, a political scientist at Stanford University. Although the two met each other for the first time when we gathered in 2004, they obviously enjoyed sparring over matters that each of them cared deeply about. It was my good fortune to know both of them well already; I had been the beneficiary of many useful conversations about contemporary Islam with each of them: with Don Emmerson at Stanford University, where I had been a visiting faculty member during the winter and spring quarters of 2003; with Dan Varisco at several conferences over the past decade. The idea for a book about the use and usefulness of the term *Islamism* in public discourse was born at that moment in 2004, among Dan Varisco, Don Emmerson, and me. Their friendly but firm disagreement would become primary to the new project we envisioned—a volume that would clarify and sharpen their positions.

It was decided that my role would be to edit such a volume. I am grateful to my colleagues for inviting me to serve the project in this way.

Although the argument between Varisco and Emmerson had the appearance of a debate, it was clear at the outset that the debate could not be contained in a simple pro-and-con format. There is no shortage of sharply formed opinions about Islamism to be found in academe, on the Internet, in broadcast and print media, on op-ed pages, or among politicians and public policy talking heads inside the Beltway. Some find the term demeaning because of its gratuitous implication of terrorism. Others opine that Islamism and terrorism are synonymous. Therefore, we decided to invite others into the discussion to place the differing positions of Varisco and Emmerson into a broader, though more complex, perspective. Those who accepted the challenge include both Muslims and non-Muslims of differing religious and political points of view, academics, public intellectuals, men, women, Asians, Middle Easterners, and North Americans. Their voices and concerns have enriched and complicated the debate in Part 1. Their responses to the essays by Emmerson and Varisco appear in Part 2.

Halfway toward the completion of this book I was joined by my friend and Emory colleague, Abbas Barzegar, who at the time was an advanced graduate student in the West and South Asian Studies Program of the Graduate Division of Religion. During the last year of preparing the book for publication, Abbas brought to this project broad knowledge of the literature and social movements of modern Islam, sound discernment between good and bad scholarship in Islamic and religious studies, competent editing skills, and indefatigable work habits; his ideas and labors are clearly evident in the final form of this work. It therefore seemed both wise and fair to ask Abbas Barzegar to be the coeditor of record. In January 2009, Anthony R. Byrd, also an Emory University graduate student in West and South Asian Religions, became editorial assistant in the final stages of preparing the book manuscript. Tony worked closely with Abbas and me to perform the countless chores that blanket the desks of those editing such a volume.

Valuable support for the publication of this book was provided by the Sohaib and Sara Abbasi Program in Islamic Studies at Stanford University. I am indebted to my former colleague at Stanford, Robert Gregg, director of the Abbasi Program and professor emeritus in Religious Studies, for his assistance in arranging support for this project. I would also like to thank Dean Robert Paul of the College of Arts and Sciences at Emory University and

Professors Laurie Patton and Gary Laderman, successive chairs of the Department of Religion at Emory in the course of preparing the manuscript, for funding research assistance associated with the book.

On behalf of Abbas Barzegar and myself as volume editors, I would like especially to thank Dan Varisco and Don Emmerson, the two chief essayists in Part 1 of this volume, for their wisdom, patience and support. I also appreciate the good ideas and professional competence that Kate Wahl, executive editor at Stanford University Press, and her staff brought to the making of this book. Kate encouraged the project when it first came to her attention and was helpful all the way through. Emily Smith, production editor and Joa Suorez, assistant editor guided us expertly through the complex tasks of making a manuscript into a book. We also want to thank Deborah Masi and Wendy Schlosberg of Westchester Book Group for providing and reviewing copyedits and author responses.

To all of those named above, the co-editors are grateful. We accept final responsibility for any imperfections that remain.

Richard C. Martin
Creston, North Carolina
May 10, 2009

Islamism

INTRODUCTION: THE DEBATE ABOUT ISLAMISM IN THE PUBLIC SPHERE

Richard C. Martin and Abbas Barzegar

SOME PRELIMINARIES

On August 29, 1966, Sayyid Qutb, one of the original theorists of modern *Islamism*, was hanged in Egypt. The event was recorded on the inside pages of the international press and soon forgotten. Some sympathizers protested, as did former members of the Muslim Brothers, an organization dissolved in Egypt twelve years earlier and already consigned to the past by the world's newspaper editors and diplomatic corps.[1]

Thus begins the first chapter of Gilles Kepel's popular book *Jihad: The Trail of Political Islam*, which links a multivalent concept of Muslim religious practice (jihad) to the cluster of activist Muslim social movements in different parts of the world. Taken together these groups and their hastily assumed shared ideology have come to be known in global public discourse as the sociopolitical phenomenon of *Islamism*. Given that Sayyid Qutb was at first simply a little-known local Egyptian dissident, it is all the more ironic that after the Iranian Revolution of 1979 and more so after the events of September 11, 2001, he received considerable attention from editors, diplomats, and the scholarly world, which earlier had dismissed him. In response to translations of his prison writings, such as *Milestones*, Western writers began to label him the "philosopher of terror," the "Marx of global jihad," and the veritable "ideologue of 'Islamism.'"[2] For policy makers, academicians, and public intellectuals, he was the perfect piece in the puzzle: As the Soviet Union crumbled, what other than the "green menace"[3] of Islam would fill the adversarial void in the imaginations of Western leaders and pundits left by the failure of Communist ideology?

1

The extent to which Qutb actually influenced the vast and multifaceted dimensions of Islamic resurgence in the modern world is as difficult to answer as the question of whether or not disparate Muslim activist movements around the world represent a distinct and unitary phenomenon in the first place. If they do, does it then not follow that together they warrant a single label? If not, what is the need for an all-encompassing label in the first place? These questions, movements, and the term *Islamism* itself have generated considerable debate among pundits and politicians, Jewish and Christian religious leaders, and Muslim and non-Muslim scholars. More important, however, is the fact that these intellectual debates and the ways in which they are resolved deeply influence the policy decisions and orientations of major political actors around the world.

Because the appropriateness and usefulness of the terms *Islamism* and *Islamist* are the very subjects of this debate, the reader might well ask: Is it even permissible for us to use concepts about whose meaning there is no consensus? Are we presuming the legitimacy of concepts and labels whose accuracy and validity have yet to be established? Does the debate itself already assume too much? What about alternative terms that might carry less baggage? Unfortunately, widely circulated substitutes for Islamism such as *fundamentalism*, *Jihadism*, or *Islamic extremism*, are themselves subject to even greater ambiguities. Rather than obfuscating what is to be done by dwelling on the lack of linguistic clarity, the immediacy and inevitability of such conceptual problems are the very motivation behind this project.

Regardless of semantic preferences, Islamism is a neologism that has come into popular and pervasive use. It usually refers to those Muslim social movements and attitudes that advocate the search for more purely Islamic solutions (however ambiguous this may be) to the political, economic, and cultural stresses of contemporary life. Islamists share the label *Muslim* with more traditional, liberal, modernist, mystical, and secular Muslims, with whom they may agree on many theological points but with whom they are often in vital disagreement on others. Those disagreements usually take place beyond the view and comprehension of Western reportage on Islam, often in Arabic and other Muslim languages, and in discourses and ways of arguing that are unfamiliar to most non-Muslims in the West. Ironically, much of what Islamists have to say is nonetheless only a few clicks away for readers of this book who are able to access the Internet (albeit many such Web sites are written in Arabic, Persian, Urdu, or other Muslim languages). However, despite being a limited group within (but not the whole of) Islam, the strength of those referred to as Islamists in some areas, such as the Muslim Brotherhood in Egypt and the Taliban in Afghanistan, gives them a disproportionate voice that has brought them to global attention in the public sphere. It is for this reason that the debate about Islamism in the public sphere draws our attention and compels us to reflect upon not just the term but the sociopolitical phenomena it purports to name.

ISLAM AND VIOLENCE IN THE DIGITAL AGE

Mention of violence in connection with Islam is, in many ways, at the heart of the debate about Islamism and is seen very differently by various contributors to this volume. Although there is no necessary correlation, and in an ideal world it would be desirable to avoid any link between *Islam* and *violence*, such a move would simply ignore the elephant in the room. The fact is that Islam *is* seen by many non-Muslims in the West to be a religion of violence, and that identification has to be addressed.[4] What, then, do these terms— *Islam* and *violence*—mean when they are made to qualify each other in the same phrase? For many journalists and writers, particularly in Europe and the United States, the reference is often to acts of violence by militant Muslims against non-Muslims, such as the attack on the World Trade Center and Pentagon on September 11, 2001; the beheading of the *Wall Street Journal* reporter, Daniel Pearl; and the London train bombings in 2005. For most Muslims and many empathetic non-Muslims, the reference is to Western violence against Muslims, such as the wars in Afghanistan and Iraq, as well as the desperate situation among Palestinians living in the occupied territories, particularly Gaza, in Israel. For some writers and commentators, the mental association of Islam and violence also refers to violence between Muslim groups, such as in Darfur, Sudan; Sunni and Shia Muslims in Iraq; and among Pakistanis and Afghanis in Central and South Asia. Although not bearing a clear correlation, the concepts of violence and Islam nonetheless are regularly embedded with one another in various realms of public discourse today. Such verbal associations and linkages affect the ways we teach, read, write, and speak. Because value judgments are deep seated in the public arena in which people around the world talk about Islam, we hope that this volume will inspire reflection and criticism by engaging one of the today's most imposing media and public concerns through the very names we use to describe it.

The appearance of the film *Fitna* by the right-wing Dutch politician Geert Wilders in March 2008 is but one of many clear recent examples that the debate about Islam and violence has become globally entrenched.[5] Taking its title from the Arabic term for discord, strife, and temptation, *Fitna* appeared on the heels of the 2005 Danish cartoon controversy. Wilders' disturbing pictorial essay juxtaposed militant-sounding verses from the Qur'an with gratuitous images of violence and destruction throughout its sixteen-minute duration. The message was clear: Muslim political violence is the product of Islam's religious texts and such violence is fueled by the ideology of Islamism; the film ends with the words, "In 1945 Nazism was defeated in Europe. In 1989 communism was defeated in Europe. Now the Islamic ideology has to be defeated. Stop Islamisation."[6] Although many saw the film as nothing more than one politician's media stunt, *Fitna* and its message and the way in which the film was widely distributed and viewed electronically on the Internet remains emblematic of a deepening public concern about the perceived conjunction of Islam and violence.

Of course, the fact that the issues of Islam, violence, and freedom of political opinion were brought together in cyberspace is nothing new. The blogosphere is now teeming with sites that purport to identify Islamist groups and individuals that are considered to be dangerous to non-Muslims and to other Muslims. One such is IslamistWatch.org, which in 2008 announced on its home page that its purpose is to present a "catalog of the writings, beliefs, motives, and methods of the Islamist movement. While Islamists have many goals, the ultimate one is establishing a worldwide Caliphate (Islamic state): to overthrow and destroy democratic governments accross [sic] the globe and replace them with a single Taliban-style Islamic fundamentalist theocracy." The introduction to the site goes on to state that the "overall goals for Islamist groups like Al Qaeda, Al Fuqra, Islamic Jihad, Abu Sayyaf, the Muslim Brotherhood, Lashkar Jihad, Jemaah Islamiyah and many others are represented here, in excerpt and, where possible, in their entirety."[7] Visitors to the Web site are then able to click on "What is an Islamist?" and find the following:

> Non-Muslims throughout the world should be put on notice that whatever they may think of the arguments for or against Jihad as presented by the works reprinted on IslamistWatch.org, the Islamists themselves believe the arguments are valid, and have taken and are taking appropriate actions. Namely, to kill the infidel wherever and whenever they have reasonable opportunity.[8]

Setting aside the alarmism and hyperbole of this statement, similar Web sites, related publications, and associated think tanks constitute a virtual industry of "anti-Islamist" political action and public advocacy.[9]

Anti-Islamist advocacy on the Internet however is only the latest development at the intersection of Islam, politics, and the struggle to shape and control public opinion. Muslim political and religious groups have long made use of the Internet and other digital technologies to promote their ideas and provide a forum for an increasingly dispersed network of global sympathizers. Such technologies have been used by liberal, moderate, conservative, and radical Muslims alike and serve various functions.[10] For example, whereas it is well known that Osama bin Laden and Al Qaeda have regularly used the Internet for getting their messages to the world, the Muslim Brotherhood of Egypt has a highly accessible English Web site that virtually doubles as a news service that retails a message of increasing moderation. The controversial Iranian President Mahmood Ahmedinejad made headlines in 2006 when he announced that he would begin to maintain a regular blog, but he was a latecomer in a country with one of the highest per-capita rates of Internet use.[11] One organization that uses the Internet for international coordination, The Center for Islamic Thought, describes itself as the intellectual center of the "global Islamic movement," whose aim is simply "to re-establish Islam as a source of power and justice in all Muslim countries, and throughout the world."[12] The Center for Islamic Thought is an outgrowth of the activism inspired by Dr. Kalim Saddiqui, the late founder of the Muslim Parliament of Great Britain and lifelong grass-roots Muslim activist.

Muslims have also used the Internet to challenge radical Islamic agendas as well as raise awareness about "Islamophobia." In seeming response to sites such as Islamistmonitor.com, Islamophobia-Watch.com describes itself as a "project to document material in the public domain which advocates a fear and hatred of the Muslim peoples of the world and Islam as a religion."[13] The site catalogs instances of anti-Muslim discrimination throughout world and is increasingly becoming a site of pan-Islamic activism. As such digital interactions approach infinity, the dizzying nature of this hall of mirrors demonstrates just how pervasive and globally interconnected the debate about Islam, Muslims, and politics has become.

. . .

Of course the debate is much wider and more consequential than what can be seen and heard in cyberspace. In fact, the debate over what exactly Islamism is, and how it should be dealt with, reaches the level of national security policy, where the U.S. government has long been an active participant. Certain Muslim groups and elements of Islam—often referred to as Islamist—have been identified by various branches of the U.S. government, as well as by leading public policy institutes and lobbying groups, as requiring reform. This general interventionist trend often begins with a positive assertion that most Muslims are good citizens and neighbors and their practice of Islam is a constructive force in the modern world. This kind of approach to Muslim societies is by no means a new phenomenon, and it is often dubbed the good Muslim/bad Muslim theory.[14] The implications of the theory are that good Muslims (liberals, modernists, progressives) should be supported in their conflict with bad Muslims (Al Qaeda, Salafis, and Islamist groups in general).

Perhaps one of the most prominent examples of this rhetoric, as Donald Emmerson points out in Part I of this book, has been President George W. Bush's consistent distinction between Islam as a "great religion" and the actions of terrorists who represent "evil and terror."[15] Amir Hussein, one of the contributors to this volume, in his response to Emmerson is quick to remind us, however, that under politically expedient conditions, what might be considered a "bad Muslim" today might very well have been a "good Muslim" before—for example when mujahideen in the 1980s were willing to accept CIA training and fight the Soviets' military occupation of Afghanistan; in that context they were seen, at least inside the National Security establishment in Washington, as good Muslims—or at least contingently "useful" Muslims.

Such interventions in, and delimitations of, the good/bad Muslim dichotomy are an important and expensive part of U.S. foreign policy. In 2005 as a result of months of investigative reporting, David Kaplan of *U.S. News and World Report* announced the ambitious U.S. grand strategy to win the hearts and minds of the Muslim world:

> The U.S. government has embarked on a campaign of political warfare unmatched since the height of the Cold War. From military psychological-operations teams and CIA covert operatives to openly funded media and think tanks, Washington is plowing tens of millions of dollars into a campaign to influence not only Muslim societies but Islam itself. . . . Although U.S. officials say they are wary of being drawn into a theological battle, many have concluded that America can no longer sit on the sidelines as radicals and moder-

ates fight over the future of a politicized religion with over a billion followers. The result has been an extraordinary—and growing—effort to influence what officials describe as an Islamic reformation.[16]

Following the model established by the United States Information Agency (USIA) in its management of America's image abroad during the Cold War, the new program was given the name Muslim World Outreach. Among its projects aimed at Arab societies are Radio Sawa, an Arabic pop music station, and Al-Hurra, a satellite news channel with a $63 million annual budget.[17] In total, the State Department has an estimated budget of $1.3 billion annually to fund these and other programs that rely upon "working through third parties—moderate Muslim nations, foundations, and reform groups—to promote shared values of democracy, women's rights, and tolerance."[18] Such efforts seemingly culminated in February 2008, when former president George W. Bush appointed Sada Cumber, a Pakistani born American Muslim entrepreneur, as the State Department's first ever envoy to the Organization of the Islamic Conference, an international body of representatives from the world's Muslim countries.

DEBATE IN MUSLIM SOCIETIES

The reader should be warned that this book does not claim to resolve the debate about Islamism. Rather it represents an attempt to think through the usefulness of the term *Islamism*, which is now prevalent in popular and academic discourse by entertaining competing and even incommensurable points of view among leading thinkers and activists. Reasoned disagreement, however, is the hallmark of healthy intellectual activity. Contentious issues such as universal health care, the war in Iraq, and prayer in public schools are familiar culture wars on the American political landscape. Although some observers and critics believe that such debates generate more heat than light, such vitality is in fact a reflection of a society's vigor and dynamism.

In premodern times, Islamic religious leaders and other intellectuals cultivated a public appreciation of disputation and debate, with rules of engagement and canons of audience criticism. These efforts did not always ensure civility and even tempers. Nonetheless, arguing about what was important was an acquired skill, the possession of which exercised some degree of social management of the public airing of contentious issues. In this environment, schools of theology and law interacted in ways that were not unlike the ways that some Islamist, liberal, modernist, progressive, and secular Muslim groups interact today. They negotiated their differences within particular frameworks, often with sharp language and hyperbole but seldom resulting in violence. Medieval historical accounts of these debates marked off aggressiveness and narrow-mindedness in discussion by noting that such a scholar was *ta'assub fi madhhabihi*, "tenacious in imposing his views." By the tenth century and probably much earlier, a genre of literature on how to argue theological points successfully and how to appreciate a good argument, setting forth rules of verbal engagement, began to be a part of the curriculum for Muslim students studying the religious sciences, such as Qur'an, hadith (sayings of the Prophet), Arabic grammar and lexicography, and most particularly the competing school positions in theology and law.

Reminiscent of this premodern culture of debate, the famous Al Jazeera Arabic cable television network, broadcasting out of Qatar to Muslims audiences globally, features no-holds-barred debates that welcome different points of view, whether religious, secular, or nationalist. Often Israeli, American, and other non-Muslim public figures are invited to participate in the debates and do so. Although such discussions sometimes extend beyond ideal expectations of "civil" conversation, the fact that wide, even antagonistic, differences of opinion are accommodated reminds one of the medieval debates just mentioned among Muslims, Christians, Jews, atheist philosophers, Hindus, and others. The cable news format, of course, is obviously inspired by and modeled after similar Western cable networks such as CNN International and the BBC, but it also is the case that the Islamic tradition of public disputation inspires an element of cultural appreciation of vigorous debate among its Muslim audiences, which is why Al Jazeera also regularly hosts forums with prominent religious leaders.

Understanding a diverse living religious tradition like Islam is not just about naming doctrines and practices that characterize its normative, moral, and ethical practices such as the Five Pillars or the Six Articles of Faith.[19] Rather it also involves appreciating those putative religious practices and the concepts that derive from them as they inform and, simultaneously, are informed by the multidimensional human societies in which they reside. In this way it is important to remember that Islamist social movements can not be defined solely in terms of contention with non-Muslims and the West, antimodern angst, or the nostalgia of tradition. In fact, the Islamic tradition has for centuries been a sufficiently capacious mansion that has included groups that today would be labeled "Islamist." The question now before us is whether Islamism is a useful term for those Muslims who are so labeled and for public discourse about them and how best to understand their diverse claims and practices in light of the Islamic tradition more generally.

SOME MEANINGS OF ISLAMISM

Islamism, as we have seen, occupies a prominent place in the Western imagination and public discourse about the relationship between Islam, Muslims, and power. It connotes for most people who employ it stridently antagonistic Muslim attitudes toward the West, socially conservative and patriarchal attitudes, intolerance toward non-Muslims, and perhaps most fearfully for outsiders to Islamist causes, the ambition to establish Islamic law, *Sharia*, as a normative political goal. Although it should be stressed that narrow insistence on implementing such beliefs across Muslim societies has gained rather limited Muslim support around the world (with wider circles of sympathy more generally for conserving traditional Muslim values), Islamism is often a label applied broadly to some (and sometimes all) Muslims. This rhetorical move is known by the Greek term of art *synecdoche*—letting the part stand for the whole, as when Athens means all of Greece or Osama bin Laden is made to characterize all Muslims. The term *Islamism* has been used in common parlance since the latter decades of the twentieth century, but it has enjoyed wide use in the West since September 11, 2001. Its popularity and the ideas it evokes among those who explain it, and those who fear it, have become part of the culture of 9/11.

In the lead essay of this volume, Donald Emmerson cites and revises James Piscatori's definition of Islamists as "Muslims who are committed to public action to implement what they regard as an Islamic agenda."[20] Emmerson goes on to define Islamism, then, as "commitment to, and the content of, that agenda."[21] In Part II of this volume, Graham Fuller, citing his own 2003 book *The Future of Political Islam*, offers similarly a definition of Islamism, linking it to political Islam: "[A]n Islamist is one who believes that Islam as a body of faith has something important to say about how politics and society should be ordered in the contemporary Muslim World and who seeks to implement this idea in some fashion."[22]

Interestingly, Islamism is not a concept derived from traditional Islamic theological discourse: It is not a term derived from the Qur'an, or the sayings (hadith) attributed to the Prophet Muhammad and his closest companions, nor was it in the vocabulary of any of the classical jurists, such Ahmad ibn Hanbal (d. 855) or Muhammad al-Shafiʿi (d. 820), or any of the great theologians of the Middle Ages, such as Qadi ʿAbd al-Jabbar (d. 1024) or Abu Hamid al-Ghazali (d. 1111). In fact, the modern Arabic term for Islamism, *islamiyya*, has been adapted to this usage by contemporary Muslim writers and intellectuals when writing about political Islam. In its classical and modern standard sense, *islammiya* refers to things pertaining to Islam or to the status of being Muslim—in which case it is merely an adjective. Thus, even in Arabic, Islamism it is not a classical Islamic religious or political term, such as *Sharia*, *ibadat* (religious duties), or *jihad*.

Nonetheless, as noted above, many of the characteristics associated with Islamism today have been present among Muslim groups and movements throughout Islamic history and particularly among those that drew the most impervious boundaries around their Muslim identities and practices. In medieval times, for example, activist groups affiliated with the Hanbali school of law among Sunnis or the Zaydi sect of Shiism were quick to take matters into their own hands in fulfillment of the Qurʾanic injunction to "Command Right and Forbid Wrong."[23] Such vigilantism may have ranged from smashing unlawful musical instruments and wine barrels prized by Muslims in bacchanalian moods to promoting open rebellion against an unjust ruler or, more passively, judging in one's mind that an act or moral failing was contrary to the teachings of Islam. Thus, public action or private personal moral judgments against wrongdoing, even if such efforts form an interpretation of religion in conflict with other Muslims, has moral and legal import within the Islamic tradition, which becomes the social framework for debate.

Consider another definition of Islamism as simply *Islamic activism*. In this case it may simply be an integral part of the Islamic tradition more generally. Indeed, such is the opinion of Oliver Roy and Antoine Sfeir in their *Dictionary of Islamism* published in 2007.[24] However, several commentators in this book, such as Bruce Lawrence, believe that contemporary formations of religiously motivated political activism in Muslim societies have a distinct relationship to the modern world. Groups commonly called Islamist, such as the Muslim Brotherhood or the late Ayatollah Khomeini's Islamic Republican Party, it should be remembered, have doubled as populist, anti-imperial social movements and are thus embedded in the dynamics of modernity in differing Muslim and European colonial and postcolonial experiences—the colonizers versus the colonized. Such Islamist movements that have arisen out of this experience have insisted that "Islam is the Answer" to what they regard as the failures of world systems and worldviews hostile to Islam, such as Western democracies, socialism, communism, and secularism, albeit in ambiguous or merely rhetorical terms. In this vein, Nadia Yassine, a Moroccan Islamist, activist, and respondent writing in this volume, offers a contemporary correction to a more common notion of an of East-West conflict: "The debate and the proper understanding of the term 'Islamism' can only progress by looking beyond these clichés and instead should be attributed to a North-South relationship underpinned mainly by economics, and not to a civilizational confrontation between Islam and the West."[25]

For many critics, such an approach is decidedly apologetic. They often have legitimate complaints, but what is at stake in the discussion of whether or not the alleged phenomenon of Islamism is modern or ancient, religious or political, economic or ideological, is identifying the role of the historical tradition of Islam in the diverse contemporary political practices of Muslims. It is on this axis that much of the discussion about Islamism takes place.

THE BOOK AHEAD

The following essays and responses are framed as a debate. In Part 1, two senior scholars of Muslim societies, Donald K. Emmerson (a political scientist at Stanford University) and Daniel M. Varisco (an anthropologist at Hofstra University) open the debate with essays that take opposing positions. They are then followed in Part 2 by a series of critical responses by several prominent Muslim and non-Muslim scholars, policy analysts, and activists who engage claims made by one or both essayists. In the final section, Part 3, the two original opponents take the stage again to restate their positions and engage criticisms advanced in the two preceding sections. The goal of the three parts as a whole is to provide an opportunity for readers to engage and reflect upon the implications of the language used in framing contemporary discussions about Islamism—whatever that might ultimately be determined to be.

In their respective openings, Professors Emmerson and Varisco argue the pros and cons of the proposition that, when properly qualified, understood, and sorted out, the terms *Islamism* and *Islamist* connote meanings that justify their continued use. In their opening statements, Emmerson and Varisco agree that "the term 'Islamism' should not be linked exclusively with political violence and militancy."[26] Arguing for the affirmative, Emmerson holds that the term *Islamist* can be applied in a non-pejorative way to some Muslim groups and movements. Why? Because it does not in fact refer to extremists only, but also it refers to Muslims who valorize Islam in public space as a source of tolerance, moderation, and democracy. Varisco argues against the proposition. He maintains that Islamist and Islamism have come to be monopolized in the media, the Internet, and all forms of public discourse by those who impute to them a purely extremist content, which is easily identified with violence. No other major religious tradition (e.g., Christianity, Judaism, Buddhism), he avers, has a form of its name that carries the notion of violence and extremism in common parlance.

The arguments pro and con in Part I have both epistemological and ethical dimensions. Is Islamism a coherent and verifiable category available to public understanding and recognition? Does John Q. Public grasp what it is on its own terms? Equally important, several of the essays in Parts 1 and 2 ask: Do scholars, students, and journalists have ethical obligations to the human subjects they are writing about and to the audiences they are writing for? Are the obligations identical in relation to each audience?

Ranging from philosophers to policy analysts and tenured academicians to political activists, the respondents to the debate in Part 2 constitute, as noted already, a diverse group of thinkers. It is no surprise therefore that they bring to the table a great range of criticism, agreement, and disagreement. The respondents seem generally to feel that the concern over the proper choice of language in the current political moment also has important ethical implications. However, it is precisely their divergent interpretations of current events that inform their ethical postures. Some respondents feel that the debate is futile: either because it is an entirely (Western) Orientalist practice or because it is simply impossible to put the genie back into the bottle and return to the status quo ante when thinking and speaking about Islam. Others feel that tampering with the term would be to invite false consciousness about the political dangers of some expressions of Islamism and thus be detrimental to national security. The great diversity and intensity of opinions from our respondents reflects in fair measure, we believe, the passion and tenacity of global debates on Islamism.

We earlier suggested that readers who would like to find in these pages a solution to the problem of labeling and thus defining activist political Muslim movements will necessarily be disappointed, because that is not the purpose of this book. Many competing assertions, opinions, and definitions concerning Islamism are available in the public realm for readers of these pages to consult; the suggested readings in the back matter of the book aid this endeavor. This volume, however, has aimed precisely at unsettling the conventions embedded in the variety of those existing positions in order to promote critical reflection on the public debate about Islamism. Nonetheless, we hope such conversations across differences as those found within this text will serve the purpose of greater public interest in framing and grasping the premises and reasons for the debate. We further hope the book will help to promote better understanding of why the debate exists and open pathways to more productive conversations.

OPENING POSITIONS

Part 1

INCLUSIVE ISLAMISM: THE UTILITY OF DIVERSITY

Donald K. Emmerson

The most beautiful names belong to Allah: invoke Him by them.
Qur'an 7:180

> —Seen on a poster at the Jamil Mosque, California Avenue,
> Palo Alto, CA, November 20, 2004[1]

Islam is the most hated word in the country at this point.

> —Edwin Bakker, a terrorism expert at the Netherlands Institute
> of International Relations, quoted a week after the 2
> November 2004 murder of Dutch filmmaker Theo van Gogh,
> apparently by a Muslim extremist[2]

I acted purely in the name of Islam.

> —Mohammed Bouyeri, speaking to the Dutch court that
> sentenced him in July 2005 to life in prison for killing
> van Gogh[3]

Islamists are Muslims who are committed to public action to
implement what they regard as an Islamic agenda. Islamism
is a commitment to, and the content of, that agenda.

> —James Piscatori, a scholar of Islam, as slightly amended
> and extended for use in this essay (below)

IN THESE POST-9/11 TIMES, how should we—English-speaking students, scholars, journalists, policy makers, and interested citizens—talk about Islam, about Muslims, and about violence in relation to Islam and Muslims? What words should we use? Why? Why not?

SPEAKING OF ELEPHANTS

Language tells us and others what we are talking about. But as they travel around the world through usage, words acquire baggage—connotations, implications, valuations. When we choose to use a word or phrase, its luggage comes along.

Such accompaniments are mostly unheard or unseen. Consider the phrase *the global war on terror.*[4] It is about what it does not name. Its five words include neither *Muslims* nor *Islam.* Yet *the global war on terror* would not have existed, in discourse or in practice, had certain self-described Muslims not engaged in violence justified (by them) with reference to Islam. To the extent that the phrase calls to mind what it omits, the effect is like hearing someone say, "Don't think of an elephant!" One can hardly think of anything else.

In *Don't Think of an Elephant!* George Lakoff tells his readers that they can oppose "right-wing ideologues" more effectively by choosing words and phrases that favor a "progressive" agenda. Lakoff's words are also luggage-laden, but to him that is not only unavoidable; it is also desirable. He wants to replace conservative language with words that carry liberal baggage—to defeat one built-in bias by popularizing another. The book ends by advising those who would take up his cause to do four things: to "show respect" toward opponents; to "respond by reframing" subjects in "progressive" terms; to "think and talk at the level of values"; and to "say what you believe."[5]

Transposed into a discussion of Islam, Muslims, and violence, Lakoff's recipe could be perverse. Just how, in such a conversation, would a secular or Christian speaker show respect for his or her Muslim listeners by reframing the topic in secular or Christian terms, talking about secular or Christian values, and *saying exactly what she or he really thinks*? Depending on what the speaker's Muslim audience believes, Lakoff's fourth counsel, far from winning hearts and minds, could harden them instead—as President George W. Bush did when he called the war on terrorism a "crusade."[6] Conversely, obeying Lakoff's first rule—*showing respect*—could tempt the speaker to violate the other three: by framing the subject along "Muslim" lines; by thinking and talking about "Islamist" values; and by shunning candor for the sake of rapport.

What price respect? What price not giving offense? What about respect for the facts, however elusive and open to interpretation these may be? A heart or a mind won over on false pretenses may be a false victory—based on deception, unlikely to last.

This book is not a prescription for replacing one set of partisan word-baggage with an opposing set that is no less partisan than the first. It is a discussion in search of language whose semantic weight—denotations and connotations—

can balance two potentially contrary objectives: veracity *and* regard. Central to the search, in my view, is how poorly or well two increasingly common words, *Islamism* and *Islamist*, facilitate a discourse on Islam, Muslims, and violence that is both critical and constructive.

In this chapter I define and recommend Islamism and Islamist as helpful terms in such discourse. But words alone cannot protect their users from making errors or giving offense. In contrast to Lakoff's purpose, mine is less to endorse a particular vocabulary than to illuminate the larger contexts in which word choices take place. Awareness of these wider implications and repercussions can, I hope, serve the goal of free but fair discussion beyond the choice of any single word. I save the terms *Islamism* and *Islamist* for last so that, in reviewing them, I can refer back to these larger themes.

ISLAM, MUSLIMS, AND VIOLENCE

I do not know whether, in 2004, *Islam* really was the most hated word in the Netherlands, as Edwin Bakker claims in this essay's second epigraph. But we would probably have to ransack history back to the Crusades to find a time when Muslims, and therefore Islam, were in Western eyes more closely identified with violence than they are now.

As the Crusades remind us, juxtapositions of Islam and violence long predate Al Qaeda's attacks on America in 2001. But even an incomplete map of the phenomenon, dating only from the Twin Towers' fall, yields dozens of sites of carnage in a swath running from North America to Western Europe, down through North, West, and East Africa, up through the Middle East, and on through South and Southeast Asia.

For an analyst who empathizes with the plight of many Muslims, this is painful cartography. It comes uncomfortably close to illustrating Samuel Huntington's (in)famous remark that "Islam has bloody borders."[7] It risks suggesting that all this violence is the fault of Islam, or at any rate of Muslims—a monolithic accusation belied by the great diversity of causes and reasons underlying all these incidents.

Apples and oranges are being lumped together: terrorist suicides blowing themselves up to kill non-Muslims but often killing Muslims as well; Muslims attacking non-Muslims who may or may not have attacked them "first" (a term that means less and less the longer the chain of reprisals goes on); violence between Muslims, as in the Iran-Iraq war, the massacres in Darfur (Sudan), or the Sunni-Shii bloodshed in Pakistan and Iraq; and the burning of cars by Muslims or people of Muslim origin in the riots that swept the gritty, ghetto-like outskirts of French cities in November 2005. It makes no sense to impute a religious motivation to any act of violence that anyone who happens to be a Muslim might commit. Disconcerting in Islam-focused views of violence committed by Muslims is the typical omission of arguably secular concerns—oppression, injustice, invasion, occupation, displacement, alienation, and Israeli-American complicity in or indifference toward these conditions, whether real or alleged.

Unfairly or not, Islam has been and continues to be linked to violence in Western media. On November 6, 2004, for example, the *New York Times* ran an item entitled "Dutch Charge 7 Muslim Men in Killing of Critic of Islam." Reading it led me to wonder how many other stories about violence in that same issue involved Muslims. Of the twenty-two news items under the page-heading "International," fourteen mentioned violence or the threat of violence. In eleven of these fourteen reports—78.6 percent—the violence involved Muslims. Muslims were the sole (actual or feared) perpetrators in two of these eleven items; in the other nine they were both perpetrators and victims.[8]

In a poll conducted a month earlier, Americans were asked what came to their minds when they heard the word *Muslim*. Most—67 percent—responded neutrally. But 32 percent made negative remarks, and a mere 2 percent responded favorably. More than a fourth of the respondents agreed with statements such as "the Muslim religion teaches violence and hatred," "Muslims teach their children to hate," and "Muslims value life less than other people."[9] Further research would probably yield comparable or even more disturbing evidence from at least some other Western societies. And if a perceived "clash of civilizations" really is under way and has a long way to go, these figures could in future seem small.

How might a more careful use of language slow the growth of false stereotypes and attendant prejudice?

CONTEXTUALIZATION

Routinely in life people sacrifice accuracy for consideration. In a delicate conversation between two parties, one may choose to be tactful rather than factual to avoid triggering the other's anger and thus possibly ending the conversation. Other things being equal, however, the higher the ratio of tact to fact, the greater the risk that the parties engaged in such a conversation will debase even its diplomatic value by ignoring real differences between them. Conversely, in such an exchange, if one side insists from the outset on comprehensive accuracy—no euphemisms, no omissions—the conversation may be broken off soon after it begins.

Such dilemmas are routine in diplomacy. Negotiation lies at the heart of that occupation. But that is hardly true of scholarship. Professionally inclined to notice the negotiability of truth in the discourses of others, academics rarely admit to practicing such selectivity in what they themselves write and say. From the viewpoint of a scholar who prizes accuracy, diplomacy resembles self-censorship.

That said, most diplomats and scholars could probably agree that language meant to slow—ideally to reverse—the growth of false stereotypes and attendant prejudice should both rest on facts and not give offense.[10] In Diagram 1, this combination is called *contextualization*.

A persisting caricature of Muslims occurs when they are depicted as violent, that is, when a propensity toward violence is imputed, in effect, to all of them. Opposing that stereotype means placing the small number of Muslims who do engage in violence in the *context* of the overwhelming majority who

Diagram 1. Four ways of juxtaposing Islam, Muslims, and violence—contextualization, denial, candor, and stigmatization

ACCURATE?

		YES	NO
CONSIDERATE?	**YES**	**CONTEXTUALIZATION** E.g.: Among all billion-plus Muslims in the world, radicals are a small minority. Within that small minority, violent radicals are an even smaller minority.	**DENIAL** E.g.: Islam is a religion of peace, so any "Muslim" who commits violence must not be a Muslim.
	NO	**CANDOR** E.g.: Conventionally in the West, freedom of religion includes the freedom to change one's faith—any faith. Conventionally in Muslim societies, freedom of religion excludes the freedom to leave Islam, an act that risks severe punishment.	**STIGMATIZATION** E.g.: Islam is a religion of war, so every Muslim must engage in violent jihad.

do not. A further distortion occurs when violence by Muslims is said to be motivated solely by their religion. Countering that assertion, too, calls for contextualization: accurately explaining violence by Muslims with reference to non-religious as well as religious conditions, concerns, and motivations. The point in both instances is factually to refute the fallacy of composition whereby only one part or one aspect of something is made to represent or explain the whole.

This strategy will not persuade everyone. Distinctions can appear invidious. The case for differentiating Muslims who are violent from those who are not may be seen as an effort to split and weaken the ranks of the faithful. Some Muslims may wish to defend the unity of their religious community (*umma* in Arabic) against any separation of "good" from "bad" believers, even if the distinction is drawn only to show how few the latter are. Some Muslims may justify violence by co-believers against the "enemies of Islam" as self-defense, not just in religious terms, but historically, socioeconomically, and ethically as well. Arguably, in their eyes, the statements in the upper-left box in Diagram 1, by omitting the reasons for violence, do not contextualize it enough. Some of these critics may even feel insulted by the idea that the violent vanguard is so small a minority of all Muslims, as if their laudable struggle were being dismissed.

Yet no analysis is possible without distinctions of some sort. Divide-and-rule imperialists may invent, broadcast, and manipulate a dichotomy to nefarious ends, but that does not prove the dichotomy itself to be intrinsically deadly. As for suppressing a distinction—ruling it out of acceptable discourse—that may indeed increase the chance of its being misused.

The presumption that nonviolent Muslims are "good" and violent ones are "bad" may be challenged by contextual explanations of violence by Muslims that make the phenomenon more understandable. Yet there is nothing about merely noticing the proportional scarcity of violence in the *umma* that rules out such larger accounts. Acknowledging the nonviolence of the majority does, however, help thwart the polarization associated with the demonization of one's perceived enemy across the board ("Muslims are violent") and the comparable overgeneralization of one's own position ("Westerners are peaceful").

In this sense, diversification—recognizing nonviolence in the Other and violence in the Self—is a requisite to what Mahmood Mamdani has called "the third response":

> Both the American establishment led by President [George W.] Bush and
> militants of political Islam . . . are determined to distinguish between "good
> Muslims" and "bad Muslims," so as to cultivate the former and target the lat-
> ter [even as the administration and the militants reverse each other's appli-
> cation of these labels]. . . . Both Bush and bin Laden employ a religious lan-
> guage, the language of good and evil, the language of no compromise: you are
> either with us or against us. Both deny the possibility of a third response.[11]

If stereotyping and prejudice toward Muslims are to be reduced, we need
to make more not fewer distinctions. The upper-left-hand statements in Diagram 1 are compatible with accurate accounts of Muslim violence that locate
it in different contexts and explain it with reference to colonial and other
settings that implicate Western actors. However unconvincing or annoying
it might seem to a Muslim who endorses violence in Islam's name, contextualization as recommended here is constructive in its aim to discourage the
exaggeration of Muslim violence by non-Muslims—and to do so with factual
statements that should appeal to the nonviolent but sensitive (if not downright
defensive) Muslim majority.

DENIAL, CANDOR, AND STIGMATIZATION

If contextualization desirably combines veracity with regard, and if these
are lamentably absent in stigmatization, diplomats and scholars are likely to
disagree on the relative (de)merits of the two intermediate, mirror-image responses in the diagram, namely, *denial* and *candor*. They are mirror images in
that, in relation to Muslims, denial is more considerate than accurate, whereas
candor is more accurate than considerate. It is not noteworthy in this context
that the Bush administration, however undiplomatic some of its actions
may have been, should have opted for denial by assuring audiences again and
again that "Islam is a religion of peace"—or, in the president's shorthand,
"Islam is peace"[12]—implicitly denying that it could be "a religion of war."

The semantic domain of the sentence "Islam is a religion of peace" runs
between two polar possibilities: closed and open. The closed or flatly exclusive
reading of the statement is that Islam disavows war—full stop. Islam is essentialized as nonviolent. The open and potentially inclusive reading is more
strenuous. It requires some creative intervention on the part of the reader
to interpret "a religion of peace" as "a religion of peace *and war*"—a religion
whose texts include statements that abjure violence but also statements that

recommend it (under various more or less specified conditions). By comparison, the closed or exclusive understanding is both more obvious and more likely. It requires less interpretation. "Islam is a religion of peace" is taken at face value, as a full description not an incomplete claim.

The two understandings differ in another way as well. Excluding war is not accurate. Including it is. In the Qur'an and the sayings of the Prophet, both kinds of statements—peaceable and belligerent—can be found. It is the combination of flattery and fallacy that causes "Islam is a religion of peace" to illustrate denial in Diagram 1, whereas the statement "Islam is a religion of peace *and war*" would illustrate candor.

Note also the rest of the illustration of denial in Diagram 1. From the assertion that "Islam is a religion of peace" an inference is drawn: that anyone who claims to be a Muslim but commits violence must therefore not be a Muslim at all. This logic sets up a cognitive-ethical firewall—an insulation of being Muslim from being violent that can be used to fend off personal and collective responsibility. A self-defined Muslim who thinks that *Muslim terrorist* is an oxymoron thereby sequesters his or her religious identity from violence done by other self-styled Muslims in the name of Islam. If Islam is a religion of peace and peace alone, such violence is quarantined—sealed off from the faith itself and from its community of necessarily peaceful believers.

Self-described "true" Muslims who engage in this form of denial may thereby also deny any connection with, let alone even indirect or partial responsibility for, terrorism committed in Islam's name by other ("falsely") self-identified Muslims. Deniers may distance themselves from such acts by labeling them "not our problem." Although the logic of collective denial was particularly common among the immediate responses by some Muslims to 9/11, such reasoning could still be heard following suicide bombings in Islam's name more than four years later.[13]

Some scholars have contributed their own versions of denial. They have made a case for peaceable Islam by quoting appropriate phrases from Islamic sources. Favorites for this purpose include a quotation from the Qur'an, "There is no coercion in religion" (2:256), and an ostensible remark by the Prophet Muhammad distinguishing war-making and self-improvement as, respectively, "lesser" and "greater" forms of jihad.[14]

Other scholars have countered this interpretation by acknowledging the martial rhetoric that also occurs in Islam's core texts and traditions. In some interpretations, that recognition is pushed to the point of *stigmatization* (see Diagram 1) in more or less explicit suggestions that "Islam is a religion of war"—an assertion that is both readily and inaccurately taken to mean that Islam is opposed to peace. Still other scholars, appalled by such denigration, have overreacted by shifting—diagonally in Diagram 1—from candor toward positions that verge on denial. Opposition to stigmatization has thus tended to encourage among those who study Islam an inclination to downplay harsh truths in order to promote dialogue with Muslims and help defend them from victimization.[15]

Herein lies an ambiguity in the scholars' task of "understanding" Muslims and their religion. Is the purpose comprehension—or compassion? It is in this second sense of understanding, as in "being understanding" toward Muslims and Islam, that one can imagine a dialogue—believing Muslims in conversation with believing Christians, Jews, Hindus, Buddhists, and/or secular persons (including secular Muslims)—that succeeds by skirting divisive truths of the sort that illustrate candor in the lower-left quadrant of Diagram 1. I am surely not the only scholar who has taken part in such dialogues who has felt uneasy when, for example, participants jointly endorse *freedom of religion* without specifying what that phrase means. As noted in the example of candor in Diagram 1, even mainstream Muslims may not include in religious freedom the freedom of a Muslim to cease being one.

It is easy to see why an inter-religious dialogue, seeking amity and consensus, might want to address such a stark difference only if doing so does not trigger misunderstanding in the sense of discord among those present. Avoiding conflict by applying this criterion, however, invites misunderstanding in the sense of deception. If the Muslims present really do believe in two-way religious freedom for everyone, they are not typical of their community and thus belie the representative role they have been asked to play. If, instead, they believe that the absolute truth of their own religion makes renouncing it heinous and punishable, then they do not really agree with their secular-Muslim or non-Muslim dialogue partners as to what religious freedom is.[16]

ISLAMISM?

In the light of these difficulties, what words should we choose to use when speaking or writing of Islam and Muslims, and of violence in relation to them—contextualizing words that are at once accurate and considerate? Not least among the answers to this question, I believe, involves using the word

Islamism, defined broadly to include, without being limited to, the possible use of force.

Some words are centripetal. Their semantic fields gravitate toward a single core. *Islamic* is such a term. *Islamic* drains attention from a multiplicity of differently living Muslims and concentrates it on the definitional uniformity of the singular noun *Islam* as one monotheistic faith—one God, one book, and by implication one community as well.

The transcendental and absolutistic doctrinal connotations of *Islamic* tend to pull that term inward (and upward) toward an abstract Allah. In contrast, the plural term *Muslims* is centrifugally humanizing—oriented outward (and downward) toward millions of uniquely lived individual lives. Other things being equal, when discourse shifts from *Islamic* to *Muslims,* the infallible Word of God gives way to a welter of human imperfections. In usage, compared with *Islamist, Muslims* makes it harder for the user to reduce real diversity to ideal uniformity—and easier to entertain contextualization as an antidote to stigmatization. Deleting the final *s* from *Muslims* does narrow its scope. But the dual-purpose, adjective-cum-singular-noun *Muslim* remains more ambiguous—more inclusive—than the formal, faith-naming adjective *Islamic.*

Fearful stereotyping will not be thwarted simply by renaming *Islamic* terrorists as *Muslim* terrorists—or by choosing to speak of *Muslim* militants instead of *Islamist* ones. But a preference for the terms *Muslim* and *Muslims* can help. If *Islamic* terrorism invites us to infer violence from religion deterministically, as a matter of preordainment, *Muslim* violence in the sense of acts performed by individual Muslims connotes a researchable range of other possible motivations. If *Islamist* is normatively closed, in effect, *Muslim* is empirically open.[17]

When variety is misperceived as unity, homogenization occurs. Some scholars have tried to avoid homogenizing the already singular noun *Islam* by coining its plural, *Islams,* as a diversified complement to *Muslims.*[18] But most Muslims think of Islam as one religion. To speak of multiple Islams is to acknowledge real variations of doctrine, belief, and behavior, but at the cost of offending mainstream Muslims for whom the thought of many Islams is uncomfortably close to polytheism, to the sin of *shirk* (in Arabic). Yet the analyst who accepts *tawhid*—the unique (and also Arabic) oneness of Allah and the implied singularity of Islam—as an empirical description of the religion as it is believed and practiced allows heavenly doctrine to occlude earthly diversity. Trying to escape that mistake by subdividing Islam into Islams may simply decentralize the fallacy of homogenization, as one grand essence is replaced with smaller ones—Egyptian Islam, Moroccan Islam, French Islam, and so on. At the extreme, Islam could be atomized into so many contingently different Islams that Islam as a category threatens to disappear, leaving little or nothing distinctive to research or discuss.[19]

BEYOND VIOLENCE

What is Islamism? A good definition is this one, offered by a well-known student of Islam and Muslims, James Piscatori: "Islamists are Muslims who are committed to political action to implement what they regard as an Islamic agenda."[20] By extension, I would add: Islamism is a commitment to, and the content of, that agenda.

In the following sequential discussion of the three parts of Piscatori's definition, I hope to highlight its virtue. I will also, however, amend it in one small but important respect.

.   .   .

Islamists are Muslims . . . This may sound self-evident, but it has a key implication: An Islamist who engages in violent political action on behalf of an ostensibly Islamic agenda is still a Muslim. The definition rules out denial. At the same time, however, it usefully rules in both subjective and objective answers to the question: What constitutes a Muslim? An analyst can choose to define a Muslim either as someone who claims to be one or as someone who meets certain descriptive criteria—and still remain faithful to the definition. The question of essence is avoided for the sake of utility.

.   .   .

. . . who are committed to political action . . . Violence is, first and foremost, an action, and terrorism is an instance of political violence. But terrorism is only one among a great variety of other political actions—voting, for example—in which hundreds of millions of Muslims engage. To equate Islamism with terrorism alone would limit the term to a tiny sliver of the world's Muslim population.[21] This would massively underestimate the extent of Islamism in the broader sense of Muslim support for subjectively Islamic agendas—the sense used here. Thus, while avoiding stigmatization, the definition realistically—accurately—recognizes Islamist political action as a larger category including behaviors far more common if not also more important than terrorist ones.

Excluding from the scope of the term *Islamism* all commitments save violent ones would be inaccurate and invidious toward Islam, as if its doctrines were exclusively and inherently lethal. Such a narrow definition would also leave unnamed, and thus invisible, the millions of Muslims who peacefully support Muslim political parties that are peacefully trying to advance Islamic agendas by peacefully competing in elections. If these political Muslims are not Islamist, what are they? Secularist? Not in their commitment to agendas that are at least said to be Islamic.

Calling them nonviolent Islamists acknowledges these Muslims' existence and helps to recognize their importance as a large potential counterweight to the violent Islamist minority. As for non-Islamist Muslims, these include secularists whose political commitments are not said to be Islamic and quietists unattracted to political action of any kind.

A major argument against using the term *Islamism* is that it demonizes a religion by associating it exclusively with violence. Piscatori's definition avoids this pitfall. But instead of naively—inaccurately—refusing to acknowledge that some Muslims are politically violent on behalf of Islam as they understand it, the definition expands the concept of Islamism beyond violence to include diverse additional actions and orientations that favor declaredly Islamic agendas. Judged by the quadrants of Diagram 1, *Islamism* in this broader usage involves neither demonization nor denial, but allows its user to contextualize the relations between Islam, Muslims, and violence—and thus to speak or write about them with veracity and candor.

A commitment to act and the action itself are not the same thing, and Piscatori's definition is usefully inclusive in this respect as well. His wording expands the scope of Islamism while diversifying its content to include Muslims (1) who engage in nonviolent political action on behalf of self-reportedly Islamic goals; (2) who support ("are committed to") but do not themselves engage in nonviolent or violent political action toward such goals; and, last and far fewest, (3) who do use violence as a means to achieve such ends.

But what constitutes *political* action? If political action is taken narrowly to mean only what government does, and what individuals and groups do to join or become the government or influence what it does, we cannot call Islamist those Muslims whose commitment to realizing ostensibly Islamic objectives is expressed in other ways. Many Muslims endorse or engage in: social work to improve the welfare of Muslim communities; economic activities,

such as opening banks that are considered Islamic insofar as they avoid charg-
ing or paying interest; cultural undertakings to Islamize literature, theater,
film, music, and other media; or evangelical efforts to convert non-Muslims
to Islam or turn secular or nominal Muslims into fully practicing ones. Alongside political Islamists, why not call these people social, economic, cultural,
and evangelical Islamists, respectively?

For too long Islamism has been viewed by outsiders through a narrowly
political lens. Such a focus is not surprising. It fits with, and may even imply, a
thoroughly political priority on preventing, circumventing, or somehow co-
opting the rise of Islamic states. But like the tendency to caricature Islamism
as necessarily violent, rendering it essentially political reflects a perception of
threat more than a knowledge of reality—the reality that committed Muslims
can and do express their Islam-ness in a variety of ways. Broadening the scope
of *Islamism* beyond what is narrowly political to include other modes of action,
and using adjectives to differentiate among them, should help make discourse
on Islam and Muslims more realistic, more comprehensive, more nuanced,
and less unnecessarily adversarial.

This is not to recommend expanding Islamist action to include everything
from terrorism to prayer. The term should not be applied to purely personal
agendas—one's own effort, for example, to resist temptation during the fasting
month of Ramadan. The *-ist* in *Islamist* points toward collective action and
ideology, not individual piety. So do the illustrations of social, economic, cultural, and evangelical Islamism given above, involving as they all do the public sphere. I would therefore slightly alter Piscatori's definition to call *Islamist*
those "Muslims who are committed to public action."[22]

•   •   •

. . . to implement what they regard as an Islamic agenda. This qualification
helps to assure accuracy while avoiding stigmatization and denial. It acknowledges what is beyond dispute—that an Islamist *claims* to support an Islamic
agenda—while avoiding any implication that the claim is true. If an Islamist
essentializes that agenda as violent jihad, the analyst remains free to disagree.
As for the counter-essentialism that a violent agenda cannot possibly be
Islamic, the definition helps the analyst escape that inaccuracy as well.

That said, the question remains: What constitutes an Islamic agenda?

BEYOND THE STATE

Consider the goal of establishing a supposed Islamic state. Militant Islamists and militant anti-Islamists have more than just their vehemence in common. They also tend to share a preoccupation with building Islamic states, including the prospect of a caliphate that might someday encompass the Muslim world. Except for the fact that he was appalled by that prospect, U.S. Vice President Dick Cheney's description of such a caliphate could have come from Osama bin Laden himself. "The terrorists," said Cheney, "believe that they will be able to target and overthrow other governments in the [Middle East], and to establish a radical Islamic empire that encompasses a region from Spain, across North Africa, through the Middle East and South Asia, all the way to Indonesia."[23]

The currency of this specter, among both those who detest it and those who welcome it, makes understandable the tendency to define Islamism simply as *political Islam*,[24] and to read that phrase as meaning that there is but one Islamist agenda with but one item marked "to do" on it: total, radical regime change. Understandable, too, is how the sheer revolutionary magnitude of this Islamist task—transforming the whole Muslim world—fits the idea that Islamism must be violent. How else could one accomplish such a drastic project? How else to implement Cheney's nightmare? Violence or threatened violence is implicit, for instance, in the description of Islamism offered immediately after 9/11 by Daniel Pipes: "a *totalitarian* ideology," akin to "fascism and Marxism/Leninism," with "a blueprint for establishing a *coerced* utopia [emphasis added]."[25]

Again my concern is for what language rules out and rules in. Conceptions of Islamism that make it both synonymous with political Islam and necessarily violent at the same time preclude tolerance of the right of Muslims to engage in peaceful political action on behalf of what they regard as an Islamic agenda. Equating violent Islamism with political Islam effectively shrinks the range of admissible Muslim behavior to activities that are not political at all.

Blinkering one's vision in this way has disturbing implications: First, it is counter-empirical in refusing to acknowledge the sheer ubiquity of peaceful yet political actions by Muslims on behalf of Islam as they understand it—actions that dwarf in frequency and variety the terrorism of a few. If something is not named, in language and to that extent in perception and policy as well, it does not exist. A broader notion of Islamism allows the naming to occur: Nonviolent political Islamists and social, economic, cultural, and evangelical Islamists can be acknowledged alongside the far scarcer, violently political kind.

Second, a refusal to countenance the legitimacy of nonviolent political action linked to Islam, including action merely meant to protect the equal rights of Muslims to exercise their faith, is undemocratic to the point of abridging religious freedom. Third, by privileging violence among all other forms of political action, an exclusive identification of Islamism with terrorism encourages the mistaken belief that all of these other, nonviolent activities must be geared to the imposition of an Islamic state as the sole sincere item on Islamism's agenda. A corollary of that exaggeration is the essentialist cliché that Islamists must believe only in disposable democracy: one man, one vote, but for only one time if the Islamists win, for then they will show their true colors, abolish the ballot, and decree the caliphate. Fourth and last, a cognitive map and vocabulary whereby the only Islamist is a politically violent Islamist invites the very outcome it is meant to prevent, as Muslims learn to live up to— violently to enact—the stigma that the definition implies.

Piscatori's definition of Islamism is no panacea, not even as amended by broadening "political" into "public." Language is at best a partial influence on behavior. But compared with the alternatives—Islamism narrowly and invidiously defined, or another term altogether[26]—an inclusive understanding of Islamism is most likely to maximize both accuracy and consideration, the two axes of Diagram 1.

The linguistic strategy outlined here may be summarized as "Islamism with adjectives." Qualifiers would be chosen based on evidence: "violent," "radical," "illiberal," or "authoritarian Islamism," for example, depending on the actual case, but also, with different evidence, "nonviolent," "moderate," "liberal," or "democratic Islamism," among other possible designations. *Islamism* in this inclusive sense allows for differentiation and precision to fit diverse circumstances, while avoiding the word *Islam* and thus not getting trapped in one interpretation of what the religion itself really and truly means.[27]

Nor, finally, has the term *Islamism* been so tainted by bloodshed in recent and current usage as to render quixotic any attempt to define it more broadly. Numerous scholars and journalists have already broadened the scope of the term and its derivatives to include nonviolence, compromise, and moderation.[28]

At the 2004 convention of the Middle East Studies Association of North America (MESA), for instance, "Islamism," "Islamists," or "Islamist" appeared in the titles of nine papers on as many panels. Three of these titles implied that Islamism could be compatible with democracy (in Egypt, Jordan, Kuwait, Morocco, and Turkey). Five titles were neutral, imputing to Islamism and its adherents neither militancy nor moderation. Only one paper title linked Islamism to violence.[29]

Daniel Pipes might reply to this enumeration that MESA panelists are more likely than other observers to harbor Islamophilia, and thus to think more wishfully than clearly about the involvements of Muslims and Islam in carnage. But clarity lies neither in denying that such violence can occur nor in allowing it to narrow the meanings of Islamism down to nothing else. Constructive clarity, neither wishful nor blameful, lies in language that allows us to be simultaneously faithful to the facts and agnostic about the truth of faith.

The approach advanced here does not guarantee that speech and writing on Islam, Muslims, and violence will be accurate and considerate. But it could make such discourse more likely. In these polemical times, that would be no mean achievement.

INVENTING ISLAMISM:
THE VIOLENCE OF RHETORIC

Daniel M. Varisco

LET ME BEGIN with an etymologically inspired thesis: Islam, I submit, is being *ismed* to death. In Arabic grammar Islam is indeed an *ism*, which is a noun that defines the religion that Muhammad proclaimed as messenger of the one God. In English, however, the use of -ism as a suffix is suffused with rhetorical intent, in no small part because English readers long ago may have failed to realize the satirical import in Montesquieu's popularization of *despotisme*.[1] By the middle of the last century *Islam* was liberated from its baggage -ism when the pure Arabic term finally supplanted *Muhammadanism* in academic book titles. I view that as a major victory for fairness to Muslims, scholarly integrity, and common secularly induced sense. Yet, in the past decade Islam has been unequally yoked by media pundits and university professors alike with *Islamism*, which is viewed by many as a euphemistic alternative to the apparently bankrupt coinage of *Islamic fundamentalism*.

I suggest that the rationale for coining Islamism has more to do with finding a replacement for fundamentalism that still captures the extremism and terrorism that so many commentators in their analysis*ism* wish to ascribe to Islam. I fully recognize that there are violent streams in the politicization of Islamic practice, hardly a new phenomenon, but I find no precedent for creating a new negative sense of Islamism when this neologistic innovation has been done for no other religion. Judaism is not a violent form of religion; nor should we hold the linguistic door open for radical *Christianism*. Why do we need a term that uniquely brands Muslims as *terrorists* rather than just calling them terrorists and militants, the way we could easily do for followers of any religion or any ideology? As scholars and students of religion, should we not be doing all we can to refute the notion that Islam is intrinsically more violent than other religions?

The problem is not just one of words and labels. Whatever non-Muslims call the religion Muslims themselves recognize as *din* and Islam, outsiders looking in often target the spiritual faith as one spread by the sword and pre-served by war-thirsty jihad. Opponents of Islam, especially in the Christian West, have tended to follow the eighth-century sentiments of the allegedly Venerable Bede, who condemned invading Muslims of his time as "a very sore plague."[2] Not only were these Saracens thought to be warlike by nature, but even in literary hell on the heels of the Crusades, Dante damned Muhammad, Islam's prophet, to a Sisyphian de-gutting for eternity.[3] Following the 9/11 disaster, President George W. Bush's own gut reaction was to use the c-word, acknowledging that a war on terrorism would essentially be a crusade, before invoking the h-bomb, the trope that a religious faith called Islam could be hijacked. For many in the American Bible Belt, Islam *is* violence and Muham-mad *is* the Devil. To paraphrase one of our dearest pre-Patriot Act American values, to be a Muslim today is to be guilty of nascent terrorism until proven innocent. In the public eye most Muslims might as well be Muslimists.

COMING TO TERMS

The use of the new term Islamism to refer to militancy done ostensibly in the name of Islam is a particularly pernicious use of language. It merges the faith of Islam with modern political movements in such a way as to make non-Muslims think that Islam itself is the source of the militancy.[4]

—Imam Feisal Abdul Rauf

To be blunt, I do not think that a linguistically resurgent Islamism is an ad-vance over the neo-illogic of Islamic fundamentalism. Both conceptualiza-tions are not worth perpetuating in academic writing, unless we are willing to throw in our critical towel and parrot journalistic suit. I begin with a verbal attack on Islamism, the word rather than the conceptual target of many non-Muslims, so that I may end up properly with Islam, both the word and the richness of the perspectives such a single word can still evoke. It is fitting in an age when Islamism has emerged as an important Internet presence to look for definitions through a Google word search.[5] Regardless of the virtue in this virtual reality check, the sophisticated search engine I chose directed me immediately to an article on Islamism written in 1998 by Daniel Pipes, founder of Campus Watch and outspoken critic of Islam in the world today.

> Islamism is an ideology that demands man's complete adherence to the sacred law of Islam and rejects as much as possible outside influence, with some exceptions (such as access to military and medical technology). It is imbued with a deep antagonism towards non-Muslims and has a particular hostility towards the West. It amounts to an effort to turn Islam, a religion and civilization, into an ideology.[6]

In Pipe's politicized sense, Islamism is ideological Islam, contrasted to a quiescent "traditional" Islam molded by the past. But there is more to connote: "Islamism is, in other words, yet another twentieth-century radical utopian scheme. Like Marxism-Leninism or fascism, it offers a way to control the state, run society, and remake the human being. It is an Islamic-flavored version of totalitarianism." As a radical ideology that has no chance of succeeding in the real world (I am glossing "utopian" here), Islamism for Pipes is no different from Marxism-Leninism and fascism, yet another variant of totalitarianism.[7] What I find distressing in Pipe's rhetoric is the range of negative isms to which Islamism is likened. Before the end of his essay, he also mentions "terrorism," which is in my mind the prime factor for the invention of contemporary Islamism as a rhetorical convention. Indeed, on his weblog, Pipes praises Frank Gaffney of the Center for Security Policy for admitting that the "War on Terror" is really a "War on Islamism."[8]

A lexical variant of the above dia[bolical]tribe is provided by the *American Heritage Dictionary of the English Language* (2000 edition), which I found cross-linked on several Googled Web sites. I say "variant" for a good reason. Read what this dictionary says about Islamism: "NOUN: 1. An Islamic revivalist movement, often characterized by moral conservatism, literalism, and the attempt to implement Islamic values in all spheres of life. 2. The religious faith, principles, or cause of Islam."[9] A naive reader of this accessible dictionary might wonder how these neutral-sounding meanings justify the Islamism linked by Pipes to fascism and terrorism. Revivalists generally try to revive a religion rather than deprive others of their religion. Moral conservatism, literalism, and Islamic values are hardly the ideological counterparts of fascism. But the big surprise comes in the second, and older, sense. Islamism has been a synonym for Islam in general since at least the first edition of Webster's American dictionary in 1828.[10] As of 1993 the first meaning above was not even referenced in the authoritative *Oxford English Dictionary*.[11] In *OED* English, Islamism simply equals Islam and the related term *Islamist* refers either to "an orthodox Muslim" or "an expert on Islam." Let me put it this way. For Daniel Pipes the icon of an ideological Islamist is Osama bin Laden; for those who follow the *OED*, an Islamist could either be the supreme shaykh of al-Azhar or John Esposito. I recognize that this nuance might very well be unacceptable to Mr. Pipes.

Ironically, the established dictionary sense of Islamism became obsolete as an unsuccessful competitor of *Mohammedanism* in late nineteenth-century writing. If you go through the catalog of the Library of Congress, you will find a reference to Frederick Arthur Neale's *Islamism: Its Rise and Its Progress*, published in London in 1854 (but originally printed in 1828). Neale was no sapient Nostradamus predicting the fall of the Twin Towers more than a century and a half later. At the time Islamism was another way of saying *Islam* when Western writers totally ignored the straightforward Arabic term, *Islam*.[12] The highly unoriginal synonym Mohammedanism, following in the linguistic wake of *Mahometanism* and before the seemingly more astute *Muhammadanism*, was eventually rejected by Muslims and Western scholars alike because it conjured up the medieval Christian apologetic that Muhammad was worshipped by Muslims.[13] Yet, the historian H.A.R. Gibb maintained the term as the title of his well-known survey as late as 1953, arguing that the "well-informed person" no longer believed 'Mahomet' was an idol.[14] Gibb failed to realize that negative views of Islam were so deeply entrenched in Western scholarship and popular culture that virtually no separation is allowed between the Islamic faith and intolerant violence. Words do matter.

The popularization of Islamism as a term reserved for a specific kind of intolerant Islam is relatively recent. The earliest use I have found is in an article by Fazlur Rahman, who in 1970 applied the term to Muslims on the right who were primarily opposed to socialism.[15] His primary examples were Sayyid Qutb (1906–1966) and Mawlana Mawdudi (1903–1979). This is Islamism as an ideology with political intent overriding theology.[16] Graham Fuller, a former CIA officer turned Islamist expert, puts it this way: "In my view," he argues, "an Islamist is one who believes *that Islam as a body of faith has something important to say about how politics and society should be ordered in the contemporary Muslim world and who seeks to implement this idea in some fashion*."[17] It is hard to imagine anyone but a secular Muslim who would not be an Islamist by this definition. Yet even secular Muslims believe that Islam has something important to say about politics and society, whether or not they agree with all the doctrines. Few Muslims consider themselves social hermits or fail to think about how their faith applies to politics. Fuller, like many Western commentators, would prefer that contemporary Islam follow suit with the political trajectory of contemporary Christianity in the West. In the United States, church is constitutionally separated from state so that the individual can be religious on Sunday and secular the rest of the week. I suppose if Muslims were to post the *Fatiha*, the oft-recited brief verses of the first chapter of the Qur'an, in their courtrooms with no overt religious motive, then that would be acceptable. As long as not becoming secular in the American or European sense is a major criterion for being labeled an Islamist, the faith of Islam will continue to be misread as political rather than moral.

BEYOND FUNDAMENTALISM

> *All blanket words such as revivalism, reformism, or*
> *fundamentalism are arbitrary invocations of the English*
> *language; they do not, and cannot, describe the varying*
> *degrees of Islamic loyalty and protest.*[18]
> **—Bruce Lawrence**

The rapid acceptance of Islamism follows a debate over the usefulness of the term *fundamentalism* applied to Islam. Before the relatively recent warming over the East bloc-West bloc Cold War, right-wing Christian fundamentalists saw red: atheist *Communists* coming over to destroy a God-blessed America. Many of these same fundamentalists, since the unprophesied collapse of the Soviet Union and unforetold attack on the Twin Towers, are now seeing green in the threat of Islamism as terrorism. As author Salman Rushdie has reason to observe, in much of Western culture an "Islamic Peril" has now been placed alongside the racy Yellow and Red ones.[19] This clearly colors the perception of those Evangelical Christians who see Muslims as profaning *their* Holy Land, where, some aver, Americans store "their" oil and harbor a large part of their religious nostalgia. Not unlike Rushdie, conservative Christian spokesmen such as Pat Robertson and Jerry Falwell have reverted from the missionary zeal for converting Mohammedans to the medieval invective against Mahound as a great Satan surrogate.[20] In this ongoing Bible Belt passion play, the medieval evil characters remain the same; only the names have been updated. The Jews, God's "peculiar people," have become Zionists and Israelis;

the Saracens and infidel Turks are now expanded to include Iranian students, Muslim Brothers, Hamas, the Taliban and Islamists; but, significantly for some Bible believers, the "Whore of Babylon" is still Catholicism.[21] In short, no childish apocalyptic idea has been left behind in avowedly Christian fundamentalist preaching.

Fundamentalism seemed a comfortable fit because it was, after all, *our* term, a word coined almost a century ago within American Protestantism to define a self-proclaimed reformist religious movement opposed to a liberal shift in mainline denominations.[22] In millenarian fashion, the conservative controversy began with a popular text, *The Fundamentals*.[23] This is the title of a book series published privately, but with a widespread public debut, between 1910 and 1915 by two wealthy Los Angeles brothers. Their financial underwriting brought the views of sixty-four conservative Protestant writers to some three million Americans in positions of public or religious authority. What was fundamental in *The Fundamentals* was hardly new to the catechism. Of all the doctrines elaborated in the volumes, the top five fundamentals—or dare I say pillars—of the faith continue to unite born-again evangelicals in principle more than any ecclesiastical body has ever managed. Fundamentalist Christian "Fivers" believe in the verbal inspiration of the Bible, virgin birth of Christ, atonement of Christ as the Son of God for all men, bodily resurrection of Christ and *His* imminent Second Coming. These are essentially doctrinal points, but they were directed a century ago at a rapidly changing cultural context in which the established church itself was seen as failing to enforce respect for the fundamentals. Ironically, most Muslims miss being Christian fundamentalists only by rejecting two of these pillars. For Muslims the Qur'an, not the existing Bible, is the divinely inspired text to follow; they believe the Qur'an corrects the early sacred texts in a similar way to Christian thinking that the New Testament revises the Old. The Qur'an comes close to Christian thinking, agreeing that Christ was born of a virgin but stopping short of saying this great prophet was the Son of God. Indeed, as historian Richard Bulliet has recently argued, there is a strong case for rethinking our shared history as Islamo-Christian civilization.[24]

Up until the late 1970s, the only fundamentalists in linguistic sight were Christian, although many who favored the five fundamentals had begun to abandon the popularly tainted label for less negative terms such as *evangelical* and *neo-evangelical*.[25] The earliest appropriation of fundamentalism to describe Muslims is hard to document. In 1964 Morroe Berger, in his widely circulated *The Arab World Today*, applied the concepts *modernism* and *fundamentalism* to Islam in a generic comparative sense.[26] One of the first scholarly efforts to define a specific Islamic fundamentalism was made by R. Stephen Humphreys in 1979, although he considered it "more a tendency than a current social reality."[27] Its use became common enough to appear in book titles by the mid-1980s.[28] I suspect, however, that the stimulus for transferring fundamentalism began among journalists due to the low esteem held for both the rising Moral Majority in the Reagan landslide and newsworthy Islamic terrorism of the Iran hostage crisis rather than from scholars in Islamic Studies.

Historians of Christian fundamentalism did little initially to dispel the expansion to an Islamic context. In 1980 George Marsden pointed out "striking" similarities and differences between the fundamentalisms of the two faiths, but he still agreed that it was appropriate "to borrow" the American term in view of Islam's "militant opposition to much of modern culture."[29] He argued, quite ethnocentrically, that Muslims have been more prone to combine "religious militancy and actual military force" than has been the case in Christianity. While there is little to be gained in quibbling over who started the Crusades, the premodern history of European Christianity is anything but pacific. European imperialism under a Christian banner has resulted in more destruction of peoples and cultures around the world than Muslims wielding scimitars. Marsden, a scholar of Christianity, shows a lack of understanding about how Islam spread through Africa and Asia via missionary activity rather than overt military conquest. When Marsden wrote, Islamic fundamentalism was portrayed metaphorically in the American media as a religion of bearded clerics wielding Kalashnikovs and shouting "Death to America." This link between fundamentalism and militancy was perpetuated in the rationale provided by Marty and Appleby for their massive *The Fundamentalist Project*. "It is no insult to fundamentalists to see them as militants," claim the editors, "whether in the use of words and ideas or ballots, or in extreme cases, bullets. Fundamentalists see themselves as militants."[30] Why is it that so many observers find it so easy to view fundamentalists as militants?

To approve a terminological transfer under fundamentalism because of Islam's touted "extremism" actually disguises what most Islamic reform movements share with the origins of Protestant fundamentalism: a call within a formally educated middle class for reform from within rather than riots in the streets. But this should not be seen as a rejection of modernity. The broad appeal of Islamic fundamentalism among many Muslims today is precisely because it offers a program to modernize in an indigenous Islamic mode. Earlier Islamic revivalist leaders, such as Muhammad ibn ʿAbd al-Wahhab (died 1792), eponym of the Wahhabi religious social movement, may have preached a golden-aged return to Muhammad's Arabia, but that has not stopped Saudi Arabia from importing the most sophisticated technology from Europe and America. Modern reformists such as the Egyptian Hasan al-Banna were not Amishlike escapists running away from technology and murmuring about modernity, nor should they be conflated with the recent Taliban in Afghanistan. Their concern was not with internal deletion of the fundamental pillars of their faith, which no mainstream Muslim authorities were advocating, but with the encroachment of Western cultural hegemony that generally supported corrupt local politics and challenged the moral order of local culture.

Until Islamism forged ahead, fundamentalism had become ubiquitous in discussions about conservative Muslims who rejected Western values. More than a decade and a half ago, Martin E. Marty and Scott Appleby argued that the term fundamentalism is "here to stay."[31] I note that the same rationale was once used for terms such as *Mohammedan* and *Negro*. Despite the important analyses in the volumes of *The Fundamentalism Project*, books still are published in which "leading Islamic fundamentalists" include intellectuals such as Jamal al-Din al-Afghani, Muhammad Iqbal, and Ali Shariati alongside Khomeini and Sheikh Omar Abd al-Rahman.[32] I agree with Barbara Metcalf, who observes: "ʿFundamentalism' has been applied as a blanket term to describe virtually all modern Islamic movements that use a religious vocabulary and encourage fidelity to Islamic practice. This imprecision, coupled with the term's pejorative connotations, make its use in relation to Islam particularly problematic."[33] If this is true for defining a specifically Islamic fundamentalism, there is good reason to cast the same critical eye at the rhetorical range now subsumed under Islamism.

A case has been made for resurrecting fundamentalism as an analytical category, but only with a flurry of caveats. "There is an urgent need to decode the rampant sloganeering that clouds Islamic fundamentalism," argues Bruce Lawrence.[34] He proposes a heuristic use of the term *fundamentalism* to compare ideological responses in diverse faiths to secularized nationalism in the modern context. Unfortunately, all the academic writing in the world has not been able to remove the pejorative stain of the term in public discourse. The problem with fundamentalism is not that it is theoretically incapable of being de-sloganized, but that its rhetorical force as a slogan will not go away. Most references to fundamentalists remain negative, because most people do not like what they think fundamentalism stands for. As Michael Williams argued for the baggage-laden term *gnosticism* in religious studies, that concept had "become such a protean label that it has all but lost any reliabily identifiable meaning for the larger reading public."[35] Unfortunately, fundamentalism is similarly flawed. "Awesome power resides in the terms we employ," Richard Bulliet reminds us.[36] Some words need to be buried and not exhumed so that we can get on with understanding the issues behind and beyond the words.

There is much to be said for rejecting the baggage-laden term *fundamentalism* outside of its Christian context. The most powerful argument, in my mind, is that of Muslim scholars themselves. As Fadwa El Guindi reminds us, this is "an imposed notion deriving mainly from Western Christianity that is conceptually inappropriate, ethnographically inaccurate, and ethnocentric."[37] Akbar Ahmed, another anthropologist, similarly laments the misuse of the term by Western commentators, who have a habit of labeling Islam in Christocentric language. For Ahmed, fundamentalism may be useful in a Christian context, but it confuses his own religion "because by definition every Muslim believes in the fundamentals of Islam."[38] In this respect fundamentalism is of a piece with the term *Orientalism*, which no longer comfortably defines the range of scholars who interpret the Middle and farther reaches of the East. If indeed, as Edward Said and others have fervently argued, we create the "Orient" in contradistinction to how we perceive our superior, modern "West," then the idea of a Muslim fundamentalist might best be judged against how we categorize and fear Christian fundamentalists in America.[39] Is it not difficult to say what makes a Muslim—or even a Hindu—a fundamentalist when in fact we have a complex rhetorical history invested in the conceptualizing of religious fundamentalism in our own society? This is not just the case for the tabloids and talk shows but also for those of us who speak from the secular bully pulpit of an academic setting.

RESISTING THE -*ISM* IMPULSE

> For –isms do not simply designate anything whatever. Indeed the range of possible meanings intimated by a term in –isms is enormous and undiscriminating. And whatever may be the reasons why such terms find ready, not to say universal, employment in scholarly as well as polemical speech, it is certainly not because their referents and connotations are clear

> *and unequivocal. A no doubt libelous suggestion would be that*
> *such terms owe their popularity precisely to the fact that they*
> *do not require a decision about what it is one is talking about.*[40]
>
> **—H. M. Hopfl (1983)**

Meanings of words change all the time, even if dictionaries are slow to document the process. In theory fundamentalism could shed its Christian origins and Islamism could be reserved for a militant and intolerant form of Islam. But the social grounding of recent etymological -isms suggests a different path. All -*ists* are not linguistically equal. This useful morpheme has a relevant history for understanding how word choice is inevitably part of a power play. First, the English sense of an -ist stems from French adoption of Latinized Greek ecclesiastical terminology, such as *evangelist* and *Baptist*.[41] Evangelist entered English less than a century after the call for the first crusade. A second wave of -isms occurred in the development of modern English after the early sixteenth century, again under French influence. I note with irony that the term *atheist* appears in English twenty years before *humanist* and thirty years before the world ever heard of English *imperialism*. Although -ist and -ism words did not necessarily have religious connotations, the differing viewpoints of the Reformation separated the world into the mutually antagonistic heresies of papists, Calvinists, Jensenists, and the like. The French Revolution jump-started a slew of significant secular -ists, with terrorists (first noted in 1795) coming only three years after the invention of *capitalist*.[42] Thus, constructing -isms has not evolved as a neutral or objective process. Words are created to solidify differences as well as define things.

Second, for the past several decades the coinage of new -ists has shifted from signifying group labels (as in *Calvinist*) or a sense of expertise or skill (as in *dentist*) to negative characterization (as in *sexist*). Linguist Adrienne Lehrer, reviewing this modern shift, argues: "Thus the current meaning of 'ism' is 'the unjust and unjustified belief of superiority of one group (of persons or things) and the corresponding inferiority of another group or other groups.'"[43] The gist of -*isting*, if I may add to the neological jumble, is really besting the other. World War II bequeathed a legacy of *Stalinism*, but without a counterpart of *Rooseveltism* or *Churchillism*, at least not on the side of the victors. The demonized other in my own youth was the Communist, following my father's generational nemesis of *Fascism*; that of my teenage son is now the Islamist. This semantic shift, I suggest, renders Islamism an irredeemable term, since it is linguistically prone to be negative.[44] We should beware of ideological frameworks that introduce new -isms as euphemisms. Otherwise we are forced to deal with monstrous tabloid creations such as *Islamofascism*.

This trend is well illustrated with the popular moniker *Jihadism*, semantic overkill for an Arabic term that had been taken wholesale into English more than a century ago.[45] On Internet sites such as jihadwatch.com and dhimmiwatch.com the term *jihadist* has become routine. The site called NoJihad directs you to a Web page that shows what would happen to your home community if the jihadists were to nuke it.[46] One Internet site I Googled equated Jihadism with World War IV![47] Shifting to jihadist is significant, because it both accentuates the negative sense of violence and ignores the previously borrowed Arabic term, *mujahideen,* for those who engage in jihad. Apparently the term *mujahideen*, widely used in the media for the Muslims who fought the Soviets in Afghanistan, needed to be *-ismized* for an American audience when those same fighters started targeting American soldiers rather than the Communists.[48] "The greatest threat facing the United States today is terrorism by Muslim jihadists," exclaim Monte and Princess Palmer.[49] "The jihadists are a self-appointed collection of religious fanatics who have launched a holy war, a jihad, against the United States and everything American." The devil here is in the linguistic detail, demonizing the Muslim other through a halfway ismhouse of language.

VIOLENCE AND ISLAM: DO WE NEED A TERM?

> *I repeat therefore . . . that the Moslem population of India,*
> *amongst who[m] Panislamitic ideas are spreading from day to*
> *day, will not remain inactive in the future should the Christian*
> *West continue to indulge in the sport of modern crusades.*[50]
> **—Arminius Vambéry (1877)**

There are no historically preserved religions that have been immune to manipulation for political violence. Yahweh was a jealous war god untamed by a fertility goddess; Constantine wielded the sword to Christianize the Roman Empire; Muslims slaughtered fellow Muslims on the plain of Kerbala. Despite centuries of internal European bloodbaths in the name of Christ, no one has yet to suggest a need for Christianism. Christians such as St. Francis of Assisi were peaceful; Charlemagne was militant. The long-standing *-ity* in *Christianity* lacks a pejorative sense. Christianity has long had its sectarian -ists, but none of these sullies the term *Christian* itself as inherently violent. Likewise Judaism, Hinduism, and Buddhism define major faiths without connoting violent expressions of belief or intolerance for other creeds. We could theoretically create *Judaists* and *Hinduists*, but consider the irony of reserving Buddhist for a militant path to nirvana. My argument is that the use of *Islamism* violates the range of engrained linguistic usage in English. The question then becomes why we need a unique packaging of violent religion in the baggage-laden label Islamism.

Until Islamism exploded in the writing of media pundits and academics alike, a number of other labels were touted to explain away aspects of Islam that Western commentators found problematic. Other mutating monikers in the haphazard essentialization of contemporary Islamic socioreligious change range from *militant, reformist, revivalist,* and *traditionalist* to *reassertion* and *resurgence.* In an influential study, first published in 1988, John Esposito adopted the term *revivalism* to cover the ideological worldview commonly called fundamentalism at the time.[51] In a volume looking at the big three monotheisms, Richard Antoun and Mary Hegland defined religious resurgence as "rising importance and visibility of religion; increased impact of religion in political life."[52] Both revivalism and resurgence have the merit of not being attached to a specific religion. Significantly, neither term predetermines a focus on militancy and political violence. These generic terms, relatively free of the pejorative connotations inherent in fundamentalism and Islamism, have the additional value of closely approximating the indigenous Arabic vocabulary of *islah* (generally translated as reform) and *tajdid* (renewal).

The media adoption of Islamism says more to me about a need to sound-bite the news than to understand the motivation and nuanced views of those who make, and more often do not make, the news. There are in fact militant and radical Muslims who promote terrorism in suicide missions; there are made-for-Internet beheadings conducted to shouts of "Allah Akbar"; there are atrocities committed by Muslim terrorists that fly in the face of basic humanitarian values. I do not ignore the current wave of violence propagated in the name of Islam, but neither do I think ideological rhetoric (whether for or against) should single out one of the world's most widespread and profound religious faiths as uniquely prone to be violent. Because it took non-Muslims so long to accept the simple fact that the *din* of Muslims is Islam rather than Mohammedanism, I question the haste with which the current din of indignation justifies an idiosyncratic and contradictory term such as Islamism.

In an ironic sense, the history of Islamism in the old synonymic sense of Islam is pre-adapted for the modern ideological usage. In a lecture delivered in 1883 by the savant Ernest Renan, the depiction of the Islamism of his time rings all too closely to the present tenor of ideological pundits and bloggers. "Every person . . . ," declared Renan, "sees clearly the actual inferiority of Mohammedan countries, the decadence of states governed by Islam, and the intellectual nullity of the races that hold, from that religion alone, their culture and education."[53] "The liberals who defend Islam do not know its real nature," continues Renan. "Islam is the close union of the spiritual and the temporal; it is the reign of a dogma, it is the heaviest claim that humanity has ever borne."[54] The heavy burden in such rhetoric for us today is the ongoing legacy in which most Westerners continue to view Islam, Islamism, or Mohammedanism as inferior and as a threat. History erodes any attempt at academic neutrality, no matter which term you pick. Given the historical baggage, I believe Islamism is the kind of term that perpetuates the prejudice so well articulated by Renan.

·   ·   ·

It is often said—or said to be said—that "sticks and stones may break my bones, but names shall never hurt me." Oh, but how names and labels can hurt people. This is perhaps one of the schoolyard myths Salman Rushdie flaunted in turning Islam's prophet into Mahound, the devil's namesake for an English audience. Islamism is a term we should abandon not just because it is inappropriately conceived, but because it is harmful to the ongoing public perception of Muslims. If we who study Islam in academe allow a single word that defines Islam as such to be born again in ideological fervor as a special kind of religious extremism, then we might as well be hurling sticks and stones at our Muslim colleagues. Whatever advantages a retooled Islamism might have in idealized print, the views of Muslims themselves should be respected by those who observe them observing their faith.

I do not wish to end only by talking about words, because there is a more important question that I think few scholars have yet to probe. Why is it that we need one special word to link Islam and violence? I agree with the recent dismissal of wordage drift such as Islamic fundamentalism and *Hindu* or *Jewish fundamentalism* as fundamentally flawed in coercing a term for a specific kind of Christian movement in the United States to serve cross-culturally. The lack of political violence in the emergence of *Christian fundamentalism* is reason enough to reject importing the term to the political forum of warmongered religious talk on terrorism. What is labeled fundamentalism or Islamism is in effect an ideology, not a theology or philosophy. As an ideology that cloaks terror with religious rhetoric, the only thing new in religious terrorism is the choice of weapon, swords beaten into car bombs. But surely the enemy is intolerance that compels violence, and this is not unique to any religion or political ideology.

Perhaps our willingness to accept Islamism with a capital *I* parallels the tendency to idealize Islam with a capital *I* rather than probe the multiple ways in which Muslims interpret and act on their faith. In a perceptive critique of anthropological studies of Islam through the 1970s, Egyptian-born Abdel Hamid el-Zein argued that it makes more sense, at least for anthropologists, to study "islams" rather than accept the essentialized notion of one Islam. "'Islam,' without referring it to the facets of a system of which it is part, does not exist," observed el-Zein. "Put another way, the utility of the concept 'Islam' as a predefined religion with its supreme 'truth' is extremely limited in anthropological analysis."[55] El-Zein, a devout Muslim, was not denying the value of his faith but challenging the ease with which we accept our analytical concepts as given realities. His point was the need to start from the diverse viewpoints of Muslims holding the faith rather than classify Muslims according to a hierarchical scale on how close they come to an ideal divorced from everyday life.

The umbrella of Islamism, like the ideal of a universally valid Islam, over-conceptualizes observable reality. Like adherents of any religion, Muslims cannot escape politics. But surely it is absurd to argue that contemporary Muslims as a whole are more political today than in the past, or even that a particular set of Muslims (such as Al Qaeda or Hamas) is more militant than a historically known group such as the eleventh-century Assassins. Of course, the underlying assumption in contemporary use of the term *Islamism* is that the violent behavior of certain Muslims is directed against Western targets. When Saddam Hussein bombed Iran in the 1980s, his brutal actions were not labeled terrorism, except by the Iranians. When Osama bin Laden and other mujahideen fought against the Soviets in the Afghan jihad, they were called *freedom fighters*, not terrorists.[56] I suspect that if violence had not been directed at American embassies in Africa, the U.S.S. Cole in Aden harbor, and the World Trade Center, the word *Islamism* would still be a quaint dictionary synonym of Islam.

So what term should we choose, if the ones discussed above all seem to be found wanting? I suggest we desist from essentializing Islam as we also resist problematic neologisms such as Islamism. What is wrong with adjectives? Muslims who advocate violence and call for blanket jihads are militant Muslims; Hindus who burn down mosques in India are engaged in terrorist acts. Individuals should be labeled violent or peaceful; ideological rationale and legitimization may very well be violent, inhumane, and brutal. We have a range of adjectives in any language to qualify ideas too broad to be summed up or glossed over in a single word. Perhaps we should take a page from Muslims, who believe in one God but revere that God through ninety-nine names. It is important to know that a Vengeful God is also a Merciful God. I argue that calling the ideological interpretation of Islam by Bin Laden as something essential to the Islamic faith denies a fundamental historical reality: All religions exist only as they are interpreted in a given place and time. Modern Jews and Christians have been able to come to terms with the intolerant interpretations that plagued their history; so have most Muslims.

Were Islamism only a word, then my argument here would be little more than a pedantic footnote. I am aware that the points I have raised in this essay will not affect the reportage of CNN, Fox News, or the usual run of Islamist-bashing media pundits. Journalists embedded with terrorist-hunting coalition squadrons in Iraq will be spinning tales of Islamist suicide attacks as long as American troops physically occupy Iraq. My goal is far more modest. I ask fellow scholars and students to examine the term critically, consider the implications of using a single word that uniquely associates Islam and violence, and exercise their own rhetorical agency; consider this a call for the greater jihad, if you will—what most Muslims and some jurists refer to as struggle within oneself. For myself, I will cease to use the term in my future writings without drawing attention to why it is the wrong term. I am proud to be an Islamist in the OED sense, a scholar intent on understanding Islam from all sides. However, I see only danger in continued use of Islamism for politicized Islam at a time when Muslims are so misrepresented in America.

CRITICAL RESPONSES

Part 2

THE SPECTRUM OF ISLAMIC POLITICS
Graham E. Fuller

DEBATE OVER USE OF THE TERM *Islamism* is as controversial as the concept of Islamism itself. For some it is an ideologically laden term, for others an analytic description. The rough outlines of that debate are well covered in the two major essays here by Professors Emmerson and Varisco, who review the historic origins of the term; its traditional and contemporary usages; its ambiguities, potentially pejorative implications, and analytical accuracy; its potential hindrance to fruitful dialog; and a search for reconciliation.

Both lead essays share a number of common analytical perspectives that I too share. Both point out the highly selective Western usages of this term, depending on whether a group is viewed as a positive or negative actor on the geopolitical and social scene, or, more simply, whether the group members are seen as "good guys" or bad. The term *Islamofascism*, for example, represents a term designed almost exclusively with pejorative, even malign intent. Indeed, *fascism* can be applied to ethnic and religious chauvinism almost anywhere, and the phenomenon exists in nearly all cultures—why then don't we talk about Christian fascism, Jewish fascism, Hindu, even Buddhist fascism (as in Myanmar)?

The two essays, however, end up drawing quite different conclusions about the desirability or value of using, or avoiding, the term *Islamism*. In this essay I defend the *analytic* value of retaining and employing the term.

• • •

Central to my argument is the observation that Islamic politics exist along a spectrum, manifesting a variety of forms. These forms can be set along a number of axes: whether peaceful or violent; democratic or authoritarian; engaged or not in party politics, openness, transparency, and pragmatism or ideological rigidity. In the end it matters less exactly *what* term is employed— although they may evoke differing emotive responses—than that *some* term be selected that will identify the full range of phenomena that objectively exist along this Islamist spectrum.

Whether or not the term is pejorative, the reality is that it is now widespread and accepted by a broad spectrum of analysts and observers, non-Muslim and even Muslim. Indeed, the term now exists and is regularly used in many Muslim languages, such as *al-Islamiyya* in Arabic, or *İslamcılık* in Turkish. For some Muslims the term is basically a Western construct; they will argue that "there is no Islamism, only Islam." Yes, there is "only Islam," but Islam has many forms, including a contemporary interpretation and application applied to politics. That broad interpretation needs a name.

The term is used with both approbation and disapprobation within Muslim societies. The same applies to the term *fundamentalism*, clearly of Christian origin. I agree with Varisco that fundamentalism may be pejorative to some Muslims but hardly to all: It is used in Arabic (*al-usuliyya*) and in Turkish (*köktencilik*), although the latter also suggests elements of *radicalism*. (I even found myself riding in a tuk-tuk in Lahore, Pakistan a few years ago that sported an English sticker that read, "Fundamentalist, and proud of it." So much for political correctness.)

•   •   •

In my book *The Future of Political Islam* (New York: Palgrave, 2003), I offer my own definition of Islamism, which I use somewhat interchangeably with *political Islam*: There I say that an Islamist believes that *Islam as a body of faith has something important to say about how politics and society should be ordered in the contemporary Muslim World and seeks to implement this idea in some fashion*" (p. xi). It is a deliberately broad definition (and I note that it parallels a definition of James Piscatori's in several respects as well). There are several reasons for casting such a broad net.

It is striking, incidentally, that the shrillest voices in the West against the very phenomenon of Islamism or political Islam are those who are most fearful of a rising geopolitical clout of the Muslim world, either in its challenge to the hegemonic reach of U.S. power across the Muslim world or in relation to Israel's security. Few analyze the term in its implications for political evolution within the Muslim world itself. Just as with the term *caliphate*, anxiety seems strongest among those who basically do not welcome a more powerful Muslim world in any respect. Some of the most prejudicial uses of the term spring from these sources. And yet political Islam is of course all about restoring the power of the Muslim world, among other things. Negative observers of Islamism tend to use the term *Islamism* strictly to apply to negative and reprehensible actions, particularly the use of violence or authoritarian means.

The issue can never be a simple one. Muslims themselves, including Islamists, do not agree on what the role of Islam in politics should be. Is Islam compatible with democracy? Can Islamism be imposed? Should it ever employ violence in the struggle? Who are its targets? Should it engage in politics? With what platform? It is simplistic to state that Islamists simply seek to establish a *Sharia state* or a caliphate. These two terms too, are notoriously ambiguous and open to different interpretations. More important, they don't begin to capture the domestic agendas of so many Islamists who seek to change ruling authoritarian regimes and bring about greater social and economic justice. And of course, even these worthy goals must be viewed against the means by which they are achieved.

In the end, then, we require some term that analysts can agree upon that will embrace this entire spectrum of Islamist political activity, running from Osama bin Laden to Prime Minister Tayyip Erdoğan in Turkey, Hamas to Hizb al-Tahrir, Fethullah Gülen to Tablighi Jamaat, Muslim Brotherhood to Nahdlatul Islam in Indonesia, the violent Jamaat Islamiyya in Egypt to the nonviolent Jama'at-i-Islami in Pakistan, Hizbullah in Lebanon to Jaysh al-Islam in Iraq. There are perhaps several hundred such movements around the Muslim world, each differing in structure, leadership, ideology, goals, methods, and political and social environment.

If it is to have validity, Islamism must be a neutral term. It cannot be reserved solely for reprehensible acts and "the bad guys." Yet this is often the tendency among numerous observers: If an Islamist group operates in a peaceful, tolerant, and more pragmatic way, then it is excluded from the category of Islamism. Islamism must apply to the "good guys" too when they demonstrate a more tolerant, pragmatic, and moderate understanding of political Islam.

Varisco too observes that the term *Islamism* is regularly used to denote an association with violence. But of course there is no reason that it should; violence is at only one end of the Islamist political spectrum. No doubt, many Islamist groups engage in violence, and some are truly murderous. The same can be said of many secular and nationalist groups as well. But most Islamist groups are not violent. Islamism should not be associated strictly with violence, any more than with nonviolence. Islam may be a "religion of peace," but no more or no less than most other religions—some of whose followers can often be quite violent and brutal in the name of the faith. If one demands some analytic term that specifically refers to violence in Islam—and I agree we need one—then we can perhaps speak of *violent Islam*, or better yet, as Emmerson suggests, "violent Muslims in the name of Islam."

At the same time, there are those Muslims who complain that it is the Western press that invariably rushes to apply the adjective Muslim or Islamic every time there is a violent act in that part of the world. Why drag in the Islamic adjective? they ask. But of course many of these organizations themselves insist on the association with Islam—sometimes even with God—in naming their movements, whether violent or not: we have Hizbullah (Party of God); Jamaat-i-Islamiya (Islamic Association), Jaysh Allah (Army of God), Jaysh al-Mahdi (Army of the Guided One, Redeemer), Jaysh al-Islam (Army of Islam), Fedayin (Sacrificers of) al-Islam, and so forth. Others adopt the clearly Islamic terms of Dawa (Propagation of the Faith) or jihad. Interestingly, Bin Laden chose not to link his organization with either God or Islam in designating Al Qaeda (The Base.)

As with all definitions, a major risk lies in the concretization or freezing of a term or phenomenon for all time. Yet the striking fact of the Islamist world is its very dynamism and pace of evolution, the range of discussions it maintains, and its use of new terminology and political concepts. Twenty-five years ago, for example, there were serious doubts among Islamists about whether democracy was at all compatible with Islam. Today that debate is largely over; only a small group of Islamists now believe that democracy contradicts Islam; the majority embraces it. (They may differ about precisely how democracy and its institutions should be constituted.) And again, it tends to be those who instinctively fear the power of the Muslim world and any power it may wield who insist on essentialist and unchanging definitions of what Islamism is; they quote passages from the Qur'an as if they were the clinching argument to what Islam is all about. Yet these observers should instead look at what Muslims actually say and do in their practice.

The phenomenon of Islamist evolution arises most vividly, for example, with the Justice and Progress Party (*Adalet ve Kalkınma Partisi* or AKP) in Turkey. Its leading figures all come out of an earlier, more orthodox series of

Islamist parties (although all rather moderate by Muslim-world standards). Some refer to the AKP as a party with Islamist roots. But the AKP has since evolved through the forge of political experience into a highly moderate party—some would say no longer even Islamist. An interesting debate revolves around that very question as to whether it still can be considered Islamist. Still, whatever the exact term used, any broad-spectrum definition of Islamism must capture this party too within its very dynamic of gradual change, increasing moderation, and greater breadth and sophistication of outlook. It is a key argument among numerous observers of Islamist movements, me included, that we cannot deny the possibility or even probability of just such an evolution among many Islamist groups.

Thus, extremism is not a defining characteristic of Islamism but merely one end of the Islamist spectrum. If Islamist organizations evolve and moderate through political experience into newer, more moderate and pragmatic organizations, we cannot suddenly deny their Islamist character, however moderate and evolved. Such a process of moderation is part of the very dynamic of evolution. (Evolution in the direction of greater radicalism, as the Taliban did before 9/11, is also possible, although less common.)

All of this has direct political and policy ramifications. If we deny the very real possibility of Islamist evolution in the direction of greater moderation and pragmatism, then we close the door to dealing with Islamism. At that point we are instead launched into a "Long War" or a "World War IV" with Islamism so regularly invoked by neoconservatives and hawks in Washington. The "enemy," by definition, then becomes implacable and unchanging; there is no alternative but to circle the wagons.

Finally it is important to understand that Islamism increasingly has less to do with religion and more to do with other political, economic, and social imperatives. In its behavior vis-à-vis the West, Islamism basically behaves more like *nationalism* than a religion. Ethnic nationalisms, such as Arab and Persian, of course exist right across the Muslim world. But in the face of overwhelming Western and now American military power in the Muslim world, does it not make more sense for Muslims to make common cause under a broader banner? Arab nationalism may be potent, but an appeal to Islam itself conjures with a higher calling; it invokes a flag that can inspire and unite a vast body of people to resist the Western invader. Why should the Muslim world not respond by framing their resistance struggle in the highest, most transcendental and moral civilizational terms possible?

As long as Western policies maintain a high degree of political and military intervention in the Muslim world, we can be certain that some ideological vehicle for response to that challenge will predictably emerge. If that vehicle is not Islam, then some other ideology will replace it to carry on the anti-Western resistance struggle. Islamism—at least in its dealings with the West—is the *response* to, and not the *cause* of, Western interventionism.

The reality is that Islamism represents a phenomenon that today has no serious political rival in the Muslim world. It will be with us for a long time to come. It will only begin to fade as the leading ideology when elements of it patently fail to meet their mission. But of course, denied public office, Islamists and their ideas remain untried and therefore enjoy indefinite immunity from being faulted for failure. Only when they are tested in office and demonstrate either success or failure—some measure of responsibility and accountability—will these movements ultimately rise or fall. (In Turkey's case, they have risen through political success in ruling.)

We therefore require a term to grasp the concept of an Islamist spectrum that is in constant motion and evolution. If analysts don't like the term for this broad spectrum, then they can create another. What is important is that the *spectrum* be captured by some single neutral term. Other terms are then required to describe various places along that spectrum: *violent, radical, quietist, democratic, reformist, moderate, pragmatic, ideological*—whatever. But in the absence of a term to describe the full spectrum of the Islamist phenomenon we in effect close our minds analytically to the encouraging evolution of Islamism in more positive directions. These movements are not likely to become more pro-American, but they can become more pragmatic and open to interaction.

TERMINOLOGICAL PROBLEMS FOR MUSLIM LIVES

Amir Hussain

> To turn insults into strengths, whigs, tories, Blacks all chose to
> wear with pride the names they were given in scorn; likewise,
> our mountain-climbing, prophet-motivated solitary is to be the
> medieval baby-frightener, the Devil's synonym: Mahound.
>
> **—Salman Rushdie, *The Satanic Verses***

I BEGIN WITH A QUOTE from Sir Salman Rushdie, a colleague of the editors
of this volume at Emory University, on the power of words. As someone who
sees himself more as a teacher than a theorist, I am concerned about the impact that our words have on our students and the broader communities in
which our universities are situated. There is something to be said for reclaim-
ing words, as Rushdie's quote illustrates. However, I do not think that *Islamism*
is one of those words that need to be (re)appropriated.[1]

I am both a Muslim and a scholar of Islam in North America. Wearing
either or both hats, it is clear that these are dangerous times to be an American Muslim, as John Carpenter anticipated in his 1996 film, *Escape from L.A.*
In the film, set in 2013, Los Angeles has become a penal colony for those who
do not conform to the high moral standards of the American president. One
of the residents is a young Iranian woman named Taslima, who tells the pro-
tagonist: "I was a Muslim. Then they made that illegal." I used to think that
line was very funny. Now I'm not so sure. In the 2006 film *V for Vendetta*, set
in a future neo-Fascist Britain, one of the characters (Dietrich) is taken away
by the authorities for owning a copy of the Qur'an. As a Muslim who is also an
academic who teaches about Islam, I have seen the changes in American Muslim life since I came to Los Angeles from Toronto in 1997.

After the terrorist acts of September 11, 2001, American Muslims came
under attack from their fellow citizens. Of course, the hate crimes were not
simply against Muslim Americans, but their targets included anyone else
who "looked the part." Indeed, the first person killed in a hate crime after

the attacks was a Sikh gas station attendant in Mesa, Arizona, Balbir Singh Sodhi. American Muslims and American Muslim groups, who had repeatedly condemned the terrorist acts, were seen to be potential agents of terrorism. The Council on American-Islamic Relations (CAIR) has documented the rise in hate crimes against Muslims in the years since the attacks. I have spoken in hundreds of different settings in the past eight years about Islam and Muslims in America. I continue to be amazed at the hatred, misinformation, and ignorance that are out there. Every single time that I have spoken—every *single* time—there has been at least one hateful question directed to me as if I were personally to blame for the evils that Muslims have done.

Let me be explicit here about my position lest people think that I am oblivious to the violence that has been committed by Muslims. I was privileged to spend July 4, 2007, in Pacific Palisades, California, as a guest of my friend Ann Kerr who works with Fulbright scholars at UCLA. Ann's husband was the late Malcolm Kerr, the president of the American University of Beirut who was assassinated outside of his office in 1984 by members of Islamic Jihad. Every time I look into Ann's face it is a chilling personal reminder of the horrors of terrorism and violence committed by Muslims. It is also a wonderful example of reconciliation, for rather than being consumed by bitterness and hatred, Ann continues their joint work, tirelessly promoting cultural interactions between America and the rest of the world. My point in relating this story is that, as a Muslim, I am deeply concerned about the violence committed by Muslims, especially when it has been done in the name of Islam. However, I am also aware that there is much more to my religion than violence. Sadly, for many Americans, violence seems to be the sine qua non of Islam.

After the terrorist attacks of September 11, many of us who teach courses on Islam made curriculum changes. I used to start with a standard historical introduction that introduced the Qur'an and the Prophet Muhammad. I did this because my students, whether or not they were Muslim, knew very little about Islam. Post 9/11, my students had a great deal of information about Islam, but almost all of it a) came from the popular media and b) was, at best, incorrect. Since then I have students start by reading a book that describes how the news media construct reality.[2] Most of my students get their information about Islam and Muslim lives from television, so I think it is important to begin with how the television news works. I also use a videotape of Bill

Moyers interviewing Jon Stewart and talking about the latter's popular *The Daily Show*. My students are admirers of Stewart's work and agree with me that the "fake" news that he presents is much better than the "real" news. I have also had colleagues from local television stations come to my class to talk about ratings and how important they are to the local news.

Having discussed media constructions of Muslim lives, I sometimes then move to something of a case study. In the American media, Palestinians—whether they are Muslim, Christian, or secular—are constructed as "Muslims." I next ask students to read a graphic novel (i.e., comic book) that describes something of the realities of Palestinian experience and contrast that presentation with the ways in which Palestinians are perceived in America.[3] There is a great advantage to using a comic book in class (aside from the reactions of students who are delighted or appalled to have a comic book on the reading list). Some students still think that a photograph is objective, that it tells the truth. They do not consider how it is composed. It is much easier to show this with drawings, where it is obvious that someone has made the drawing and someone else might do it differently. From there, it is easy to talk about the power of words, especially the use of words to describe something. This helps to introduce my students to the bias in words and the bias in pictures.

My students are conditioned by the media to think of Islam, primarily, as a religion of violence. Of course, there is a long history to this in the United States. Donald Emmerson seems to neglect this in his chapter. There is no mention of the way in which Islam was viewed, say, in 1979, when the revolution in Iran presented us with "bad" Muslim violence (because it was directed at "our" ally, the Shah), whereas the Soviet invasion of Afghanistan presented us with "good" Muslim violence, as it was directed at our enemy. There is no mention of the fact that the modern American Navy was created to fight Muslim pirates off the Barbary Coast. This is reflected in the first lines of the Marines' Hymn: "From the Halls of Montezuma / To the shores of Tripoli." Most of us are aware of the connections to Mexico and Montezuma, but how many know the reason that Tripoli is mentioned?

I do appreciate the question that Emmerson raises at the beginning of his chapter, how should we talk about Islam, Muslims, and violence? I also appreciate his call for contextualization, of examining the bigger picture when it comes to Muslim lives. However, with all due respect, let me raise a few critiques of Emmerson's chapter.

First, I take issue with his opening assumption that "*the global war on terror* would not have come into existence had certain self-described Muslims not engaged in violence justified (by them) with reference to Islam." I submit that instead, the global war on terror is a convenient rhetorical device to link together various ragtag Muslim groups while at the same time ignoring the very contextualization that Emmerson calls for. Do we pay attention to the role of our government in supporting repressive regimes, or do we simply criticize the citizens of those countries when they act in what may be their best interests but not in ours? Certainly a small group of nineteen Muslims was able to do horrific damage in the United States on 9/11, but it is we who link them with other Muslim groups, and not, say, to other terrorists like those responsible for the Oklahoma City bombing or suicide attacks in Sri Lanka. How many of us remember that the car bomb was invented in Europe, by Christians, and not the Middle East? And I wonder what role we play in the spreading of terror and creating terrorist groups. The United States invaded Afghanistan and Iraq but not North Korea. It was only after our invasion of Iraq that Al Qaeda began to operate in that country.

Second, I am not sure at all what Emmerson means when he speaks of "showing respect" in reference to the work of George Lakoff. In the summer of 2008, I was able to teach a course on reconciliation and interfaith dialogue with another friend and hero of mine, Derek Evans. For much of the 1990s, Derek was the deputy secretary general of Amnesty International. For me, as an academic, a bad day at work is when the Internet is down or the photocopier is broken. For Derek, working with Amnesty, a bad day was when prisoners of conscience were tortured or executed. In our course, Derek articulated six principles of dialogue:

- Listen to understand (not to convince, correct, refute, re-load)
- Mutual (a dialogue, not a monologue)
- Rooted in recognition and respect (disagree agreeably)
- Honest and real
- Open to the possibility of relationship
- Functions by declaring and testing assumptions[4]

Conflict exists—it is a natural element of any relationship or community or system. The question is whether it is destructive to the relationship, community, or system or whether it leads to health and understanding; to stronger relationships, communities, or systems; to reconciliation.

And what do I mean by reconciliation? In his 2004 book, *Before the War*, Derek Evans gives these beginnings of a good definition of reconciliation:

- It is not about enemies coming to like each other.
- Instead, it is about recognizing, whether we like it or not, that we are in each other's future.
- It is a move from agreeing to terms of separation to creating conditions for collaboration.
- Practicing reconciliation involves finding ways, and helping each other to find ways, to build our necessary relationship on a new foundation.
- The new relationship is based on our authentic identities, instead of ones defined by our mutually perceived roles as victim or perpetrator.
- Reconciliation may or may not involve measures such as compensation, punishment or forgiveness, but will certainly require acknowledgement of suffering and well-founded assurance that it will not happen again.[5]

In examining any conflicted relationship, Derek uses these three basic questions: What do I know? What do I admire? What do I fear or hate? These are crucial. Often, we know very little about our conflict partners. We may admire in them things that we admire in us. We may also fear or hate in them things that we fear or hate in us. Think of these three questions as applied to the issues of Islam and violence. Showing respect in dialogue is not the same thing as avoiding candor or not giving offence.

Third, Emmerson falls into the easy trap of linking together violence in separate parts of the Muslim world as if there were a connected strategy or a coherent pattern at work among various Muslim groups. One could talk about the same thing, for example, with Christians in Africa. However, one rarely sees the rubric of *Christian violence* or *African violence* even though the death tolls in Rwanda and the Congo (where there are very few Muslims in either country) in the last two decades have been of an order of magnitude greater than all the deaths combined at the hands of Muslims during the same time period. There is indeed no mention of the disproportionate number of Muslims killed by non-Muslims, or for that matter, *any* reference to the murder of Muslims. It would be interesting (and, of course, obscene) to do a rough calculation of the number of Muslims killed by non-Muslims (and vice versa) in the last few decades. Emmerson, curiously, does not mention unpleasantness involving the United States, whether it is our disregard for the Geneva Conventions, the use of military prisons and tribunals to hold civilians without charges, rendition, or the acceptance of torture by our government.

Fourth, in his discussion of diplomacy, negotiation, and scholarship he makes no mention of the work in cultural anthropology and ethnography in the last twenty-five years. True, this is more Daniel Varisco's territory, but there is a large body of literature, beginning with works such as James Clifford and George Marcus's *Writing Culture*, Ben Anderson's *Imagined Communities*, or his own Stanford colleague Renato Rosaldo's *Culture and Truth*.[6] All of these books tackle the notion of "objectivity" in the human sciences.

Finally, there is a problematic discussion of "freedom of religion." There is no mention in the body of his text of the work of a number of Muslim scholars (myself included) who are working to challenge commonly held assumptions (by Muslims and non-Muslims alike) about apostasy and Islam.[7] Although he does make reference to this work in a footnote, the body of his text presumes that Muslims who favor religious freedom are atypical. I would challenge this assumption, particularly in the North American context.

Varisco, by contrast, recognizes the problem of the ways in which Muslims have been understood to be inherently and ontologically violent. There is a tremendous power to our words, particularly for the words that we use to describe things or people. Varisco captures this in his chapter, and I too will try to follow his lead of not using Islamism without drawing attention to the problems associated with this term.

ISLAMISM: WHOSE DEBATE IS IT?

Hassan Hanafi

THE DEBATE ABOUT *ISLAMISM* is basically an argument among Western Orientalists who seek to find the best technical term to refer to contemporary Islamic movements using violence to implement their goals. Their concern is to find suitable expressions using the languages of their own culture to define problems in another. In spite of all efforts to establish correspondence of meaning in theories of translation, each term in one language, which at one level has synonymous terms in another language, is still limited because terms in different languages do not exactly correspond to each other. They are translated or translocated into another language that operates with a different system of reference. Translations are not done through dictionaries or computers, but they are a process of understanding and expression. Each language has its own world and means of expression depending on the degree of concentration and the level of imageries, regardless of human emotions, passions, and inclinations of interpreters transposing the content of peoples and cultures into the language of other peoples and cultures.

The problem of applying Western terms such as Islamism to social phenomena in Islamic societies is not merely an academic one. It is also related to the larger problem of mass media, the provenance of communications theory, which transcends the focus of Islamic studies. One of the concerns of theories of mass communication is how the language used by scholars is transformed when it is appropriated and circulates in the mass media. In this form it clearly reveals the mindset of the translator as well as his attitude toward the topic translated, namely, *Sachen-Selbst* (things themselves) in phenomenological terms. Therefore, differences in views concerning the best term to express a thing in a different language is not based on academic research, but sometimes it is also a struggle involving power in choosing this word or that word or another one, to translate this meaning or that one, to push toward a special action or toward another one. The translator is not an innocent conduit of meanings from one language to another; he or she is like a fighter on a battlefield where one's weapons are the content expressed and the forms of expression. Images prevail as powerful signifiers in the mass media, and there are many familiar examples on cable television and the Internet. Scholars such as Donald Emmerson and Daniel Varisco work more at the conceptual level in attempting to resolve the terms of debates, such as usefulness of such terms as *Islamism*.

Thus, the debate about Islamism is a dispute within Western Orientalism, between different Orientalists. Each shows his choices and preferences, which reveals also his inclinations and attitudes. This is clear in the number of Western references by Western scholars writing in Western languages compared with studies done in Western languages by Muslim scholars living in an Orientalistic world. No endogenous references (Arabic, Persian, Turkish, etc.) have been used. Islamism then is a Western invention as well as *fundamentalism* and all *-isms* native to Western systems: Cartesianism, Kantism, Hegalianism, Marxism-Leninism, Maoism (derived from names); or rationalism, empiricism, existentialism, positivism (derived from doctrines); or Mohammedanism by analogy to, Buddhism, Confucianism, Zoroastrianism, Manichaeism (derived from the names of the prophets).

Western thinkers have been accustomed since the Enlightenment and the rise of secular worldviews to reject the traditional worldviews of the past, to build alternative ones called systems: idealism, realism, rationalism, empiricism, existentialism, classicism, romanticism, formalism, materialism, voluntarism, nihilism, modernism, post-modernism, deconstructionism, and so forth. Many of these systems came as reactions to other Western -isms. This mentality has been projected on other cultures, namely Islam, to discover Islamism, an invented term and concept from the Western mind. The indigenous names of Islamic movements are *harakat* (movements), *jamaat* (groups), and *tayyar* (current). Therefore, it is better not to translate but to transliterate as did the early Arabs who translated the Greek legacy, especially Aristotle's, as well as modern Arabs who transliterated some terms of Western philosophy such as Descartes' Latin *cogito ergo sum* and Immanuel Kant's concept of the *transcendental*. The problem is in the mind of the translator not in the data translated.

It follows that debating Islamism is a case of formal linguistic argumentation concerning Western Orientalism that deals with the means of expression and communication rather than things themselves. It does not touch the hearts of peoples who belong to the culture studied by Western Orientalism. It is an in-house debate that does not transcend Western discourse. However, Muslim scholars knowing the two cultures can help in clarifying discrepancies between the term used and the content expressed, to discover not only theoretical and academic inaccuracies but also human attitudes and inclinations and the degree of sympathy or antipathy toward the thing studied. The debate as stated by the two main essayists creates a false problem and tries to solve it, as an empiricist might accuse an idealist of throwing up dust and then complaining of not being able to see. This leads to general judgments on dissimilar subjects.

The problem is a power struggle on the level of language and technical vocabulary, which reveals conflicting wills and interests. It has no theoretical and academic solution. It can be resolved through "ethics of science" such as neutrality, disinterest, integrity, purity of the heart, and primitive innocence. That is why the debate becomes highly apologetic, offensive, or defensive. Every position begins by legitimizing itself by a famous quotation, pro or con. It is clear from the different quotations inside each essay that the author selects sects supporting his view but neglects others against his view. Also clear is the difference of degree in sympathy or antipathy of each disputant, between absolute sympathy and absolute antipathy. Some who write about Islamism link Islam to terror or violence, using phrases such as *Islamic terror* and *Islamic violence*. Others are more neutral, speaking of terror or violence as such, recognizing that such phenomena exist in every culture and not only in Islam. However, some ideological background appears surreptitiously, such as the Orientalist reference to the impetus for the spread of Islam as an Islamic desire for empire and the caliphate. But what about the contemporary American spread of influence and violence in Iraq and the Middle East? Is President George W. Bush any different than Osama bin Laden?

Definitions of invented terms such as *Islamism* are biased, heavily loaded by prejudgments and ideological presuppositions, pro and con and mostly con. Islamism is linked to terrorism, violence, backwardness, fanaticism, oppression, and so forth. These pseudo-definitions are oriented and formulated by security forces and intelligence services. They have practical purposes, usually negative, to caricaturize the adversary and to legitimize possible aggressions. "Clash of civilizations" is the global and umbrella theory for this type of strategy, but pejorative images and literary devices are also common. Take for example the medieval Mahound or Mahoun, a play off of the name Muhammad, used in popular western literature to conjure up images of demons or devils. Little need to mention, of course, the Danish cartoons episode. Sometimes transliteration is used to put forward some names that have negative connotations such as *jihad, jihadist,* and *Jihadism* rather than using terms such as *decolonization, liberation, resistance, freedom fighter,* and so forth.

The two essays are extremely significant. They are symptoms of auto-critiques of Western disciplines that study Islam (and that I prefer to call *Orientalism*), to answer the external criticisms of Orientalism from the likes of Edward Said. His moral courage deserves honor and respect.

Important in this media debate about Islamism is the recognition of some analysts, such as Donald Emmerson, of the need for contextualization. Each phenomenon has its sociopolitical and historical context. Comparison is done not between abstract and essential entities but between similar and dissimilar circumstances. Contextualization can even be analyzed with a mathematical quadruple diagram, as in Emmerson's essay, with three other categories (denial, candor, and stigmatization) and with two positions (yes and no). Some axes measure attitudes such as candor. Some should look for more neutral vocabulary, such as *political Islam*, or try to pave the way for a third attitude between two conflicting ones. Scholars who think and work within both the Western and the Muslim worlds and who know the languages and concepts of each are well situated to contribute to this debate.

BETWEEN ETYMOLOGY AND REALPOLITIK

Nadia Yassine

JUL, A FRENCH COMICS AUTHOR, in his production entitled "The Crusade Having Fun," caricatures a summit meeting with President George W. Bush presenting to his staff a globe composed of four axes. You can find an axis of evil, an axis of good, an axis of "not so bad," and an axis of "could do better."[1] Humor can serve as therapy against the latent anxiety inhabiting the post-modern world, but it does not exorcise evil, real evil, the one that pulls out of the sleeve of global imperialism the trump card of "Islamism" to fabricate a clash of civilizations at any cost.

In this essay, I address the concept of *Islamism* and the influence of this appellation on the dialogue between the two antagonists who now seem to shape the world, namely, the West and Islam. However, it is impossible to establish a diagnosis about the right or wrong use of a term without regarding it also as a conveyor of a concept, for any given concept is bound to have a history that is not only etymological but also and above all social and ideological. The particular concept in question must be delimited, insofar as since September 11 it has become what I would call an alibi concept that not only animates public debates among Orientalists and other Western elites but also serves as a formidable weapon in the hands of those who seek to manipulate Western public opinion.

For Ferdinand de Saussure, father of modern linguistics, the *signified* forms an indissoluble unity with the *signifier*. Hence, when talking about Islam, we must ask: who speaks and what is spoken of? Who does the signifying and what is signified? Political neologisms can be oriented by and be even more prone than other new expressions to a dialectic between signifier and signified. In this sense, the history of concepts, including that of Islamism, cannot be linear and subject to a purely terminological approach.

When one takes time to analyze the appellation within the ideological framework inherent in an international policy of north-south domination, where the Islamic world happens to be in a geostrategic epicenter, it becomes obvious that Islam receives interrogation in every sense, especially in the etymological sense. Neocolonial discourse is imbued with this conflict and adversity. That is, Islam is seen as the very expression of a latent violence inherent in religious faith, rather than seeing violence and conflict involving Muslims as having a dialectical explanation that is purely political and that takes place within a framework of postcolonial struggle. It is therefore important to question the use of the term *Islamist*. What is "the situational context," or to return to the semiological register, "the paradigmatic context" or "the syntagmatic context"? No concept has ever been as undermined and in more dire need of contextualization as Islamism then.

ISLAM: REMINDERS ON TERMINOLOGY

The word *Islamist* has been used in Orientalist terminology since the eighteenth century. Voltaire had already applied it to Islam and its Prophet in terms that were anything but gentle. Stigmatizing Islam was nothing new, however. Voltaire and the philosophes sought to usher in political modernity with the Enlightenment. What came with the Enlightenment was the ideological foundation that would justify the economic expansion caused by the Industrial Revolution, which inevitably led to a colonial system. It is not necessary for our purposes here to go back in history to the Crusades of the eleventh to thirteenth centuries, as, many have proposed, to show that Islam has always been the focus of Western disquietude and its extreme otherness.

The nineteenth century witnessed an increased interest in this otherness. Islam, which was linked to the image of the Orient, was seen through a continuous swing between fascination and repulsion. If approaches at that time were still tinged with a certain naiveté, mistrust, however, was well in place and the alleged violence of Islam was already being highlighted. Consider a few brief examples. Alexis de Tocqueville (d. 1859), however conciliatory he was toward religions (he was by far the most indulgent toward Islam), regretted the violence that originated from the Qur'an according to his understanding of it (which was far from being objective, exhaustive, or contextualized). Much more radical was Ernest Renan (d. 1892), who already cited the term

Islamism in his systematic judgment that Islam had rejected the Enlightenment and was thus incapable of modernity.

Thus, although the term *Islamism* appeared in eighteenth- and nineteenth-century Western literature, its current definition today had not yet crystallized and the confusion between *Islam, Islamism, Muslims,* and *Islamists* occurred very often. The term *Islamism* was often an etymological usage, which indicated a rather weak, even shy, cultural approach. It was thus quite often synonymous with Islam.

The current political connotations, such as the one advanced by James Piscatori, cited by Donald Emmerson above, and which links the notion to a political agenda or action, were only adopted by the advent of the Muslim Brothers in the twentieth century. It is important to note in this regard that Islamism as a designation and concept took shape in a context of adversity, where it has been debated and motivated by an acute identity crisis. One of the most powerful catalysts of this process has been colonization. The fall of nationalism following the infamous *nakba* (calamity) and the Six-Day War in June of 1967 promoted Islamism as a liberation alternative, which introduced a kind of complexity in the choice of the different tendencies of this trend—a trend that had become more political than ideological. It was at this precise dialectical turning point that the semiological changeover occurred.

This confusion was to be resolved as the result of a power struggle that sought to situate religion at the center. Nonetheless, its primary and even exclusive momentum was economical because a major factor had made its appearance in the meantime: oil, known otherwise as the "black curse." Islamism was *the* enemy to eliminate because it was likely to create a force of cohesion too dangerous for a desire for power that was no longer hidden except behind words. An all-out war was then launched, and among its maneuvers were a war of words and manipulation of consciences. September 11, 2001, was a turning point that, had it not existed, would have had to have been invented (to paraphrase Voltaire) in order to perfect and legitimize the demonization of the Other. It now carried an effective ideological instrument: the reference to the immutable Islamic identity that goes beyond ethnic and geographical differences. The manipulation of terms such as *Islamism* had become an indispensable tool of aggression meant to challenge an Islamic Other that would oppose the claims of Western liberalism.

Orientalism supported colonization but did not at first articulate a broad spectrum of propaganda insofar as the discourse was that of a narrow elite.

Later, the neocolonial expansion developed a massive and radical linguistic weapon: mass media. This influenced public opinion and an electoral base that has proved to be quite malleable and impressionable. The polls are there to feel the pulse of public opinion. Noam Chomsky has demonstrated in *Media Control: The Spectacular Achievements of Propoganda* (2003) the processes used to forge a broad public reaction against Islam, a phenomenon that is bothersome mainly for its blatant political manipulation of public opinion.

Consequently, the etymological problem is not simple. The confusion between Islam and Islamism is no longer what it was in the time of Voltaire, but it has become an inherent strategy of the clash of civilizations that was to become a self-fulfilling prophecy. Since September 11, violence is the ingredient that this conceptually loaded cocktail can obviously not do without anymore, and another term has been automatically attached to this fog maintained by a mass media that is not only biased but also exceptionally superficial, namely, *terrorism*.

ISLAMISM: CONCEPT BEYOND CLICHÉS

The debate and the proper understanding of the term *Islamism* can only progress by looking beyond these clichés and instead should be attributed to a north-south relationship underpinned mainly by economics and not to a civilizational confrontation between Islam and the West. The approach that exclusively analyzes religion as the problem is a caricature that ignores the fact that Islam is as multiple as the West is plural. The vagueness of concepts overspills as a diversionary maneuver. The caricature is even easier to pass for truth because, historically, self-centered Western public opinion, until September 11, saw Islam through different prisms ranging from indifference to esotericism, fed by curiosity and distrust, but nothing more insightful. Since September 11, an emotional upgrade based on irrational fear goes along with another one that operates at the level of word usage. Only very few circles of intellectuals and few independent academics have resisted these increasingly misleading trends.

Therefore, it is futile to try to effect a positive understanding of the concept of Islamism at the level of mass audiences. It would require clear strategies that lamentably are lacking in the Muslim world for political reasons relating to anti-democratic state powers. The best move to make at this point is to encourage intellectual resistance that explains the complexity of the concept of

Islamism by linking it to an entirely different reality than the imposition of Western political goals on Muslim societies.

In Western public perception, Islamism has become the face of Islam or, for some, an aberration produced by a rebellious and violent segment of the Islamic world. It is a trend that is more or less elaborately or subtly presented as breaking the smooth course of a stable political reality. Islamists are thus seen as the violent squatters of a society, destabilizing factors, but above all inveterate enemies of democracy and modernity. Another characteristic of the term *Islamism* in the discourse of this single-minded thinking is that it is a catch-all concept that raises Osama bin Laden to the same level as the respected jurist Yusuf al-Qaradawi and Al Qaeda with the Palestinian resistance movement Hamas. If for enlightened minds this is a salad whose ingredients are difficult to discern, then for laymen it is a real compote whose feared significance is violence.

Beyond these clichés shaped by the superficiality of the biased information, the real history of Islamism is very different. We will nonetheless start from a point of convergence with the current understanding of this concept by using the common synonym of Islamism, which is *political Islam*. We retain the primary sense of the term *politics*, which is *management of the city*, for Islam has always combined spirituality with the management of the city, and the constitution of the Prophet Muhammad's city, Medina, is a tangible proof of this commitment. It is therefore preferable not to consider Islamism as a recurrence of a political will that opposes a purely spiritual one, the latter being the true identity of Islam, but rather as a liberating dynamic force within an Islam that has always been and can only be political. Its main feature would not be violence but its existence in a framework of crisis.

Once we learn a little more about Muslim history, we understand that Islamism or *self-identification in relation to the original texts* is not a passing fad but a modern phenomenon directly connected to the period of great *fitna* (civil strife), a moment of political and communal crisis in the generation after the Prophet Muhammad died. It all started with a coup d'état by the Umayyad clan, successor dynasty to the Rightly Guided Caliphs who immediately followed Muhammad. The Umayyads hijacked sacred texts and established thereby their own official history of Muslims. Islamism has ever since been the recurring attempt to release these texts from the "official" interpretation. Islamism is this arm-wrestling between marginalized and official interpretations of Islam. If it is perceived as a novelty proper to the twentieth century, it is not because it is new but because the colonial political economy has propelled this recurring attempt from the endogenous field into an exogenous one. That is, the opponent is not internal anymore but external in the form of north-south dominion. Since colonization and even more so since the fall of the Ottoman Empire, references to the Islamic identity in an attempt to find a source of sociopolitical cohesion no longer pertains to a revolutionary internal struggle but to an external liberation.

It is important to emphasize, going back upstream in our history, that Islamism is this movement of redefinition vis-à-vis the central power usurper. It is interesting to note that since early in Islamic history, one could discern these two trends that are currently identified as *reformers* and *radicals*. Historically, there have always been those who advocate rebellion and those who advocate peaceful resistance. Husayn, the Prophet's grandson, icon, or even idol of the Shia, was Islamist when he rose against the Umayyad power. The Sufis who withdrew from the secular world and advocated the education of the ego to face up to the impossibility of living under the tutelage of a corrupt power were also Islamists. Islamism, or self-identification in relation to the Muslim identity, was so natural that even the usurping autocracy upgraded (and still does, for example, in Morocco) to recover this second nature and become more Islamist than the Islamists by reestablishing its legitimacy on foundations more Islamic than Islam itself. We can trace this recurrence regularly throughout the history of the Arab-Muslim world. Islamism is the permanent reverse side of our history and the expression of the original liberating values of Islam. It is rather the expression of a dynamic that refuses to desist and a capacity for readjustment quite natural to the strength of a nation. Current drifts that bear this fierce desire for violence should not be attributed to Islam as such but to a context of globalization. Colonialism was a destabilizing factor that marked a rift between a victorious Islam and a defeated one. It has provoked considerable dissension. Globalization with its media process completed the changeover and drove Islamism to extremes in the trenches. The dominant discourse in the West, however, has only grasped the marginal radicalism of the social movement I am referring to. Hence, Islamism was seen as this one-dimensional form of radicalism. Yet, seen from within the tradition, contemporary Islamism is the bearer of a genuine reflection and realistic proposals quite compatible with the modern world.

In conclusion, I would like to reiterate my point that whether or not a term such as *Islamism* is offensive to Muslims is not the real issue. My argument has been that Realpolitik not only produces the use of unclear terminologies but also actually inhibits the awakening of an enlightened Islamic conscience that will be a vehicle for a genuine process of democratization. The problem, therefore, is not primarily etymological but rather political.

ACADEMIC WORD GAMES

Hillel Fradkin

IS THE WORD *ISLAMISM* APPROPRIATE? This is the apparently scholarly question that the scholars and professors Dr. Varisco and Dr. Emmerson pose and answer. The former says no and the latter says yes. But of course to answer this question properly one must identify first what phenomenon it might or might not be appropriately applied to. But alas and strangely, neither begins with a reference to that distinct historical movement within the contemporary Muslim world to which the term *Islamism* has been applied. Nor do they really describe it later either. In the case of Varisco, he proceeds effectively as if the phenomenon were nonexistent altogether, though here and there he refers to individuals and organizations connected to the movement. He attacks, he says, "*Islamism*, the word rather than the conceptual target of many non-Muslims, so that [he] may end up properly with *Islam*." Emmerson is not so cavalier. His treatment implies that it exists—most directly in endorsing a definition proposed by James Piscatori. But he finds that definition somewhat wanting partially because it is too abstracted from important concrete contemporary Muslim phenomenon and hence revises it. But in the end, his revision leads to the conclusion that almost anything Muslims do of a public nature may be described as *Islamist*. With this, Islamism almost ceases to be a useful term of distinction.

This strange result—strange at least in an ostensibly scholarly context—is not accidental. For despite their differences, Varisco and Emmerson share one concern that is different than the concern with the subject of Islamism as such. They are concerned with what Americans may or may not believe about Islam. In particular they are concerned with the alleged fact that most

Americans have a negative view of Islam and associate it particularly or "essentially" with violence. Both agree that the latter is untrue and hence the former is unjustified. It is also by their lights dangerous both for Muslims and non-Muslims alike. Hence they regard their task as not merely academic but rhetorical and one might say public-spirited.

For Varisco this task turns out to be not only an additional one but the primary one and eventually the only to which he and others should bend their efforts. For him it is important to use the "secular bully pulpit" of academia to this end, though the result is anything but academic. His intemperate essay is a mixture of homilies, apologetics, and diatribes whose two moving spirits are concern that Muslims—especially his Muslim colleagues—be respected and indignation with all who might not, which seems to encompass the entire non-Muslim American world. Emmerson is also concerned with what he calls "regard." But he believes that what he calls "veracity" also has its claims and that the two need to be combined even if they are "two potentially contrary objectives." This mode of proceeding has the net consequence for the commentator in that he must address two subjects: first, Islamism or at least that phenomenon to which the term has been applied—whether appropriately or not; second, the propriety of their description and analysis of the state of our public discussion of this matter, as well as Islam more generally, and their rhetorical strategies.

Let me begin briefly with the latter. It is of course a fine and indeed appropriate thing for scholars to perform a public duty. Indeed and despite what the authors, especially Varisco, sometimes imply, since the terrorist attack of September 11, 2001, the public has looked to them for guidance in the belief that it is precisely "experts" who could and should guide them. But I doubt very much that these two efforts will achieve their goals. Indeed, at this point in time, the problem is that the public has already heard much of this before—in some form or other—and has found it wanting and unhelpful. It has even come to distrust the academic community's motives or its alleged devotion to public duty.

The difficulty is this: The public can see with their own eyes that something distinctive and momentous is going on within the Muslim world and it hears numerous Muslims declare that this has something to do with Islam. Contrary to what at least Varisco says, a great many non-Muslim Americans were disinclined to take that at face value and perhaps still are. In this they were supported by the highest public authority—the pronouncements of

President George W. Bush. But they are not prepared to hear that this "something" is a figment of their imagination whose source is their own nasty prejudices and that their concern is much ado about nothing or worse. Nor should they be.

For that "something" does exist and in my opinion Islamism will do as a term to describe it. It is a movement that at a minimum can be traced back eighty years to the founding of the Muslim Brotherhood and that for approximately the last thirty-five years has been the dominant ideological movement and sometimes the only real ideological movement in the Muslim world. It is perfectly true that during the same thirty-five years it has also ceased to be identical with the Muslim Brotherhood and now embraces a wide variety of tendencies and organizations that disagree with one another—frequently strongly—often about the issue of jihad or violence. It is thus appropriate and even required to make the proper distinctions. But it is also necessary and indeed obligatory to appreciate such commonalities as they share: The first is the belief that the Muslim world requires a thoroughgoing reform and even Islam itself as it is commonly understood by contemporary Muslims. Second is the view that such reform must take its bearings by, if not pursue an absolutely faithful imitation of, the founding generation of Islam—Muhammad and his colleagues—the *al-Salaf al-Salih* or *Salaf* for short. The third is that this reform will realize its ultimate objective—however long it may be delayed—through the founding of a so-called Islamic state or states that at a minimum will be defined by the authority of Islamic law or Sharia and its effective implementation. Fourth is that this program of reform is not only intrinsically superior as an interpretation and application of Islam but is also *the* condition of the restoration of Islam's worldly fortunes. As noted above, over the last thirty-five years various groups have arisen which disagree among one another regarding the proper strategy and tactics for implementing these principles and achieving these goals. As also noted, it is important to recognize these differences—differences say between the Muslim Brotherhood and Al Qaeda—and take them into proper account. But the principles and goals remain common. One is not entitled to forget the forest for the trees. Anyone of any competence should know these facts.

Does this forest deserve the name of Islamism? Varisco says no and says moreover that it is specifically designed to link Islam with violence. But he offers no real proof either that it was so designed or that it even has had that effect. Instead he takes on a tour of all the ways in which Westerners—even the

"Venerable Bede" of eighth-century England—have misunderstood and denigrated Islam and then claims that the term *Islamism* is all of a piece with this. He further objects to *-ism* and *-ist* and claims that this very linguistic usage is invidious and invidiously meant. He asserts that we need to get behind words to the issues they reflect. But he also claims that word choice is inevitably a power play. If the latter is simply true, then this whole exercise is perhaps irrelevant. The issue will then be settled by the greater power however arbitrarily.

In the welter of alleged facts that Varisco offers, there is at least one true and actually relevant one that belies his claims and, if he had dwelt upon it, might have assisted his reflections and even chastened his indignation had he not been so bent on indignation and on following in the dishonest footsteps of Edward Said, who tailored facts to suit his own indignation. It is that in its contemporary usage—and not the irrelevant usage of the past—Islamism was apparently first used in English by the late Fazlur Rahman, who referred in that instance to Sayyid Qutb and Mawlana Mawdudi, two of the absolutely most important figures of the Islamic reform movement described above. No dastardly anti-Muslim Westerner he. In fact, as any reasonably competent scholar of contemporary Islam should know from his extensive publications and the story of his life, Rahman was an observant Muslim theologian of Pakistani birth who was devoted to the contemporary health of Islam. Among his reasons for using the term *Islamism* was precisely to distinguish the radical movement from Islam lest Islam be identified with it. It is also easy to see if one has eyes that its subsequent usage by non-Muslims has been intended to fulfill the same purpose and not the evil designs Varisco attributes to them. Besides, adherents of the radical movement themselves are inclined to use the term to describe themselves precisely because they want to distinguish themselves from "ordinary" Muslims. Nor does the use of -ism or -ist have the bearing that Varisco claims. It is the normal way of translating the Arabic suffixes *-iyya* and *-iyy*, which are commonly used in Arabic—and for a very long time—to denote groups and movements and their members. Does he propose that Arabs and Muslims drop the use of these suffixes and with them words such as *Islamiyya* and *Salafiyyah*, terms commonly used in contemporary Muslim discourse precisely to make the distinctions he regards as inaccurate and pernicious?

Perhaps yes. As noted earlier, Varisco claims to want to dispense with Islamism so he may end up properly with Islam. But in the end he ends up not with Islam but *Islams* and along the way provides his own non-Muslim account of what Islam is or as one might say dictates to Muslims what they should believe. His brief treatment of this is of a piece with his treatment of Islamism but goes beyond the subject of this volume. But it is difficult to have much confidence in his understanding of Islam, and for that matter Christianity, because he makes an egregious error regarding the Qur'an's view of the Old and New Testaments as well as Christianity's when he says that Muslims "believe the Qur'an corrects the early sacred texts in a similar way to Christian thinking that the New Testament revise the Old." In fact, the Islamic and Quranic view is that the Qur'an replaces the Old and New Testaments because they are more or less hopelessly corrupt distortions of some originally true revelation. Christianity by contrast accepts the authenticity of the Old Testament and regards the New as its authentic commentary and completion. As a result Muslims do not feel obliged and have infrequently had the desire to read or write commentaries on the Old and New Testaments. Christians of course have done both extensively. Whatever merit there might be to Richard Bulliet's suggestion of an Islamo-Christian civilization, it would have to rest on grounds other than scriptural ones.

Emmerson's discussion is a different and far superior one precisely because his concern with "regard" does not lead him to dispense with a concern for "veracity." He struggles manfully and admirably to do his duty to the truth. In part, this is a function of his concern with "regard." As he says, "A heart or a mind won over on false pretenses may be a false victory—based on deception, unlikely to last." In accord with both, he recognizes, as Varisco denies, that "most Muslims think of Islam as one religion." To acknowledge this may well complicate things for Muslims and non-Muslims alike. But to deny it is disrespectful to both Muslims and the truth.

Nevertheless and despite the virtues of Emmerson's twofold approach, with regard to Islamism or its referent, Emmerson's account has one serious deficiency. As I alluded to before, this emerges from his discussion of Piscatori's definition of Islamism. I too find it inadequate, but it is not actually improved by the substitution of "public" for "political" action. For the fact of the matter is that there is not and has not been a single organization or leader belonging to the reform movement that does not conceive of its ultimate objectives in political terms. This is not to deny that some organizations and leaders may have placed a more immediate emphasis on what one may term sub-political but public activities. Such was and has been especially characteristic of the Muslim Brotherhood and its founder Hasan al-Banna who proposed the so-called "gradualist" approach. That approach dictated the progressive reform of the individual, family, and society and the institutions necessary to accomplish it. Still al-Banna looked forward in principle to an ultimate and most important political outcome. So do his present-day successors, as is made clear by the draft political program recently published by the Egyptian branch of the Brotherhood.[1]

As Emmerson more or less makes clear, the real reason for this substitution and attendant error is less the various and sundry sub-political activities in which reformers may engage. It is rather the fact that politics may suggest violence. Emmerson could and did argue that the two are not necessarily connected. And of course he is correct. But perhaps that seemed insufficient to him for the following reason: The reformist organization least inclined to violence, the Muslim Brotherhood, is not opposed to it altogether. Moreover, as the Brotherhood understands violence, it or rather jihad has a connection with its political ambitions and has had since the beginning. After all it was al-Banna who coined the following description of his movement: "Allah is our objective. The Prophet is our Leader. The Qur'an is our Constitution. Jihad is our way. Dying in the way of Allah is our highest hope." At all events, Emmerson, like Varisco, is concerned with the association of Islam and Muslims with violence, and this affects his treatment of Islamism.

But what of this concern and the debate about the term *Islamism*? Does it encourage or impede "negative stereotyping." On balance it probably impedes it insofar as it makes possible and reinforces a distinction between Islam and those Muslims currently most devoted to violence. The hope that one might protect Muslims from invidious associations with violence by dropping this term, as Varisco suggests, seems absurd. Indeed it would tend to reinforce it by suggesting that most Muslims embrace the reform movement and its radicalism.

But in truth one may well wonder whether the whole discussion of Islamism may bear the weight of this concern or is even central to such association as may now exist. For as Emmerson observes and Varisco ignores, the problem is not merely Islamist violence directed against non-Muslims but other instances of violence associated with Muslims, Islamist and non-Islamist alike, whose principal victims are themselves Muslim—in Darfur, Pakistan, and of course Iraq, where the principal violence has been between Sunnis and Shiites. In the latter case, are we non-Muslims supposed to decide who is the real Muslim and who is not or to celebrate the "diversity" of Islam Varisco tries to stress?

It is these brute and also brutal facts and not invidious word games that have raised the issue of the role of violence in Islam. Nor will word games protect Muslims from non-Muslim doubts. Indeed, worst of all, they cannot protect Muslims from themselves and above all their need to think through and address these distressing circumstances. Thoughtful Muslims, including many I count as friends, know that and do not welcome the efforts of their erstwhile academic apologists to deter them and their fellow Muslims from performing this duty.

ISLAMISM: *ISM* OR *WASM*?

Ziba Mir-Hosseini and Richard Tapper

SCHOLARS, THE MEDIA, AND PUBLIC DEBATE

Words do matter, indeed. Whatever may have been the position in the past, as scholars specializing in Islam and the Muslim world we now find ourselves studying, and called to comment on, a topic that has become a permanent focus of attention of politicians, the media, and the public. Consequently, we must be careful what we say and how we say it. We bear a responsibility, as presumed authorities, for precision in vocabulary and mode of discourse, whether in our academic articles and monographs or in our contributions to public media debate. At the same time, our interlocutors in this debate may well have both greater media skills and the ability and inclination to read our work selectively and in ways we cannot control.

This is the context for our discussion of *Islamism*, now one of the most widely used English terms not only in public and media discourse but also in academic writing about Islam. Both our protagonists start from the premise of a newly reinforced Western stereotype associating Muslims and Islam with violence; and both seek a vocabulary that will break that association and contribute to what might awkwardly be termed the *de-demonization* of Islam. But they take opposed positions: For Emmerson, Islamism is a term that "facilitate[s] a discourse on Islam, Muslims, and violence that is both critical and constructive," whereas Varisco sees "only danger in continued use of *Islamism* for politicized Islam at a time when Muslims are so misrepresented in America."

We favour Emmerson's recommendation, that Islamism (in a slight modification of James Piscatori's definition) is a useful general term for Muslims committed to public action to implement what they regard as an Islamic agenda; it must be qualified by adjectives: moderate, democratic, violent, radical, and so forth. We are troubled, though, by some of the arguments used to support this strategy.

DIPLOMATIC AND LINGUISTIC DILEMMAS

In the first place, we note that this project poses two dilemmas: the diplomatic and the linguistic. Emmerson is most concerned with the diplomatic, which he phrases as a choice between, variously, fact and tact, veracity and regard, accuracy and consideration, candour and denial. He finds a resolution in the concept and strategy of contextualization, but in our view this too often leads to apologetics. We would prefer less explanation and contextualization of "Muslim violence" and more questioning of its facticity. Moreover, it makes no sense to talk of "accuracy" when considering a statement such as "Islam is a religion of peace/violence"; either version of this is merely a slogan, as is any statement beginning. "Islam is . . ." or "Islam says . . .".

The linguistic dilemma is the perennial scholarly question of jargon versus common speech: whether to attempt to impose precise distinctions and definitions onto the vocabulary of everyday language or to construct a terminology that is intelligible only to specialists. A related question is whether it is the job of scholars to prescribe or merely to describe (and analyse the usage of) terminology. Neither of our protagonists addresses these issues directly, but again they appear to take different positions. Emmerson is happy to employ common terms, but is concerned to expose the baggage they bring with them, and to qualify them wherever necessary. Varisco, however, seems inclined to reject any term that has become tainted and ambiguous by use in public discourse—though happily he too concludes that we need more qualifying adjectives.[1]

The position one takes in trying to resolve these dilemmas depends on what audience one is addressing, and the wider the audience the more difficult the task. Both our protagonists address not only the general public and the Muslims but also polemicists with manifestly Islamophobic agendas: notably, the controversial Daniel Pipes. Emmerson avoids mentioning Pipes until his last paragraphs, but his whole essay can be read as designed to defuse an attack from this direction.

Varisco, by contrast, dignifies Pipes by allowing him to define Islamism, yet what promises to be a frontal attack turns into a retreat: Pipes equates

Islamism with *totalitarianism* and *terror*, therefore the rest of us must avoid the term altogether. Varisco lists other meanings that have been given to Islamism, and other reasons why the term should not be used, but we feel he too quickly dismisses its commonest meaning, in formulations quoted by himself from Graham Fuller, and by Emmerson in his epigraph from Piscatori, namely *political Islam*—a meaning of Islamism that the majority of scholars writing about Islam and the Muslim world today would accept.

More important, however, is the absence in either account of more than a handful of references to Muslim perspectives on political Islam. Both concede a historical association—in (Christian and Jewish?) Western eyes—of Islam with violence. Emmerson traces Muslim violence in historical events from the Crusades to the present day; yet his project is not to examine the causes of this history of violence, which he lists briefly as "arguably secular concerns," but merely to question whether it is religiously motivated. But isn't it rather perverse to accept the Crusades as evidence of *Muslim* violence?

Varisco traces the genealogy of texts associating Islam and violence, as well as the etymology and semantic history of Islamism; yet when he quotes Muslim users of the term (in English), he finds reason to dismiss them. Feisal Abdul Rauf equates Islamism with *militancy*—but we are not told what this means. Fazlur Rahman, according to Varisco, wrote of Islamism as an "ideology with political intent overriding theology," a definition elaborated by Graham Fuller; Varisco dismisses it as making *Islamists* of all but "secular Muslims," but he fails to tell us what he means by *secular*—does he include quietist Sufis, jurists, and theologians?

As for *fundamentalism*, the precursor to Islamism, Varisco finds that the baggage it now carries invalidates its use as an analytical category and wants to abandon it or to confine it to its original Christian context. But is such censorship likely to be any more successful than an attempt to prescribe an appropriate definition? Fundamentalism is no more necessarily associated with violence than Islamism; it need not even connote political activism but only belief. If carefully defined, it can be a useful comparative term.[2] Applications beyond Christianity have not been confined to Islam (a relatively early comparative study also addressed Sikh, Jewish, and Hindu fundamentalisms[3]), nor to religion: The term is now commonly applied—quite helpfully, if only because it defuses attacks on Islam as exceptionally *fundamentalist*—to dogmatic versions of non-religious creeds, for example, secularist, economic, and human-rights fundamentalisms.[4]

Varisco also takes exception to the recent proliferation of -*isms*. On the one hand, he is uncomfortable that Islamism was originally just another word for Islam. On the other hand, having traced the "social grounding of recent etymological-*isms*" to show them to be "inevitably part of power play" (though he misses *revolutionist*, the precursory of *revolutionary*, which predated both American and French revolutions), he finds the current trend is for -isms to be used to demonize Others; hence "*Islamism* [is] an irredeemable term, since it is linguistically prone to be negative." But this is far from the case, and once again takes only the outsider's perspective. There are plenty of recent -isms (as well as many earlier wasms) that are gladly if not proudly claimed by their adherents: Marxism, feminism, humanism, socialism . . . and indeed Islamism.

ISLAMISM IN CHANGING PRACTICE: POST-REVOLUTIONARY IRAN

It might be useful to reflect on how Islamism has been conceived, and has evolved, in a specific political context: post-revolutionary Iran. After all, it was the triumph of political Islam in Iran that started the process of giving the term *Islamism* new meanings and became the impetus for a range of academic responses such as the Fundamentalism Project.

For Iranians before the 1978–79 revolution, the Persian term *eslami* meant "Islamic" or "religious-minded." Suddenly it acquired a new connotation: "political activist." It was now used for—and by— anyone who adhered to an "Islamic ideology" and wanted an "Islamic state," both of which were still fluid notions, imbued with prerevolutionary discourses of opposition to and liberation from the Pahlavi regime. In the early months of the revolution, people, ideas, and positions termed *eslami* ranged from progressive to reactionary. Then the war with Iraq enabled radicals to justify the violent elimination of their opponents within the ruling coalition, and by the time the war ended (1988) the fluidity was gone and positions were polarized. The term *eslami* became part of everyday parlance, an adjective that followed people, policies, and ideas; for most people, it now implied the use of violence to implement an undemocratic agenda. It was a new way of thinking of religion: not as a faith and a way of life but as public policy and a political system. But gradually nuances returned, and differentiations emerged between democratic-pluralistic and absolutist-dogmatic versions of eslami. Many who still believed in the original project of political Islam tried to redeem it through democratizing it; these reformists, both lay and clerical, found a voice in the structures of power following Mohammad Khatami's unexpected election as president in 1997. Hojjat ol-Islam Eshkevari, for example, terms the brand of democratic political Islam he advocates *social Islam*.[5] The reformists' opponents had to find a new term in order to claim a specific kind of Islamism for themselves, and by 2003 had adopted the label *osul-geraian*, literally "people of principle." Interestingly, these Iranian neocons are anxious to distance themselves from those known pejoratively as *bonyad-geraian* (fundamentalists). In the Iranian context eslami remains a general category for anyone who advocates political Islam, but like Islamism it is no longer meaningful without qualifiers.

How can anthropologists or scholars of Islam write about such developments, about such internal differentiation within Islamism, without both using and analysing the very terms and concepts that we encounter in the field? If we avoid Islamism, however loaded the term may be in some current Western discourses, are we not doing violence to academic honesty and responsibility? Are we not silencing the voices of those who, like Eshkevari and other reformists in Iran, are trying to reclaim Islamism— political Islam—and to reconcile it with the very notions that we in the West claim to cherish: freedom of expression, pluralism, tolerance, and democracy?

As both our protagonists stress, some versions of Islamism do entail violence, intolerance, and patriarchy. Such characteristics are also widely perceived by Muslims to be associated with the democracy advocated by American neocons. They will not go away if we keep silent about them; rather they should be exposed.

Engagements with, and observations of, self-styled Islamists of different hues in different countries persuade us that we should not evade contentious issues by, in effect, censoring key terms because polemicists like Pipes have polluted them. We suggest that greater attention should be paid to the vocabularies of the Islamists—whether moderate, radical, or otherwise. Varisco favours *revivalism* and *resurgence* as nicely translating Arabic notions of *islah* and *tajdid*, whereas he rejects *Jihadism* as tainted by Western media "semantic overkill." Yet *jihadi* is widely used by those formerly self-described as *mujahideen*, and accordingly is, in our view, an appropriate term for the combination of violence and Islam, so long as we accept that Islamism has no such necessary connotation.

In the end, though, we are pessimistic about the potential of academics to change the vocabulary of public debate. We note, in conclusion, that the inevitable successor to Islamism would seem to be *post-Islamism*, yet perhaps surprisingly this term, well over a decade old, is neither yet current nor mentioned by our protagonists.[6]

REJECTING ISLAMISM AND THE NEED FOR CONCEPTS FROM WITHIN THE ISLAMIC TRADITION

Syed Farid Alatas

AS NOTED BY BOTH Don Emmerson and Daniel Varisco, there is a tendency for many to associate Islamism with violence and *extremism*. However, there is another reason for which I prefer not to use the term. This has to do with the self-understanding of Muslims regarding the phenomena that are supposedly captured by the word *Islamism*. We ought, then, to make use of both the conceptual vocabulary of the social sciences as well as that of our object of study, Islam, as sources for our terms and, more important, ideas. Islamism would then become unnecessary.

Varisco notes that *Islam* was liberated from its baggage -*ism* when the Arabic *Islam* replaced *Muhammadanism* around the middle of the twentieth century. The break from -*isms* however was never a clean one, for Muhammadanism was simply replaced with Islamism. Among the three contentious terms, *Islamism*, *Islamic fundamentalism*, and *political Islam*, the oldest is Islamism. It has had a long and not illustrious career. It probably began with well-intentioned motives but ill-informed views. According to Martin Kramer, the term was first used in French in the eighteenth century but in reference to Islam as a religion rather than the ideologies of Muslims.[1]

As the Orientalist study of Islam developed in Europe in the eighteenth and nineteenth centuries, the term *Islamism*, coined by Voltaire, gradually came to replace *Mahométisme*. Voltaire, who had a serious interest in the study of Islam, saw himself as correcting his readers when he asserted that this religion was called Islamism.[2] Throughout these centuries, the French *islamisme* referred to the religion of Islam and this influenced the English usage of the term as well. According to such usage, an *Islamist* was a follower of

Islamism, that is, a Muslim.[3] By the early part of the twentieth century Islamism gave way to the more economical Islam but was revived again in France in the 1970s, this time to refer to Muslim movements that had begun to become prominent.[4] It is likely that this usage of Islamist was established in English with the translation of Gilles Kepel's *Le prophéte et pharaon: Les mouvements islamistes dans l'Egypt contemporaine.*[5] Although the English version uses *Islamicist* for the French *islamiste*, it is Islamist that became popular in the English-speaking world of academics and journalists after the translation appeared in 1985. In this case, however, its reincarnated form appears as a replacement for Islamic fundamentalism, as suggested by Varisco.

The term *Islamism* is problematic for the following reasons. Many who use the term use it in a manner that is synonymous with political Islam as well as extremism. Islamism was officially defined as ideologies that "draw upon the belief, symbols, and language of Islam to inspire, shape, and animate political activity."[6] Although former U.S. Assistant Secretary of State for Near Eastern Affairs Robert Pelletreau himself noted that Islamists may be either moderate, peaceful and tolerant, or intolerant and violent, it is the latter sense in which the term *Islamist* is usually used by both academics and journalists. Also, the above definition of Islamism encompasses a wide variety of Muslim orientations and, more importantly, is virtually synonymous with Islam itself. It tends to be vacuous as a concept. Furthermore, it is a term that is offensive to Muslims because it is derived from a God-given term via revelation, that is, Islam, but generally refers to unholy ideas, individuals, and groups. In this way, Islamist and Islamism came to replace a term that had begun to gain currency in the 1970s and all but faded away later, that is, Islamic fundamentalism. Therefore, the question put forward by Emmerson with regard to the words we should choose when writing about the relationship between Islam and violence is important. To be more specific, what are the "contextualizing words that are at once accurate *and* considerate" of the feelings of Muslims? Emmerson suggests a more expanded definition of Islamism that included commitments to both violent as well as non-violent agendas would help to avoid the identification of Islam with negative stereotypes. It maximizes accuracy and consideration. In reality, however, this has not happened. Islamism continues to be associated with violence, extremism, and with backward, or at best, conservative ideas. As Varisco says, "Words do matter." I believe, therefore, we can go further and drop the term altogether. Muslim and Western scholars of the last century conspired to stop using Muhammadanism, resulting in the term falling out of use. Indeed, the same fate may await Islamism if we put ourselves up to it.

Non-Muslims are often puzzled as to why Muslims take offence to such terms as *Islamic extremism, Islamic fundamentalism*, or *Islamic militancy*. For many Muslims these are contradictions in terms. To the extent that Muslims regard Islam as a religion of the middle path, extremism and fundamentalism cannot be Islamic. Implicit in this attitude is a distinction between the beliefs of Islam and the orientations of Muslims. The former refers to those beliefs that are contained in the Qur'anic revelation and the sayings of the Prophet Muhammad and that are believed in by Muslims of all historical periods, regions, and communities. The distinctive feature of Islamic beliefs, as defined in this manner, is that they are independent of historical conditions and social location. It is, of course, possible to account for many Islamic beliefs in terms of sociohistorical factors. Many, Muslims as well as non-believers, may be inclined to explain the emergence of certain beliefs in terms of sociohistorical factors. Nevertheless, it is undeniable that there are many beliefs, particularly the fundamentals, among Muslims that have taken on an existence independent of any sociohistorical setting. The term *Islamic* should be reserved for such beliefs because these are the beliefs that are contained in revelation, or are consistent with revelation, and are not spatially and temporally determined. To define Islamic beliefs in this way is not to suggest that Islam at this level is completely homogenous. Any two beliefs that are opposed to each other may both be Islamic in the way that I have defined Islamic beliefs. An example would be beliefs for and against bodily resurrection. I would also hesitate to define these as the ideals of Islam because these beliefs are not merely stated in revelation but live in actually existing Muslims of the past and present.

It is here that we should avail ourselves of the many conceptual tools found in the social sciences. The beliefs of Muslims are not confined to that which is Islamic in the above sense. There are those beliefs of Muslims that are consistent with the revelation but that are nonetheless specific to particular historical and social conditions. For example, the theory of the caliphate is consistent with Islamic principles, but it is a product of a particular period and is incongruent with current realities. There are also those beliefs that are neutral as far as any judgment of their Islamicity is concerned, and there are beliefs that contradict Islamic ones. An example of the former is the belief in being vegetarian, and an example of the latter is the belief in reincarnation.

Therefore, when we speak of Muslim beliefs there is a recognition that these beliefs (1) may or may not be consistent with Islamic beliefs and (2) are products of particular historical and social conditions even where they are consistent with Islamic beliefs. Muslim beliefs, then, are orientations that Muslims have toward the world that contain within them Islamic beliefs (both undetermined and determined by social conditions) as well as extra- and un-Islamic ones. It is to such orientations that we may apply the terms *ideology* and *utopia*. My own preference is to use these terms in the sense given to them by the Hungarian-born German sociologist Karl Mannheim. Ideology refers to thought that is so interest-bound to a situation, the real conditions of society are concealed or obscured by the collective unconscious of a given group and the given order stabilized.[7] Utopian thought, however, refers to that which is not capable of correctly diagnosing an existing condition of society because those doing the thinking are not at all concerned with what really exists; rather, in their thinking they seek to change the situation that exists. Their thought is never a diagnosis of the situation; it can only be used as a direction for action.[8]

When we think in terms of ideological and utopian orientations, Islamism disappears. What is often thought of as constituting Islamism in its broader definition can be reconstituted in terms of a variety of ideological and utopian orientations such as traditionalism and modernism. What is referred to as the violent dimension of Islamism is really a form of modernism. Modernism refers to orientations that tend to neglect the centuries-old tradition of Muslim learning and cultural development. There are, broadly speaking, two streams within the modernist orientation, that is, *accomodationism* and extremism. For the accomodationists, Islam should inform public life, but it is interpreted as being congruent with Western systems and ideologies such as democracy. They advocate a return to the Qur'an and Sunna to find new interpretations compatible with modern times. The other stream within modernism is the extremist one.

Modernist extremists share with the accomodationists the relative neglect of tradition in that they limit the sources of authority to the Qur'an and Sunna. They are, however, far less accepting of Western systems and ideologies and adopt an intolerant stance toward Muslims who disagree with them. An example of an extremist orientation is the thought associated with the Wahhabi social movement (Arabic: *al-Wahhabiyya*). The main traits of extremism include the following:

- Intolerance of others, particularly Muslims who disagree with their orientations
- Over-emphasis on rules and regulations at the expense of spirituality
- Forbidding beliefs and practices allowed by the majority of Muslims
- Non-contextual/non-historical interpretation of Qur'an and hadith
- Literalism in the interpretation of texts

The founder of the Wahhabi orientation, Muhammad ibn Abd al-Wahhab saw himself as returning the Arabs to the true monotheistic teachings of Islam. In his time, the veneration of not only saints but also trees and other objects was common. These were all manifestations of unbelief (*kufr*) and polytheism (*shirk*), and Ibn Abd al-Wahhab saw his role as rooting these practices out by emphasizing the unity of God and returning the people to the true beliefs and practices of Islam. He enforced rules and punishments considered excessive even by the people of his own village, Uyayna. These included the public stoning to death of a women accused of adultery.

The problem with what is often understood as Islamism, therefore, is not that it is political but that it suffers from the traits enumerated above, that is, what I am calling its modernist orientation. The usefulness of talking in terms of orientations rather than Islamism is that it deflects attention away from Islam as a *din* (religion) to the ideologies and utopias created by Muslims. Is that not, after all, the problem?

There is yet another reason to reject the term *Islamism*. If we were to use a more social scientific term such as *modernist extremism* and inquire about what this extremism is, we would not be able to get a satisfactory answer without referring to the way in which Muslims themselves have conceptualized extremism. Examples are the concepts of *ghuluw* (often translated as zealotry) and *hashwiyyah* (deformism, which is a reference to, among other things, the anthropomorphists—those who compare and reduce God to created things).[9] Related to the study of the wider phenomenon of Muslim revival are, of course, terms such as *islah* (reform) and *tajdid* (renewal). The first theorist of Muslim revival was probably Ibn Khaldun (d. 1406), whose theory of state formation can be seen as a social theory of Muslim revival founded on the concept of *taghyir al-munkar* (lit. modifying the abominable).[10] As long as there is the failure to take into account such self-understandings by bringing this conceptual vocabulary into the social sciences, there will be the tendency to view Islam from the lenses of Christianity. For example, many object to Islamic fundamentalism because it is derived from Christianity and may result in the reading into Muslim phenomena Christian understandings.[11] There is another problem with the use of the term *fundamentalism*. Muslim scholars had made an elementary error in translating fundamentalist into Arabic as *usuliyyun*. This was then related to *usul-al-din*, the basic or fundamental principles of Islam.[12] The distinction between the *fundamentals of religion* as opposed to *fundamentalism as an ideology* that is literalist and narrow in orientation is not made and may convey the understanding that a return to the fundamentals results in a literalist and narrow interpretation of Islam.[13] Translating fundamentalist into Arabic as *usuliyyun* has given rise to the danger of associating the stressing of or the return to the fundamentals of Islam as a specifically fundamentalist project, whereas the *usul-al-din* refer to basic theological doctrines that are accepted by Muslims who may have diametrically opposed political ideologies. For example, two Muslims may both accept Asharite theology but have divergent views about the use of violence in political activism.

Concepts from within the Islamic tradition remain conspicuously missing from the social scientific literature on Islam. The Eurocentrism is such that the social sciences tend to ignore the self-understanding of the subjects that they are studying. Muslims are reduced to objects of study rather than a source of concepts and ideas for the study. This is particularly glaring in view of the fact that Muslims had conceptualized what I am referring to here as extremism from the very first centuries of Islam.

ISLAM AT RISK: THE DISCOURSE ON ISLAM AND VIOLENCE

Bruce Lawrence

AFTER READING BOTH ESSAYS, one by Don Emmerson supporting, while also qualifying, *Islamism*, and the other by Dan Varisco, rejecting, without providing a substitute for, Islamism, I find myself in a quandary. The presupposition of our collective labor is to problematize the reflex that links *Islam* to violence, but we must do so in a post-9/11 world where most readers have already prejudged the answer: Islam is violent, no matter what terms you use, and Muslims are prone to wage war, or jihad, against their enemies, no matter what context you conjure.

The problem, and therefore the challenge, for each observer is the media. Varisco rightly observes that Islamism was invented to replace *fundamentalism*. Yet it was a neologism invented by a Muslim scholar (Fazlur Rahman), in order to refute the perspectives of two fellow Muslims, Sayyid Qutb and Abu al-Ala Maududi. Islamism, like fundamentalism, came to suit the shorthand needs of journalists, commentators, and also scholars. It has become part of the popular lexicon, along with fundamentalism, and no amount of scholarly concision or protest can alter media or everyday usage. In 1996 Henry Munson wrote a brilliant essay trying to show that Islamism, already popular then, was a much more problematic category than *Islamic fundamentalism*, yet Islamism has mushroomed, along with Islamic fundamentalism.[1] Most folk do not separate one from the other. Emmerson, nonetheless, is consumed with separating Islam from violence by (1) talking solely about Islamism and (2) advocating judicious use of James Piscatori's definition of Islamism.[2] Emmerson's stance reminds us of how anthropologist Clifford Geertz typically laid out a definition. Like Geertz, Emmerson parsed subsets of the definition he advocated, in order to make the single, salient point that "an inclusive understanding of Islamism is most likely to maximize both accuracy and consideration." But that argument is tautological especially since Emmerson omits any reference to fundamentalism as an alternative term apart from an evasive footnote (n. 26), full of flimsy conjectures. ("*Islamism* is by far the more malleable noun. . . . A 'moderate fundamentalist Muslim' is a walking oxymoron. A 'moderate Islamist' is not. *Islamism* is not a blank slate, but there is more room for writing on it.")

There are two issues that need to be addressed beyond the labor, etymologically riveting but analytically stillborn, of these essays. The first is to acknowledge the power rather than bemoan the influence of popular media. More important than giving journalists credit and trying to operate in tandem with them, instead of labeling them as part of the problem, is the issue of seeing how far extant scholarship by Muslims themselves has gone beyond either label, fundamentalist or *Islamist*. In the remainder of my essay I explore the frontiers of rethinking the issue of Islamic reform(ation) from within the academy, both by Muslim scholars and by others dedicated to understanding the puzzle of post-9/11 Islam.

Let me begin with Abdullahi An-Na'im, Sudanese activist and Emory law professor. As soon as you introduce the two categories Islamism vs. Fundamentalism (or Extremism or Jihadism, etc.), you already have preloaded the dice toward engaging in what An-Na'im has called "false dichotomies and unnecessary dilemmas."[3] One must first step outside the narrow choice of linguistic convention or popular usage and look instead at language in relation to values and institutions.[4] An-Na'im has done this powerfully in his most recent book, *Islam and the Secular State*. His argument, *in nuce*, is that the state can have nothing to do with Islam qua religion, for "the state is by definition a secular political institution, especially in the context of Islamic societies."[5] Yet the major characteristic of all modern-day Muslim societies is the centralized authority exercised by the state on behalf of whichever form of Islam best suits its rulers. As one astute observer noted about the profile of statist Islam:

> This rise of "officialized, government-supported forms of Islam and Islamic ideologies is . . . one of the most important developments of Islam in Muslim countries since the mid-century. The government itself benefits from this "officialized" version of Islam because it gives a religious legitimation to the state and its politics, however hard they may be on the population. But this "official-

ized" Islam inevitably evokes responses among the population, including political and religious opponents of the established regime, and these will also be expressed in terms of Islam. As soon as the centralization of state power leads to particular state-supported definitions of Islam, its opponents will develop alternative definitions such as one finds in Islamist circles all over the present-day Muslim world.[6]

Herein lies a productive irony: Not only does the state define Islam but also its definition competes with the definition of other Muslim nation-states, because the majority of Muslims, while clinging to ideals of collective solidarity, live within Muslim nation-states that compete with one another. Most were created since World War II, often by colonial administration and imperial diplomacy. As independent nation-states they must compete with one another, for, though free from direct foreign rule, they remain separated from the political and social loyalties that characterize their Muslim neighbors. And, as independent states, competing articulations of Islam have been embedded in, and more often than not superseded, the various systems of political loyalty.

Nasr Hamid Abu Zayd, arguably one of the major victims of Islamic fundamentalist or Islamist juridical actions (he was declared an apostate for his views on the Qur'an), has also presented a cogent articulation of his own plea for rethinking Sharia, democracy, human rights, and the position of women with scarcely any mention of fundamentalism or Islamism. At the outset he declares:

> It is a fact that the fundamentalist and exclusivist trend of Islamic thought prevails in most presentations and even dominates in the media, particularly since the 11 September trauma. By contrast, the main focus of this research is on the positive, liberal, and inclusive reaction embedded in the writings of Muslim thinkers who sought to reread and revisit Islamic tradition, including the foundational texts, namely, the holy scripture, the Quran, as well as the Prophet's Tradition. And so the central question of this study is: *To what extent are these liberal, reformist thinkers engaged in genuine renewal of Islamic thought? Do they succeed in challenging the negative image of the West presented by the traditionalists?*[7]

One could dwell on the definitional slippage here, eliding fundamentalist with *traditionalist*, as though the two were not just commensurate but identical. Far more consequential, however, is the absence of either term in the analysis that follows, at least until Abu Zayd has to explain the shift of Egyptian reform from progressive to regressive under Rashid Rida. The Muslim Brotherhood in Egypt, argues Abu Zayd, was inspired by Rida's Salafi discourse. Hence, "Modern political Islamist movements, which are usually labeled as fundamentalist in Western public discourse, are all offshoots of the Muslim Brotherhood."[8]

In other words, Islamist, fundamentalist, traditionalist—all are conflated with Wahhabi/Salafi thinking, shaped, above all, by a militant anti-Western bias, traced back to Qutb, according to Abu Zayd. Abu Zayd, in turn, is critical of other reform-minded Islamic thinkers, not least An-Na'im. He feels that the latter has not moved beyond the dichotomies of Western vs. Islamic, and secular vs. religious. To the extent that An-Na'im advocates a distinctly Islamic ideology of reform, Abu Zayd claims that An-Na'im remains a traditionalist! He "attempts to integrate Western thought and Islamic norms by way of Islamizing the former and reinterpreting the latter within a highly confused and confusing hermeneutical circle."[9]

Yet this critique precedes the new book, mentioned above. Here An-Na'im invokes "civic reason" as a bridge between anti-religious secularism and religiously validating citizenship. After an extensive and detailed review of three major Muslim polities—Turkey, India,[10] and Indonesia—An-Na'im concludes that the central challenge is the rigorous separation of Islam from the state, "required for the active and legitimate negotiation of the public role of Islam *in each society according to its own context. . . .* This process of negotiation is subject to constitutional and human rights safeguards for the role of civic reason in setting public policy and legislation. A minimal secularism of separation of religion and the state is the precondition for a negotiated, richer, and deeper secularism, the substance of which will include religious discourse and which will necessarily be specific to each society in its historical context."[11] In other words, the categories fundamentalism and Islamism are irrelevant to the project of invoking then applying *civic reason* to the future of Sharia within a modern state, whether it be a Muslim majority, such as Turkey and Indonesia, or Muslim minority, such as India.

What counts, above all, in choosing fundamentalism or Islamism as a key analytical category is the disciplinary location of the analyst. Humanists, including intellectual historians and linguistic anthropologists, are wary of using the term. It is no accident that Dan Varisco is a social anthropologist with strong interests in linguistic theory. Similarly, Bruce Lincoln, a Chicago historian of religion who bridges interpretive social science with the humanities, avoids use of fundamentalism, above all because of its negative connotations, and in its place he substitutes *maximalist religion*.[12] The counterpart to maximalist religion is minimalist, which also substitutes for another odoriferous term, *modernism*. The contrast between Lincoln, Abu Zayd, and An-Na'im is minor compared with the contrast between them as a cohort of engaged humanists focused on contemporary Islam vis-à-vis another cohort, one of social scientists intent on categorizing large-scale movements, and predicting the changes they augur, in the Muslim world.

I have noted Emmerson's exclusive focus on Islamism in one of the two principal essays of this volume, but consider how other social scientists, while differing among themselves, almost invariably follow a method like Emmerson's, advocating a preference either for Islamism/*post-Islamism* or fundamentalism/*neo-fundamentalism*. In the former camp is Peter Mandaville, a political scientist interested in globalization as well as cosmopolitanism within the Muslim world. Mandaville, like Piscatori and Emmerson, is confident that the key, overriding term is *Islamism*, and he uses it with rapt certainty to its past, present, and future utility. "Islamism, it can be argued, has been a feature of Muslim politics since shortly after nation-states began to take root in Muslim lands. Its political fortunes have ebbed and flowed over the past century, but Islamism in one form or another has been a consistent feature of Muslim politics."[13] Then, after reviewing Islamism as political strategy, Islamization from above and below, Islamism in weak and failed states, radical Islamism and jihad, along with Muslim transnationalism, Mandaville raises the question: Beyond Islamist politics is there "post-Islamism and its discontents"? Here he has to discuss Olivier Roy, yet another political scientist, who initiated this debate in 1992 with his book, *The Failure of Political Islam*.[14] Others have taken up the issue, notably Asaf Bayat, a sociology professor and former director of the now regrettably non-operational International Institute for the Study of Islam in the Modern World (ISIM), who has perhaps staked out the clearest position linking post-Islamists to *progressive Islam*, that is, those Muslims who "emphasize rights instead of duties, plurality in place of a single authoritative voice, historicity rather than fixed scriptures." At the same time, however, Bayat argues that Islamism and post-Islamism can coexist, almost like pragmatic speaking positions, so that it is possible for Muslims to advocate both approaches in the public square, depending on audiences and circumstances.[15]

From Roy's perspective though, what must be understood is the radical de-territorialization of identity in the modern, meaning the post- 1979, Muslim world. Neo-fundamentalism has become the leitmotif of de-territorialization. "It has internalized and addressed the changing forms of religiosity. It deals with a westernization that is now at the core and no longer at the frontiers of Islam. Conversely, it is dealing with a religion that is no longer embedded in a given society and thus is open to reformation."[16]

Roy can, and should, be criticized for his limited understanding of formal political structures, notably, the envelope of the modern state, at once affirmed and critiqued by An-Na'im. Yet Roy himself confirms the power of the state when he admits: "The globalization of circulation networks is made possible by the weakness, but also by the stability, of the state."[17] In other words, the envelope remains in place at a time when the Information Age, via television and cassettes, Internet and cell phones, permits conversations and fosters options for a Muslim future within global culture that has yet to be imagined, by either Islamists or their successors. All religious critiques of the state, as also movements to deflect or redefine its power, arising within Muslim movements labeled fundamentalist/Islamist, have to reckon with the staying power of the post-colonial, neo-praetorian state.

NAMING TERROR

Anouar Majid

READING DONALD EMMERSON and Daniel Varisco's debate over the proper word
to use in defining those organizations, individuals, or movements that aspire
to change their world—in the narrow or broad sense—through the legitimacy
that Islam, as a living faith, confers has had a rather unintended impact on me.
In cases like this, I normally would have scoured my mind, dug deep into the
wells of language for etymological sources, tried all sorts of analogies, and
rearranged concepts to come up with some workable alternative. As if by some
cosmic coincidence, just when I was deciphering my reaction, I read an article
in *Newsweek*, adapted from a new book, on why we need to name the terrorists we are fighting *jihadists*.[1] Could this be the season for naming? Anyway,
the term *jihadist* doesn't work for Varisco, which is fine with me. In order for
me to intervene forcefully into this debate, I would have to have a rock-solid
opinion, one that would allow me to contest one view and support another.
Unfortunately, I have none. And this is why I am surprised by the effect of this
debate.

This is not to say, of course, that this debate is not important, or that it is
not long overdue; the project cannot be more timely or urgent. I guess my reaction may have something to do with my suspicion that semantic differentiations through word choice will not, in any way, alter the larger syntax of the
West. Drain the bathwater, if you will, but the baby will still be wrapped in the
ominous color of green. There was no *Islamism* (in the sense proposed by
Emmerson) in the Middle Ages; there was none in the early days of America;
and there was certainly nothing of the sort when the Europeans rolled their
artillery across the vast landscape of Islam in the early twentieth century. Yet

in each case the enemy remained one and the same. Islamism, in its contemporary sense, was no problem at all when it appeared to challenge Arab nationalism, and *Jihadism* was certainly a valuable weapon in the U.S. arsenal in its cosmic battle against Communism. Islamism of this sort was a package invented in the furnaces of other wars, engineered by shrewd politicians who somehow managed to harness the power of oil and religion to keep godless Soviets out of Afghanistan. This kind of Islam would best be named *Saudi-American Islam*. It certainly doesn't feel like the gentle Sufi traditions that prevailed in the Afghani-Pakistani fault lines before Saudi-inspired and financed madrassas made their appearance. Using Islamism may somehow help us save the Muslim baby from the darkened bathwaters of political extremism, but doing so will barely allow us to account for the term's secret history, its mutation into anti-Communist and anti-Crusader ideology.

To be sure, words, as Varsico reminds us, do matter, but, in the case concerning us here, would they really make a difference? *Muslims* are still used interchangeably with *Arabs* in other discourses, thereby adding a layer of complexity to the whole conundrum of naming. The Arab designation could have the effect of erasing faith altogether, that of Muslims and Christians alike. Or it might conflate diverse languages and nations into one ethnicity, one that is far from being palatable to Kurds and Persians, not to mention the increasingly militant Amazigh (Berbers) of North Africa who now wonder why a country with an overwhelming Amazigh heritage such as Morocco is a member of the Arab League. The very Arabs and Muslims who denounce Western hegemony and American imperialism suddenly turn suspicious in the face of this cultural revisionism, as if the reality of Arab domination is something to be swept under the rug for the remainder of history. We worry about the fate of Native Americans but not about native Africans. Here's one example of Islam being peaceful and violent, both at its inception and in our own times, but such nuances complicate—or so many think—the resolve to confront the enemy, the Crusaders. This history doesn't play comfortably into the hands of Arab or Muslim detractors, either. Morocco's great dynasties of the Almoravids and Almohads spoke the various Amazigh dialects in the nation, but they also revered the language of the Qur'an and opened or consolidated new territories for Islam. History doesn't accommodate purists easily.

Would *revivalism* or *resurgence* do the trick? I doubt it. For one thing, Muslims have been talking about the *nahda* (which might include any or both terms) for more than two centuries; the *nahda* is, in fact, somewhat of an

Arab obsession, a takeoff that is supposed to happen when all the necessary conditions, including the processes of *islah* and *tajdid* (reform and renewal) are in place. Arabs and Muslims started speaking the language of revivalism only when they awoke to their comparative weakness on the world stage. Because Islam is a lived and fluid experience, Muslims may not recognize the revivalists among them. What do they have or want that the average Muslim doesn't? Freedom, justice, and prosperity are the dream of every Muslim, with the possible exception of country folk who may still be attached to their premodern (and pre-Wahhabi) saints.

The question of naming is not a problem for Muslims. When terrorists detonated their crude explosives in Casablanca in 2003, no one seemed to worry about what to call them—they were mere terrorists inspired by deluded ignorant preachers with no serious knowledge of Islam. Such people had no hero status because they were part of a transnational terrorist organization, led by Saudis and Egyptians, out of some lunar landscape in Asia. Morocco's Muslim police and secret services did their work and collaborated with their European partners without worrying about Islam at all. But a terrorist act perpetrated by Muslims in America would have an entirely different meaning. A montage of images, as was described in Richard Flanagan's novel, *The Unknown Terrorist* (2006), would suddenly fuse shots of Osama bin Laden, veiled women, some group of Muslim men worshipping in some back alley, and riots in Kashmir and Palestine, thereby lending the visual impression that the West is confronted with a crazy, irrational faith. In this case, no words are needed, really. Call the montage what you will, Islam will be to blame in the end. There is no palliative strong enough to withstand the suspense and drama of countdowns to wars against Muslims. Muslims will not be discreetly represented; their truth will not be televised.

In early 2008, a student in Missouri asked me if Muslims cared what Americans think of them. It was an arresting question, one that led me to think—once again—about whether we who write and think about Islam from the West protest too much. A walk in the souks and medinas of Morocco would disabuse anyone from thinking that Muslims are transfixed in front of their TV screens taking note of the word usage deployed against them. No, just as the dead are the living's problem so is naming the scholar's, not the average Muslim busy with her rich daily life. Such rank-and-file Muslims know what African Americans have long known—that the Muslims who commit terrorist acts and the African American men who commit street crimes allow dominant nations and social groups to extend a long history of prejudice and discrimination while conveniently disassociating themselves from their dark pasts. Islam is too much of a necessary villain to be erased from a service economy of narratives and storytelling. If a distorted image of Islam has been preserved by the rise of print culture in the early modern period, our digital age won't budge unless the Russians or the Chinese pose enough of a threat to warrant a renewal of alliances between jihadists and American patriots. Even then, of course, Islam will not be rescued. At the risk of sounding too pessimistic, I may even declare here that it never will. Islam, like Christianity, or any other *-ism,* implicitly invites repudiation and scorn by its mere existence. Islam's mere existence constitutes an act of unbearable arrogance, if not cheap betrayal, toward Judaism and Christianity, whereas the two older monotheistic religions will remain imperfections bypassed by the last word from God, the Qur'an.

Or maybe I have spoken too fast. A sort of interfaith consensus might eventually reduce suspicions and hatred and give rise to a new vocabulary. In American history, the Protestant war on Catholicism gave birth to a mere Christian tradition, which was then married to the faith of Christianity's old enemies, the Jews. So that now America is understood to be a Judeo-Christian nation with secular political institutions. Could the blanket term of *Abrahamism* (yet another *-ism!*), tentatively proposed every now and then as a more accurate term to bring all three monotheisms together, redefine Islam in the American mind and pave the way to a more rational conversation about faith, globalization, and violence? It will take Americans reimagining their traditions for Islam to be rescued from the media's relentless bad press. If that ever happens, people will find it as difficult to speak mindlessly about Islam and terrorism as they do about Christianity and violence.

Until the West actually changes, not through the well-meaning prodding of academics but through a new reality on the ground, one that gives a new place to the faith of Islam, the latter will continue to haunt and thrill. If Muslims and their allies want change, they will have to play a role. Gilles Kepel thinks that European Muslims are Islam's last hope to break away from its debilitating impasse,[2] but I really do think American Muslims are in a slightly better position to drive this change. Just as American Christianity had to adapt to the tenets of republican thought in the eighteenth century, so is Islam in America challenged to work out a compromise of beliefs, one that combines Americanism and Islam. The literature on religion in America in immense, but impatient Muslims could avail themselves of some of Jefferson's writings and America's own scriptures—the Declaration of Independence and the Constitution—and perhaps lead the way to a global reformation, one that promotes dialogue and redefines meanings. Meanwhile, we just have to write back the best we can.

POLITICAL ISLAM, LIBERALISM, AND THE DIAGNOSIS OF A PROBLEM

M. Zuhdi Jasser

THERE IS SOMETHING distinctly orwellian about any systemic effort to direct the community lexicon. Although the term *Islamism* is already ubiquitous in the public square and despite the fact that many Muslim activists refer to themselves and their movements in these terms (*al-Islamiyya* and *al-Islamiyyun*), many academics and intellectuals still say the jury is out regarding the use of the term. Donald Emmerson's and Daniel Varisco's essays are a perfect window into the growing division between those who believe the term *Islamism* is a fair and viable term and those who prefer (at times paternalistically) to avoid its use.

As a devout Muslim, I am often as internally frustrated as the rest of my concerned coreligionists at how our own faith of Islam is perceived. But sweeping terms under the rug will not change reality. The reality of militant Muslims is that they derive the basis of their program of societal change from theocratic interpretations of Islam (political Islam). I believe in a real contest of ideas, an enlightenment society where the domain of God is separated from the domain of this world, but I fear that by avoiding a term we are simultaneously ignoring a problem.[1] It is as if a physician were to engage a patient in the treatment of a disease but refused to name it. Such treatment would probably prolong the illness rather than address the realities of the pathology.

Political Islam has both militant and nonviolent components, but to dismiss the motivations of the militants as simply extremist is to entirely ignore the large body of politically motivated theology that fuels their actions. Understanding the political change they seek and their desire to implement theocracy cannot be dealt with if it is not named. Avoiding the term *political*

Islam or *Islamism* allows the theocrats to remain without critique. The militants not labeled as *Islamists* thrive in an environment where political Islam in the West is protected from critique. Its advocates have benefited from a discourse that simply addresses militancy and is not about theology, or more important, theocracy.

How are Muslims who do not believe in political Islam (Islamism) to engage the followers of political Islam without debating the theological bases of their motivations? Many Muslims, such as the members of my family, who came to the West seeking religious freedom in fact believe that individuals are far more truly *Muslim* living in liberal secular democracies since their faith practices are all derived from free will rather than coercion of the collective body politic. Liberal democracies which truly respect individual rights based in universal religious freedom allow for a personal expression of Islamic practice which is far more real than in an Islamist theocracy that abrogates religious freedom for Muslims and non-Muslims alike.[2] No matter how democratic the scriptural exegesis of those who advocate Islamist governance might be, at the end of the day citizens of other faiths living under Islamist control are given their freedoms not at the behest of reason and natural law but at the behest of the interpretation of Islamic law by Muslims.[3] The same is true for Muslims. Their freedoms in the Islamic state are not inalienable from God but rather guaranteed by the "consensus" of the clerics or "ulemaa" (scholars) chosen in this oligarchy to interpret Islam for the nation (or the *ummah)*. A core debate about these issues needs cultivation within the Muslim community.

I can certainly understand the frustrations of Muslims who see the term *Islamism* with *Islam* in its root unnecessarily associating political acts with the faith we love. But the reality is that Islam has scriptural elements and jurisprudential precedents that serve as the intellectual fodder for many autocratic Muslim theocrats who have oppressed millions upon millions of Muslims and non-Muslims. This type of interpretation needs a name in order to be countered appropriately. Islamism is that name.

Islamism is the ideology of clerics and Muslim theocrats who believe that Sharia (Islamic jurisprudence) should be the guiding laws of society where laws are made by exegesis and not solely by reason. Although one could argue that as a movement, political Islam has been growing internationally as a response to secular and authoritarian dictatorships, such a perspective ignores the ideological implications of this line of thought.

One should read the work of Hasan al-Banna, founder of the Muslim Brotherhood and those of other Muslim Brotherhood ideologues such as Sayyid Qutb, (author of the infamous treatise *Milestones)* to understand the all encompassing transnational goals of Islamism.[4] Although the Muslim Brotherhood has reportedly recently abandoned its open endorsement of terrorism and changed its methods to include democratic means, its endgame (theocracy) is still an anathema to Western liberal democracies. Democracy is not only about the ballot box. It is about a system of law into which every citizen has access. The ideology of the Muslim Brotherhood has flourished over the past century under the toxic atmosphere of despotic dictatorships and monarchies throughout the Muslim world into hundreds of Islamist splinter movements.[5] Although some are violent and some are nonviolent, all seek some form of a theocratic Islamic state. In the atmosphere between nondemocratic authoritarianism and illiberal Islamism there has been little opportunity for non-Islamists, such as myself, to engage in a constructive debate about Islam and liberal democracies.

As an anti-Islamist or a non-Islamist Muslim, I believe in a personal (nongovernmental) Sharia and many of the ethics, values, and principles manifest in a personal modernized Islamic Sharia. But, moreover, when it comes to arguing law in public, I believe in arguing the reason of the law and not it's scriptural purity, which is only relevant at home. Similarly, I don't believe faith or any religious doctrine should be a prerequisite for legal expertise in legislation or in political leadership. Islamists believe that the president and their politicians should be Muslims and enabled to write legislation grounded in Sharia. Islamist constitutions which at minimum provide for a veto of all legislation so that it "not conflict with Islam," basically enact a theocratic construct. Their foundation in Islamic law gives clerics the ability to inject their interpretations at any time over and against the will of the population at large.

At heart I am a classical liberal in my views of the role of government.[6] Non-Islamists should be understood as devout traditional Muslims who just do not believe that government should be in the role of legislating God's laws (Sharia). We may in fact believe that the most successful societies are those where the vast majority of God's laws are left to personal choice so that the free will of faith, the central "submission" of Islam, is in fact a choice made of one's free will.

Non-Islamists believe that our Qur'an is one of the sources of law for mankind but not *the only* source of law. Islamists will certainly agree with non-Islamists that our pillars of faith—belief, prayer, fasting, pilgrimage, and charity—cannot be coerced since they are founded in free will. Similarly, the other commandments and laws from God to Muslims should also be left to free will if they are truly to be about God, faith and free will over coercion. Non-Islamists simply believe that our laws on this earth are only necessary to prevent chaos, preserve our national sovereignty, and the natural rule of law based in reason. They are not for the empowerment of a theocracy or its clerics.

A nation, such as the United States, founded upon liberty and freedom of speech should stand strong against the frustrations of Muslims who prefer to remain in denial over the realities of the ideological struggles of their coreligionists. We should especially understand this struggle in the United States, which was founded by those who stood firm against the same struggle in Christianity.

Varisco and others dismiss Islamism by saying that no other faith is tagged with a similar title such as *Christianism*. But in actuality there was no need for such a label because it was obvious that the pious Christians wanting freedom were fighting the Christian Church of England. It was a political struggle rooted within the Christian identity. A respect for the freedom of religion in nations such as the United States does not also mean a complete avoidance of critical theological discourse. Muslims need to be permitted to experience and fight for this same revolution of religious freedom.

The debate within Islam is arguably the most important debate of the twenty-first century. Those in denial dismiss militant Islamists and feel the debate is over generic forms of *radicalism, intolerance, extremism*, or *fundamentalism* not unique to Islam. These are all words that do absolutely nothing to describe the reality of the ideological sources of those who are committing the acts of terror. Militants use terror as a means to an obvious end—the Islamic state. Likewise, they use Islam as a political tool. To separate the debate over political Islam from the analysis of terrorism committed by militant Muslims is to miss the treatment necessary to counter their core stimulus.

This debate cannot be honestly waged without engaging the entire Muslim faith community. To finally truly engage the Muslim community and wake us up, we Muslims must feel that our faith is being threatened by radicals as well as by political Islam (Islamism)—which it is. Likewise, there will be no way to engage in the process of modernization or *ijtihad* (critical interpretation of scripture in the light of modern day) if we do not highlight the fact that this is a struggle within the *ummah* of Islam between those who seek to implement a societal system based upon their own narrow interpretations of Islam and those that believe in the rule of natural law derived purely from reason.

As a Muslim I am taken by the compassion of many non-Muslims who want to abort the use of the term *Islamism*, despite the central position of Islamic militancy in many current global conflicts, simply in order to respect the Muslim faith. But by refusing to use the term *Islamism* in discussing the ideological conflict taking place within Muslim communities around the world, non-Muslim academicians and leadership move themselves from being external facilitators in the debate to being one of the greatest obstacles in this critically important Muslim debate.

One of the most obvious reasons to call their ideology Islamism and its followers Islamists is because that is exactly what they call themselves. Besides, when did I as a Muslim, or for that matter the non-Muslim academics and politicians, become qualified to determine who is appropriate to call a Muslim and who is not? How do we determine who can and who cannot call their cause Islamic or Islamism? Non-Muslims cannot paternally marginalize the ideology of those who advocate for political Islam as far outside the realm of "mainstream" Islam on their own.

From a devotional Muslim perspective to dismiss Islamists as not being "true Muslims" is very problematic and in fact un-Islamic. Certainly lawful Islamists who are nonviolent but believe in theocracy are Muslims but just have ideas about clerical influence upon government that are different from mine as a non-Islamist. Even Osama bin Laden cannot ever be told he is "not a Muslim." He is certainly an evil, barbaric, inhumane, and un-Islamic man. But criminals do not lose their ability to call themselves what they think they are. To control what they call themselves is to commit *takfir*, excommunication. I believe that, as the Amman Message of 2004 states, Islam forbids such practices—those matters are reserved for God.[7]

After reading the opposing views of Emmerson and Varisco, one remains confused where to go from here. It is far too easy to dissect any term and dismiss its validity in various academic gyrations. It is also fair, however, to question whether a term that exists is adequate to represent the phenomenon it claims to represent. Varisco gives a bewildering hodgepodge of reasons for dismissing the term *Islamism*. He dismisses the militants as simply *intolerant* and leaves us with no method of engaging the ideology of intolerance or especially the ideology of political Islam.

As a Muslim who loves my faith and holds my relationship with God vis-à-vis Islam as a central part of my life, I believe the term *Islamism* affords the best way to understand the real ideological conflict taking place within the Muslim community. Islamism, as I see it, is not a nuanced distinction from Islam too difficult for the lay citizen to understand. We cannot separate nonviolent political Islam from the theocratic motivations of the violent Islamists. To do so would be at our own folly. Political Islam has its leaders and its adherents who seek domination over global systems of political power. This domination is not just a desire to inspire Islamic morals and values like other politico-religious movements, as Varisco would have you believe. This imposition is about governance, Sharia, and its incompatibility with secular liberal democracies and, from my perspective, its incompatibility with truly devotional Islam.

The path toward modernity in the Islamic community will not be easy against the infrastructure of political Islam. But delaying the inevitable is ill-advised. One of the greatest struggles of my life has been an attempt to publicly engage those Muslims who keep trying to bring their literal version of Islam into every walk of life. To avoid calling them Islamists is to keep us Muslims from having this debate at all. I can tell you from experience that relying upon this debate to happen inside the mosques or within the Muslim community with no external pressure to do so will never work. Non-Islamists can never engage and marginalize those ideas that have been never allowed to enter the conversation within Islam. To avoid calling them Islamists is to allow the continuation of two separate conversations about Islam among Muslims, which will never begin the long process of change. An anti-theocratic movement within Islam can only happen if anti-Islamist Muslims are not written off from the beginning.[8]

IDEOLOGY, NOT RELIGION

Angel Rabasa

> *It would be the greatest injustice to confuse Islam, as a pious way of life, with contemporary Islamism, which is an example of what Burke, writing of the French Revolutionaries, called an "armed doctrine"—in other words a belligerent ideology bent on eradicating all opposition to its claims.*
>
> **—Roger Scruton, *The West and the Rest***

IF THE TERM *ISLAMISM* did not exist, it would have to be invented, for how else can we distinguish between Islam as a religion and the modern ideology that derives its ideational content from that religion? In the Varisco-Emmerson debate, Varisco states that "the rationale for coining *Islamism* has more do with finding a replacement for *fundamentalism* that still captures the extremism and terrorism that so many commentators in their analyisism wish to ascribe to Islam." I would argue that, on the contrary, the use of the term *Islamism* makes the useful distinction between Islam and a religiously based ideology that has political ends and whose adherents often employ violent means. Rather than stigmatizing Islam, the use of the term *Islamism* distances Islam from the connotation of terrorism and violence that rightly concerns Varisco. It would be naive to believe that if scholars or, for that matter, everybody else ceased to use the term *Islamism* or *Islamists*, the discourse that associates Islam with violence would also cease. Perceptions can be changed not by the suppression of politically incorrect speech but by a rigorous analysis of the realities that underlie the use of the terms *Islam* and *Islamism*.

Varisco recognizes that there are violent streams in the politicization of Islamic practice, but finds "no precedent for creating a new negative sense of *Islamism* when this neologistic innovation has been done for no other religion." His objection is grounded on the history of the use of *-isms* and *-ists* in power struggles to stigmatize opponents. He cites Adrienne Lehrer to this effect: "Thus the current meaning of 'ism' is 'the unjust and unjustified belief of superiority of one group (of persons or things) and the corresponding inferiority of another group or other groups.'" Varisco then argues that the term *Islamism* is irredeemable because "it is linguistically prone to the negative." But the history of ideas cannot be reduced to what today we could call negative campaigning. An -ism can be used legitimately to characterize a religious, intellectual, or political movement without derogatory intent. Judaism, Hinduism, and Buddhism all have positive connotations. When introduced in the early nineteenth century, the term *socialism* had respectable associations. Neither are *liberalism* and *conservatism* viewed (as least by their adherents) as inherently negative terms.

This brings us to the question of why not *Christianism*? It is true that a term analogous to Islamism has not been coined for Christianity. (At least it has not in the English language. In Latin-root languages, the word for Christianity and Christianism is the same; for instance, *cristianismo* in Spanish. Are we really arguing about a quirk in the English language or about something more fundamental?) That aside, there may be historical reasons why there is no Christian analog of Islamism. Although there are political parties and sectors in the West whose agendas are informed by Christian values, there is no Christianity-based ideological movement that seeks to reconstruct society on the basis of a particular interpretation of the Christian scriptures. Of course, there have been attempts to construct theocratic Christian polities—for instance, by some of the millennialist movements such as the Anabaptist "Kingdom of New Jerusalem" in sixteenth-century Münster[1] or the more successful rule of John Calvin in Geneva—but historically these Christian theocratic movements have been the exception rather than the rule, and there have been none in modern times.[2]

ISLAMISM AS IDEOLOGY

That politics was not coterminous with religion was true not only in the Western European tradition but also in the lands of Islam. The role of Islam and religious officials in politics was a contested issue in Safavid Persia and the Ottoman Empire. Under the Seljuks and early Ottomans, the leadership of the Turkish nation and the religious class leadership were separate, with the sultan exercising political authority and the caliph performing solely religious functions. This formal separation only came to an end with the unification of the offices of the sultanate and the caliphate by Selim I in 1517.[3] In Shia Islam, the separation between religion and state has been particularly sharp, with Iraqi Shiite scholars of the Ottoman period avoiding involvement in secular affairs and denying the state any religious authority.[4]

The conflation of religion and politics—the essence of what I regard as Islamism—really came about in modern times, with the emergence of politicized tendencies within the Salafi movement that emerged in the nineteenth and early twentieth centuries. The Salafi vision represents the supposedly original character of Islam as understood and pursued by the *Salaf*—the virtuous ancestors belonging to the founding first generations of Islam, including Muhammad, his closest companions, and his early successors, the so-called Rightly Guided Caliphs. In its original formulation by reformers such as Muhammad Abduh (d. 1905) and Jamal al-Din al-Afghani (d. 1897), Salafism was not a rejection of modernity or the West. Rather, Abduh urged Muslims to unite and to draw the lessons that their contacts with the European nations might have taught them.[5]

Abduh and al-Afghani represented the tendency that evolved into what has been referred to as *modernism*—the conviction that the fundamentals of Islam could be reconciled with modernity and universal concepts of democracy, pluralism, and human rights. Another branch of evolution in the early Salafi movement (by way of Abduh's disciple Rashid Rida [d. 1935] to the Muslim Brotherhood, established in 1928) led to Islamism. Rather than seeking accommodation with modern liberal values, conservative Salafis regarded them as sources of decadence and decay.[6] Islamist ideology differs from mainstream Islam in that it is primarily a program for radical political transformation. Islamist ideology has a religious substratum that justifies its program of action and gives the movement protective coloration (because criticism of Islamist movements can be presented as attacks on Islam), but its purposes are not transcendent. They are political.[7]

But, as Emmerson asks, what is political action? As he notes, many Muslims engage in Islamic social work, economic activities such as opening banks that do not charge or pay interest, and efforts to Islamize the culture and the society that are not, strictly speaking, political. He argues, correctly in my view, for broadening the scope of Islamism to include nonpolitical spheres. The advantage of this approach is that it reflects more closely the character of some broad-based Islamist movements themselves, which are rarely purely political but encompass a wide variety of social and economic activities. However, broadening the definition of Islamism beyond the equation

Islamism=*political Islam* raises some conceptual challenges. Non-Islamist as well as Islamist groups engage in educational and social work. How can we tell Islamist from non-Islamist social work? The answer depends on the agenda of the organizations involved. For instance, in the hierarchy of objectives prescribed by Muslim Brotherhood founder Hasan al-Banna—building the Muslim individual, the Muslim family, the Muslim society, the Muslim government, the Muslim state, and the caliphate, which in turn will spread Islam around the world—the organization's social activities fall squarely within a program of political transformation. In the end, the universe of Islamist activities comes back full circle to politics.

THE VARIETIES OF ISLAMISM

Contemporary Sunni Islamism comprises a great diversity of ideological streams that adhere to a Salafi worldview. Of course, not all Salafis are Islamists. In fact, some eschew politics altogether and make religious practices the focus of their work. They often do so because they believe that political partisanship *(hizbiya)* undermines the unity of the Muslim community, the *umma*. The term *hizbiya*, in particular, is used as a derogatory term by some conservative Salafis to describe followers of the Muslim Brotherhood. And not all Islamists are Salafis. There are Sufi Islamists, not to speak of Shiite Islamists. What could be more archetypically Islamist than the Ayatollah Khomeini's innovation of the *velayat-e faqih* (rule of the jurisprudent), a concept of political Islam alien to classical Shii jurisprudence?

Within the universe of Sunni Islamism several broad categories can be identified including Wahhabis;[8] Islamist groups within the Deobandi tradition, such as Jamaat-i-Islami; the Muslim Brotherhood in its great variety; and groups derived from the Brotherhood, such as Hizb al-Tahrir. Notice that I have not yet spoken about violence. Most Islamist groups are nonviolent with regard to their methods (although there is a great ambiguity in their attitudes toward violence, as we shall see), but they pursue similar goals and view themselves as part of a single community. References to these tendencies (however denominated) as being about conservative Muslims who reject Western values are only partially right. Central to Salafism and the Salafi variety of Islamism is the rejection of centuries of Islamic tradition and cultural accommodation. Radical Salafism presents a greater threat to mainstream Muslims themselves than they do to the West, something that mainstream Muslims recognize far better than many Western academics.

ISLAMISM AND VIOLENCE

Now we come to the crux of the matter. Emmerson properly notes that Islam is a religion of peace *and war.* I do not concern myself here with the causes or sources of the violence associated with Muslims—whether oppression, injustice, invasion, occupation, displacement, alienation, or real or alleged U.S. complicity in these conditions—but with the theological justification for the violence. To say that violent Islamists distort the teachings of the religion is not scripturally accurate. There are texts in the Islamic scriptures that can be used to justify both violence and opposition to violence. The religious justification of violence has a great deal to do with the choice of texts, that is to say, with the hermeneutics—the methodology for textual interpretation used by Muslims to understand and apply the teachings of the Qur'an.

Most mainstream Muslims and Salafis may not support the extremists' justification of violence on scriptural grounds, but it is difficult for them to refute it on the same grounds because it is grounded on the texts and axioms that they share. The difference between the approach taken by mainstream Muslims, on the one hand, and extremists, on the other, is that by and large moderates tend to take an expansive hermeneutical approach, whereas radicals tend to take a restrictive approach. That is to say, mainstream Muslims rely on the whole body of the Qur'an, the *sunna*, and Islamic tradition to develop their positions, whereas many Salafis, particularly the more radical sector of the movement, make selective use of the Qur'an to support their views.

Extremists, for example, make extensive use of abrogation (*naskh*)—which is the practice by which an earlier text in the Qur'an is abrogated by a later, abrogating text. Radicals generally consider that earlier (more peaceful and tolerant) verses of the Mecca period are abrogated by later (more militant and intolerant) verses of the Medina period—the so-called Sword Verses.[9] A U.S. scholar of Islamic hermeneutics, Joseph Kickasola found a total of eight abrogations in the approved Saudi translation and commentaries on the Qur'an. Although Islamic scholarship accepts the practice of abrogation, there is no consensus on the hierarchy of texts and the method of abrogation. Most mainstream Muslims take the opposite approach from the radicals: that it is the earlier, more tolerant message of the Qur'an and not the later, more militant message that is normative today. That was the view, for instance, of the reputed Sudani reformer Mahmoud Taha, author of *The Second Message of Islam*; Taha was executed for "apostasy" by the Sudanese government in 1985.[10]

Nevertheless, the problem of explicit, religiously based rationalizations for the necessity of violence and death in some streams of Islamism, what Shmuel Bar calls *thanatophilia*,[11] cannot be gainsaid. Hasan al-Banna extolled "the art of death" (*fann al-mawt*) or "betrothal with death" (*urs al-mawt*), with their emphasis on martyrdom. Banna argued that the Qur'an commands to love death more than life, citing the Prophet Muhammad's observation, "He who dies and has not fought and was not resolved to fight, has died a *jahiliyya* death."[12] The Egyptian Brotherhood has long departed from advocacy of violence and has committed itself to long-term missionary work (*dawa*),[13] but this line of thinking is very much alive in more radical Islamist currents such as Al Qaeda.

This is not to say that violence by Muslims is motivated solely by their religion. A comprehensive explanation of the sources of violence by adherents of any particular religion would need to take account of nonreligious as well as religious sources, if any. Contextualizing the violence by the small minority of Muslims who do engage in violence or the somewhat larger population that condones it, as Emmerson recommends, is therefore important to mitigate the popularization of stereotypes. I can think of no other approach that would be consistent with the facts and would not stigmatize Islam as a religion of violence.

For those of us in the policy and analytical communities, understanding the ideational sources that animate Islamist ideology is not a mere academic exercise. It is a critical first step in developing effective policy responses to one of the most serious security challenges of our times. Those of us, Muslims and non-Muslims alike, who recognize radical Islamism as a threat to the liberal and pluralistic values can make no pretense of neutrality in this ideological struggle, but engagement does not preclude objectivity. Indeed, objectivity is essential to forge the intellectual tools that are necessary to prevail in this struggle. For this, we need a clear-eyed understanding of the phenomenon of Islamism. Neither demonization nor denial is an option.

WHY ISLAMISM SHOULD BE RENAMED

Feisal Abdul Rauf

WORDS HAVE MORE THAN IDEATIONAL CONTENT: They are colored with emotion and attitude. Muslims perceive the term *Islamism* and its close cousin *Islamofascism* as terms originating from and laden with Western negative prejudice toward religion in general and Islam in particular. They set up Islam as the existential enemy of the West, the "new Communism and Fascism." This is false and dangerous in a globalized world because Muslims are sensitive to and detect such negative valuation,[1] which stimulates a spectrum of reactive defensive responses—among which is always an element, no matter how minor, of militancy. This in turn fuels the Western perception of identifying Islam with militancy and the Islamic reactionary perception that the West is inherently hostile to Islam, sustaining a vicious cycle aggravating tensions between some Muslims and Western societies. This cycle must be broken if we are to begin a sustainable rapprochement between the Muslim world and the West, and if for no other reason than this I support Daniel Varisco's call for such terms to be deemed unacceptable and stricken from our lexicon. Having said this, the spectrum of ideational issues referred to by *Islamism* is real. They should be properly identified and named for what they are; but named with a neutral attitudinal valuation.

Two big-picture substantive issues have helped to generate the struggle referred to by the term *Islamism*. One is the global battle of ideas between antireligious social forces cloaked in an atheistic-based humanistic secularism that, for a good part of the past century in most Muslim and non-Muslim nations, eviscerated and sought to banish the role of religion from the boardrooms of society. The other is the global religious reaction to this secularism, usually called *fundamentalism*, but which I prefer to call *religionism*. What Emmerson refers to as Islamism could more neutrally be called *Islamic religionism*. In my judgment, religionism has been at the vanguard of this ideological battle between the Muslim world and the West as well as both within the Muslim world and within the West. By using the term *religionism* and the adjective *Islamic*, I identify and name a position shared by the majority of Muslims with many Christians, Jews, and other religious believers who hold that religion does and should be accorded its rightful and respectful place in the public debate on how to build the Good Society.[2]

The second referent is the struggle within Muslim societies to establish Islamic societies that would incorporate many of the values normative to secular Western societies, and which Westerners mean by their use of the term *democracy*. It is a term that when used alone falsely suggests that the ballot box alone will cause—as naturally as water flowing downhill—the specific line items implicit in what Westerners usually intend by the term *democracy*. These usually include participatory governance; economic freedoms and upward mobility; social justice and the rule of law; an independent judiciary; a check-and-balance (what Americans call a "separation") of powers, including the separation of the military from the state (not a state run by the military); separation of the economy from the state (privatization and non-monopolies, not a state-owned and state-run economy); separation of the press from the state (not a state-run press but a free press). Within the Muslim world, calling the phenomena associated with this struggle Islamism isn't always coherent. For although Muslim political parties exist in the Muslim world whose political platforms espouse some or more of these ideas, and although the term *Islamism* may work in countries whose governments are not outwardly religious, the term does not work where the governments are avowedly Islamic. In the battle between Osama bin Laden and the Saudi government, for example, whom would we label Islamist: Al Qaeda or the Saudi government? Who would be the Islamists of Iran, the wing represented by Ahmedinejad or by Khatami? Are the Iraqi Islamists those who are bombing the streets, Ayatollah Sistani with whom the Americans have been friendly, or Shii leaders of the Iraqi government such as former Prime Minister Jaafari, who clearly aspired to a vision of an Islamic state?

AMERICA'S UNFINISHED BUSINESS

In a *New York Times* op-ed piece written in 1998, the Catholic thinker Michael Novak observed that America in the twentieth century answered two out of the three "really big questions" the West has grappled with over the past five hundred years.

The first question was political: whether democracy or dictatorial authoritarian regimes (fascism or communism) provided the better blueprint for society. By the end of the twentieth century, democracy clearly proved itself to be the superior form of government, concurrent with the demise of fascism, communism, colonialism, and empire building.

The second question was economic: Should there be open markets or state-controlled economies? With the fall of the Soviet Union, it and the remaining socialist countries rushed to adopt capitalist insights, practices, and reforms to improve the economic conditions of their poverty-stricken populations. Economic infrastructures associated with open-market economies, such as banking, stock, and capital markets, have become the way to go in nations such as China, India, and Indonesia, where previously powerful attempts had been made to engineer socialist economies. The resolution of the above two questions have forged the indisputable success of what Novak calls *democratic-capitalism*.

A third very large question in America is the religious, or the moral *and* religious, rather than simply the religious question alone. In coming to this conclusion, Novak diagnoses "the present American crisis" as deeper than moral and asks the paramount questions: How then shall, and *must*, we live to preserve free societies and be worthy of the blood and the pain the West has endured? Why are our sentiments about justice so strong? Why do we long for universal amity? Why should we trust reason? Why should we be moral, especially when no one is looking and no one is harmed and no one will ever know? These questions lead Novak to confidently predict that "the twenty-first century will be the most religious in 500 years."[3]

America has demonstrated the Marxist axiom that religion is the opiate of the downtrodden, weak, and impoverished masses to be false. It has proved that the strong, empowered, and wealthy are just as much in need of religion, and it has prompted leading American voices of our age to call for greater attention to religion—and not only in our private enclaves but also in the forum of public life. The answers of secular humanism no longer seem adequate, even to the many who tried hard to be faithful to them. Today the religious question has arisen most insistently among some of the most successful and the most powerful public figures and not at their moments of weakness but during their hours of greatest triumph. Just when they have achieved everything they once thought would make them happy, they bump into their own finitude—and their infinite hunger.

America's "unfinished business of the twentieth century" is therefore about how to express a religious impulse more fully *while remaining within the guidelines set forth in the Constitution*, especially the establishment clause of the First Amendment. And serious American thinkers, Novak adds, have begun to take it up.[4]

THE MUSLIM WORLD'S UNFINISHED BUSINESS

The unfinished business of the Muslim world is just the flip side of what I have mentioned above. Muslims have lived with cycles of economic deprivation and with political disempowerment, but they can not, have not, and will not live faithlessly: Life holds no meaning without the spiritual and existential gratification Islam has provided them for fourteen centuries.

The contemporary debate in the Muslim world is about how to formulate the ideal Islamic state. The struggle waged by religionism in the Muslim world is, in my judgment, about how to develop an Islamic form of democratic capitalism *while remaining within the guidelines set forth in Islamic law*. It is an aim the West should unequivocally and unambiguously support—not oppose—and therefore should use language supportive of this effort. Using the term *Islamism* is unhelpful in this effort for it implies that the West is against these important developments and rejects the principle that Islam is consistent with democratic capitalism.

This debate therefore should focus on developing a nomenclature as part of a discourse that bridges and mediates American values and America's unfinished business with Islamic values and the Muslim world's unfinished business. How to do this takes us into a discussion of the perceived clash between Western and Islamic values and then defining what our mutual values are that can positively reshape the future of relations between Muslims and the West. A complete discussion of this takes us beyond the scope of this brief essay, but one milestone along the way is to eliminate some key false perceptions each side maintains.

THE FALSELY PERCEIVED CLASH BETWEEN
WESTERN AND ISLAMIC VALUES

Because the West historically experienced religion as a hindrance to its growth and success, it fears religion as a cause of societal retrogression. And because the Islamic world, in contrast, historically experienced religion as the cause of its greatness and historic success, it therefore fears Western secularism as a powerful corrosive of the norms and values that comprise an Islamic community's existential anchors. These fears are embedded both in the West's attitude in the use of the term *Islamism* and in Muslim reaction to *Western secularism*. And because we cannot eliminate the terms *West, Islam* and *secular* from our lexicon, this discussion on terminology is important.

The West experienced its dramatic civilizational advancements over the last five centuries as a result of severing its ties to the church and escaping the clutches of religious dogma, which ushered in the Enlightenment, the rise of reason, and the simultaneous development of democracy and capitalism. These occurred as concomitants, giving rise to the beginnings of, and thus defining, Western secular humanism as its metaphysical construct—which I strongly believe are the ethical injunctions of the second commandment stated separately from the first.[5] The Islamic impulse as defined in this essay, on the one hand, is neither anti-reason nor anti–democratic capitalism. The Islamic world, on the other hand, experienced its civilizational apogee— its "enlightenment" that boomed between 800 and 1200 CE—as a result of its religious impulse. The Prophet Muhammad urged his followers to "seek knowledge even if it were in China" and to "seek knowledge from the cradle to the grave," and an unauthenticated Prophetic teaching is that the ink of the scholar is more precious than the blood of the martyr. Muslim scholars interpreted these prophetic injunctions to mean that seeking nonreligious/secular knowledge in other cultures was a religious mandate and avidly pursued, collected, and advanced the world's trove of knowledge during the first five centuries after the Prophet, along the way developing and advancing the scientific method.

The Prophet was also a merchant, sensitive to economic considerations and commanded by the Qur'an to consult with his companions and not to rule dictatorially. His immediate followers, starting with the Caliph Umar, did not seek to force the faith of Islam on the populations they conquered, and in fact 'Umar was responsible for inviting Jews to take up residence in Jerusalem around 638 C.E. after they had been banished from it by the Romans in 70 C.E. Islam has historically supported multireligious, multiethnic and multicultural societies.

The perceived clash between the Western and Islamic civilizations is less about fundamental values both share. It is more a clash of the collective memories that were historically the founding principles of each civilization and the reciprocal fears associated with a perceived antipathy to its existential viewpoint that each side sees in the "other."

The negative connotations of the term *Islamism* are neither helpful nor conducive to strengthening the important and potentially fruitful dialogue between the Muslim world and the West—for each has achieved something that can contribute to the other's unfinished business. The task at hand is to recognize our mutual values and their role in reshaping the future discourse and to find ways to combine each side's accumulated wisdom and positively transform life in the global village.

RECONSIDERING THE ARGUMENTS   Part 3

MITIGATING MISRESPRESENTATION

Daniel M. Varisco

AS THE RESPONSES TO THE TWO ESSAYS in this volume amply illustrate, words do matter and they seldom escape the ideological veneer of politics. What really matters, for all of us, is more than the words involved. My argument for setting aside the recent usage of *Islamism* as the way to label the political dimensions of Muslims, whether militantly extremist or mildly assertive, is not a call for banal political correctness. Offensive words in themselves are not evil, but rather the danger lies in politicized rhetoric that fosters intolerance and blame labeling. I believe that rejecting the term *Islamism* should not be an end in itself, but rather a means to mitigate misrepresentation. If Islam becomes the only major religion where one highly charged word, and one that in the past simply meant the religion as a whole, defines political manipulation, it is hard to imagine how the crusader-laden trope of a civilizational clash can ever be replaced with pragmatic assessment of how religion can at times be used to justify intolerance and abuses of human rights and other times promote peace and mutual understanding.

I am pleased that the general response here from Muslim colleagues who have no choice but to bear the brunt of Islamophobic rhetoric supports my rejection of Islamism as the best way to label extremist or intolerant methods that they themselves reject as not representing the values of their faith. The heightened prejudice against Muslims, exacerbated by the tragedy of 9/11 and ongoing terror-wars in Afghanistan and Iraq, is no academic matter. As Amir Hussain knows from firsthand experience, the "the hatred, misinformation, and ignorance" about Islam is not hard to find in America. To the extent violence remains the sine qua non in representing Islam, as Hussain notes, using a term such as Islamism does little to lessen the bias. I also agree with his point that a terminological focus on Muslims as terrorists ignores the disproportionate number of Muslims killed by non-Muslims, not to mention the sectarian violence stimulated by the American invasion of Iraq. Given the extraordinary cultural diversity of Muslims worldwide, is it logical to lump all who use political means to achieve differing agendas under the convenient umbrella of Islamism? As an anthropologist, I start with the principle that it is not being Muslim that leads to violence, but the same socioeconomic and psychological factors that foster aggressive acts species wide are the catalysts. In similar agreement, Feisal Abdul Rauf states that we need to break down rather than sustain "a vicious cycle aggravating tensions" between Muslims and followers of other faiths. The negative connotations of Islamism, as he notes, do not lead to fruitful dialogue. Bruce Lawrence makes the important point that Muslim intellectuals such as Abdullahi An-Na'im and Nasr Hamid Abu Zayd are thinking outside the narrow box delimited by previous use of the term *Islamism*.

I appreciate the observation of Syed Farid Alatas that we should choose from the conceptual vocabulary of the social sciences or Islam itself for the appropriate terminology. He places the study of contemporary violence connected with Muslims on a sound footing by returning to the well-honed conceptual tools of scholarship on religion. In a comparative sense, Islam shares with other religions a variety of views that can be either utopian or ideological. The coinage of Islamism elides the important point that the attitudes covered by the term are very much a product of the modern world and a counterpoint to Western political and intellectual hegemony. The issue here, as Alatas well argues, is between extremists and accommodationists, but in the context of contemporary historical contact and not on some assumed universal interpretation of Islamic values. In a further contribution, Alatas draws on the concepts developed by Muslims to reflectively critique the way Islam is practiced. The much vaunted clash "of"civilizations is more accurately styled as a perpetual clash "within" civilizations. Muslims have not been silent in the face of atrocities any more than Christians have, nor should it be assumed that sympathy for acts of violence defines Muslim identity as much as it speaks to the perception that Muslims are oppressed by the policies of Western states and the ideologies that summarily reject Islam as a viable claim to truth. As Alatas succinctly reminds us, "The Eurocentrism is such that the social sciences tend to ignore the self-understanding of the subjects that they are studying."

I suggest that the term *Islamism* perpetuates this ignorance whether or not those using the term view Muslims as inherently more violent than members of other faiths.

As I suggest in my essay, attention needs to be paid to the reasons Muslim scholars reject the term. Alatas adds to this by noting that Islamism "is a term that is offensive to Muslims because it is derived from a God-given term via revelation." Were *Judaism* to be reserved solely for Masada-style warriors or *Christianism* coined for both Catholic and Protestant combatants in the recent political tragedy of Northern Ireland, I suspect that devout Jews and Christians would, respectively, be offended and rightfully so. None of the respondents are calling for a return to the misconceived notion of *Muhammadanism*, so why should rejection of Islamism be ignored when Muslims affected by misuse of the term find it similarly objectionable? Nadia Yassine, in her eloquent exposé of European colonial abuse of Islamic countries, concludes that whether or not the term *Islamism* is offensive to Muslims is not the real issue. I agree that the impact of word use is only the surface issue; the deeper structural problem is the way in which people react to the use of words. Yassine is right to quote de Saussure and then ask, "Hence, when talking about Islam, we must ask: Who speaks and what is spoken of?" The "who" behind the recent etymological spin of Islamism are not Muslims coming to terms with actions of fellow Muslims, but mostly they are Western non-Muslims looking for a way to describe an anti-Western attitude that many Muslims, as Yassine shows, understandably agree with. The "what" is an indelible link between one of the world's major religions and forms of violence that threaten the allegedly secular basis of modernity. Islamism should be abandoned not simply because it is offensive to many Muslims but also for the justifiable reasons that Muslims find it offensive.

One of the main criticisms of my argument is that I am naive to assume that rejecting a term solves the problem of prejudice. Angel Rabasa comments, "Perceptions can be changed not by the suppression of politically incorrect speech but by a rigorous analysis of the realities that underlie the use of the terms *Islam* and *Islamism*." I think all of the commentators would agree on the second part of this statement; the issue is never simply one of word choice. This is the point of my closing remark that I am not advocating a pedantic footnote. It would be foolish to call for suppression of the term in the media or by pundits, who often find rhetorical value in its supposed ambiguity. My point is to question the heuristic value of the term, asking why we need a single term that equates Islam and violence when no such term exists for any other religion. The term *Islamism* has been reinvented; it already existed and its trajectory of ideological baggage is hard to disguise. Yassine, in her response, shows how the negative view was inherent even in the eighteenth- and nineteenth-century uses of Islamism in European languages. The linguistic argument, which is a secondary rather than a primary support for my rejection of the term, is that most recent *-isms* tend to connote negativity. Because Judaism, *Hinduism*, and *Buddhism* all have theoretically neutral denotations, the question must be asked why Islamism should be the only exception.

Rabasa offers a confused view of the history of Christianity in claiming that "there is no Christianity-based ideological movement that seeks to reconstruct society on the basis of a particular interpretation of the Christian scriptures." Not only have such movements left a bloody sectarian legacy in Europe, but a number of contemporary Christian sects attempt to do exactly this. Although most of these groups are marginal, such as the Branch Davidians involved in the 1993 Waco, Texas tragedy, accommodating sects such as the Mormons and Jehovah Witnesses promote their unique perspectives on salvation and apocalypse through missionary activities to the entire world. Complementing Rabasa's utopian view of Christendom is the assumption that Muslims have always acted as Sharia robots. As Richard Bulliet explains, in Europe clerics were usually co-opted or manipulated to support authoritarian regimes, whereas in Muslim areas it was the role of the scholarly elite (ulema) to resist despotism and corruption.[1] Many of the great Muslim jurists were imprisoned or lost their heads precisely because they resisted the excesses of rulers, even those claiming to be commanders of the faithful.

As Rabasa notes, what is called Islamism today, including the Salafi movements, is a modern phenomenon. This is not to ignore the fact that the sacred texts of Islam have always been interpreted by some to justify violence against non-Muslims and fellow Muslims. But I do not think this makes refutation of extremism difficult for other Muslims because "it is grounded on the texts and axioms that they share." As the history of hermeneutics in both Judaism and Christianity attests, it is never the case that a sacred text has a single unimpeachable meaning. The spirited debate within the Islamic tradition of *tafsir* interpretation and hadith analysis shows that disagreement need not always result in violent opposition. The extant Sunni legal traditions can coexist precisely because they represent attempts at making sense of a common text. It is only when an existing textual rendition is rejected, as some Muslims do in abrogating certain passages in the Qur'an or denigrating the Torah and New Testament, that reconciliation becomes virtually impossible. But, as Yassine observes, it is a compote of violence to suggest that Bin Laden and Yusuf al-Qaradawi or Al Qaeda and Hamas can be disposed of with a single term, as though the only thing that matters is their anti-Western stance rather than the way they act upon it or the motivating factors.

Hillel Fradkin shares a central problem with the response of Rabasa: the underlying assumption that the greatest threat to mutual coexistence today is some concrete object definable as radical Islam and that any attempt to go beyond religious labels to motivating factors that transcend any particular faith is "wanting and unhelpful." "Anyone of any competence," claims Fradkin, after dismissing my essay as ad hominen, should know the list of facts he rattles off as so obvious that there is no need for discussion. First, as any scholar who seriously studies the history of Islam continually discovers, there has been a call for reform within Islam since the inception of the faith; it did not start with the Brothers. The only ideal Islamic state in the minds of most Muslims is the *umma* that existed at the time of the Prophet Muhammad. Second, recognizing the Prophet and his companions as sources of inspiration and guidance is paradigmatic, but differing opinions have always existed, evidenced demonstrably by the need to codify sound traditions more than a century after Muhammad's death. Third, the ideal of a particular political form of Islamic state is not set out in the Qur'an, nor have the numerous dynasties ruling in the name of Islam ever created such a utopia. Fourth, the vast majority of Muslims pragmatically recognize the diversity of political arrangements existing today. Indonesia is not Saudi Arabia. Indeed, it is the despotism supported in large part by Western powers that fuels Muslim fears more than a desire to turn back the clock to seventh-century Arabia. All so-called Islamists do not share such an outside view of their alleged agenda. Neither Hamas nor Hizbullah seek a caliph crowned in the New Mecca or old Kabul, but they were formed to resist Israeli political occupation in Palestine and Lebanon. In this sense they share more with Irish Catholic resistance in Northern Ireland than Osama bin Laden's benighted banter for a caliphate under the banner of Mullah Omar.

An author should be pleased to be corrected of any "egregious error" made in the course of an argument, but egregiousness is only compounded when the error is in the mind of the diatribalist. Contrary to Fradkin's translation lesson, the Arabic *-iyya* and *-iyy* endings do not automatically becomes *-ists*.

Thus, my Yemeni friend may be a *Yemenite* but never a *Yemenist*. *Sunni* does not deform into *Sunnist*, nor *Shiite* into *Shi-ist*. Although tangential to my argument, it is important to reiterate that Islamic teaching views Muhammad's message as the Seal of the prophets, not a totally new revelation. Thus, Adam, Noah, Abraham, and even Jesus had submitted to the one God, and Muslims consider them fellow Muslims, as Muhammad validated in his journey through the seven heavens. The Qur'an is said to correct the existing Jewish and Christian scriptures, but those who follow these sacred texts, even if in error, are allowed to maintain their faith as People of the Book. Contrary to Fradkin's casual assumption, most Christians do not believe that the existing manuscripts of the Bible are inerrant originals, even those Baptists who still believe Moses wrote the original Torah. Mainstream denominations accept a literary critical analysis of the Old Testament. The point is that in both cases the newer religions, Christianity and Islam, follow a continuing revelation from the same God of Abraham, but one that charts a new course and defines itself as closer to the divine plan.

My original essay was written as a stand-alone argument rather than a counterpoint to the essay by Don Emmerson; both were originally presented side by side at a conference. I respect Emmerson's attempt to probe the meanings behind usage of the term. His stated purpose not to "endorse a particular vocabulary" but to "illuminate the larger contexts in which word choices take place" shares the same goal as my own essay. We both agree that the term *Islamism* should not be linked exclusively with political violence and militancy. Emmerson provides an alternative way of conceptualizing political or public action by Muslims, but in the end he concedes that his strategy requires an "Islamism with adjectives." I reach the same conclusion about the need to go beyond one overarching term to specify the various ways in which Muslims promote political agendas as Muslims. He makes an important point about the semantic shift between citing "Islamic terrorists" and "Muslim terrorists," the former ordaining violence and the latter connoting "a researchable range of other possible motivations."

I agree with Emmerson that the coinage of *Islams* is problematic, but only because of the capital *I* here. I do think there is merit in the distinction proposed by Abdul Hamid El Zein three decades ago that we can distinguish Islam in the abstract sense from the lived *islams* with the small semantic *i* allowed in English. It is not just that individual Muslims vary in practice; for the critical historian there is no one set of universally agreed-upon beliefs called Islam in the quotidian pace of daily life over fourteen centuries. It is for the believer to determine what makes Islam real, but this does not stop those on the outside from recognizing multiple islams with clear distinctions that override the commonality of central doctrine. Osama bin Laden is not Yusuf al-Qaradawi, nor is he King Fahd, nor a Manhattan taxi driver named Ahmed. I suggest individual Muslims follow differing and at times oppositional islams that neither Islam nor Islamism can fairly evaluate as uniform terms.

The major problem I have with Emmerson's laudable attempt to rethink the conceptual depth of terminology used to identify a link between Muslims and violent actions is the serviceability of the term *Islamism*. If, following James Piscatori, the minimal definition of this word comprises "Muslims who are committed to political action to implement what they regard as an Islamic agenda," then there is still an elephant thundering through the rhetoric. That elephant is the association, indelibly linked in Western representation, of violence as the modus vivendi of Muslim political action. Graham Fuller attempts to salvage the term by offering the broad view that anyone who thinks the Qur'an and traditions are relevant to the contemporary context is an Islamist. Because every historical context, including the origin of the faith, is contemporary at some point, then Islamism could cover the entire history of Islam. Political use of sacred texts in Islam did not begin with the Muslim Brothers; the entire evolution of the Sharia is evidence of adapting Qur'anic passages and prophetic traditions to everyday Muslim life and politics. But such usage denies all nuances. Surely both the Iraqi Prime Minister Nuri al-Maliki and Muqtada al-Sadr are each engaged in political actions as Muslims. If both are to be styled Islamists, what is gained apart from less (or more) respect for al-Maliki by most Western observers? One might as well say that *Communists* are those committed to political action to implement what they regard as a Communist agenda. Not all Communists use violent means, but the rhetoric of the Cold War has so damaged the nature of their political action that there can effectively be no good Communists in the West. Ironically, not only have Islamists become the green menace replacing the enemy status of the Soviet red menace, but Muslims now find themselves "black-isted" even before they act.

Abdul Rauf is right to observe that the perceived clash between Western and Islamic civilizations is "less about fundamental values both share" and "more a clash of the collective memories." Anouar Majid points out that there was no Islamism when the United States supported the mujahideen fighters in

Afghanistan against the Soviets. Like Abdul Rauf, Majid conjures up the collective Muslim memories of always bearing the brunt of Western representation, seemingly resigned to an eternal standoff between Islam as the arrogant newcomer and the "two older monotheistic religions" as imperfections wielding secular power to the disadvantage of Muslims. But stepping back from the brink, he sees a glimmer of hope that America may be the place where Islam can be reimagined along the lines of reforming the sectarian squabble between Catholic and Protestant or, indeed, between Jew and Christian. I agree that this will not come about merely through the "well-meaning prodding of academics" such as myself or Don Emmerson but only if tolerance in practice trumps the memories of past sins. But I still have a role to play, both as an academic who writes about Islam and Muslims and as a citizen concerned about the rhetoric I hear daily that allows no space for Muslims to be seen as tolerant. Hasan Hanafi dismisses our debate over terms as an "in-house" Orientalist game that "does not touch the hearts" of the people defined. He misses the deeper problem: that people who link Islam and violence have pushed an agenda that abuses and kills Muslims. I reject the negative baggage that taints the term *Islamism* and insist that there is no need for one term in any language that links Islam and violence in a way not done for any other major religious faith.

BROADENING REPRESENTATION

Donald K. Emmerson

DAN VARISCO AND I share what I take to be the purpose of this book: to encourage a discourse on Islam and Muslims that reduces the incidence of, and the audience for, a mistaken and prejudicial views of the world's second-largest faith in all its variants, and of the billion-plus human beings who, no less variably, identify with it. The same goal inspires, I believe, the comments that Varisco's and my colleagues have taken the trouble to contribute to this book.

It was in order to serve that larger goal that I spent the first half of my opening essay (in Part One) not analyzing the term *Islamism*, but proposing what I called (in Diagram 1) *contextualization* as a way of helping to maximize, in discussions of Islam and Muslims in relation to violence, two different but not necessarily incompatible criteria: consideration for the feelings of Muslims on the one hand, but accuracy about the subject of discussion on the other. The definitions of *Islamists* and *Islamism* that I offered in that essay were meant to illustrate this balancing approach.

I continue to find it helpful to distinguish contextualization from three other ways of characterizing Islam and Muslims in relation to violence: the *denial* of any connection at all, a stance favored by some politicians, some diplomats, and the self-deceived; the connections' exaggeration to the point of *stigmatization* by other politicians, bigots, and the ill-informed; and the *candor* of certain impolitic scholars, undiplomatic reformers, and the well-informed. In this fourth and final category belong those who are able and willing to acknowledge the connections without overstating them, but are insensitive to the feelings of those Muslims for whom candor verges on denigration.

Consideration in this discourse calls for empathy and diplomacy to reduce enmity, gain confidence, and prevent or resolve conflict by avoiding inflammatory candor, let alone stigmatization. Accuracy, however, calls for honesty and veracity to reduce self-deceptive assumptions, false stereotypes, and simple ignorance, including the risk that ignorance could unravel agreements and understandings precariously based on denial.

I had this trade-off in mind when I adapted and extended James Piscatori's rendition of *Islamists* and *Islamism* as follows: "Islamists are Muslims who are committed to public action to implement what they regard as an Islamic agenda. Islamism is a commitment to, and the content of, that agenda." The adjective or singular noun *Islamist* applies to someone who fits this definition.

I advocate using *Islamists, Islamism*, and *Islamist*, but I insist on interpreting these terms diversely, by qualifying them with adjectives or adverbs as needed. I do so because the interpretation is accurate—the persons, groups, movements, and agendas covered by this definition really are diverse—and because it increases the likelihood of contextualization. By opening the content of Islamist agendas to a full range of political, social, economic, cultural, and evangelical actions in the public sphere, Piscatori's amended definition invites knowledge and specification of the differentiating contexts in which such actions can and do occur. By requiring qualifiers, *Islamism* in this broad sense supports a diversely situational perspective on Muslim behavior, making it harder to use the term prejudicially as a one-word synonym for violence done in Islam's name.

BORDERS AND INNARDS

In my opening chapter, I quoted the late Samuel Huntington: "Islam has bloody borders." He wrote that in 1993. Later, answering widespread criticism of this conclusion, he went even further: "Islam's borders *are* bloody and so are its innards. The fundamental problem for the West is not Islamic fundamentalism. It is Islam."[1]

How should one respond to these words? Consideration for Muslim self-respect calls for their outright rejection. But what of their cogency? One could dismiss them in anger without even trying to determine their accuracy, as if that crucial second dimension in Diagram 1 were somehow irrelevant. Yet Huntington did cite evidence to support his conclusion. Not bothering to investigate, empirically, his sanguinary image of Islam would amount to conceding the argument to him. Although his facts do not speak for themselves, that is no reason to ignore them in favor of a feel-good preference for nice words over nasty ones.[2]

I lack the space here to review and assess Huntington's evidence for "the Muslim propensity toward violent conflict"—for "Muslim bellicosity and violence" as "late-twentieth-century facts which neither Muslims nor non-Muslims can deny."[3] Nor would such an investigation fit this book's main focus on language. But his charge is utterly relevant. For if Islam really does have bloody borders and innards, if the religion really is the cause of the carnage done in its name, then Varisco and I are both wrong to defend such a lethal faith, even if we do so in different ways.

Evidence relevant to Huntington's claim includes a dataset, compiled by Professor Monty Marshall, covering the world's major armed conflicts from 1946 to 2007.[4] Although in 2007 most of these conflicts were no longer in progress, twenty-five of them, recent or old, were ongoing in that year. Twelve of these conflicts were in countries with Muslim majorities, compared with eleven in countries with non-Muslim majorities. The two remaining conflicts—Arabs versus Israelis over Palestine, Pakistanis versus Indians over Kashmir—spanned the borders between Muslim- and non-Muslim-majority jurisdictions.

Of the estimated cumulative 2,243,200 deaths in all of the conflicts that were underway in 2007, nearly three-quarters—73 percent—resulted from violence *among non-Muslims*, compared with 21 percent linked to violence among Muslims, and 5 percent attributable to violence between Muslims and non-Muslims. If we estimate that, over the historical course of all this political violence, 20 percent of the world's people professed Islam,[5] the 21-percent death rate suffered by Muslims at the hands of other Muslims—the so-called "bloody innards" of their religion—almost exactly matched their share of the world's population.

By these admittedly crude measures, taking into account all of the deaths attributable to all of the major armed conflicts still raging in 2007, Muslims were neither more nor less likely to have killed each other than were non-Muslims likely to have taken the lives of other non-Muslims. Noteworthy, too, is how the paucity of fatalities inflicted by Muslims on non-Muslims or vice versa—a mere 5 percent of all deaths—undermines *both* Huntingon's specter of global jihad waged by Muslims against their non-Muslim enemies *and* the radically Islamist conviction that Christians and Jews have been engaged in a global crusade against Islam.

Various responses to my use of these data are, of course, possible. First, one could deny that Muslims are even partly responsible for the mayhem—that Western backing for Muslim despots has left their oppressed Muslim subjects no recourse but revolt; that Muslims have been manipulated into killing fellow believers by oil-seeking Westerners eager to divide and rule; and that if the United States had not invaded Iraq, Sunni-Shii violence there would not have occurred. Second, one could say that although Muslims bear some responsibility for the violence, they have been much less bellicose than non-Muslims—that if the 73 percent figure for deaths from violence between non-Muslims were disaggregated by the faiths of those concerned, the "innards" of Christianity would appear much bloodier than those of Islam. Third, one could argue that the controversy sparked by Huntington is too complex and subjective to be clarified by recourse to "objective" evidence, that the very notion of objectivity is a myth, and that arguments over Islamism will be settled not by those who have the facts but by those have the power. Fourth, one could accept the need for empirical research, but question the use of cross-national statistics and call for a qualitative approach that relies on the in-depth investigation of the natures and causes of particular conflicts.

Had I the space to address these arguments, I would show how the first three are at least somewhat amenable to being empirically researched. As for the fourth, I agree. Scholars must be aware of the limits of empirical research, the need to seek qualitative evidence alongside the quantitative kind,[6] and the importance of careful and nuanced reasoning, especially in handling a proposition as incendiary as Huntington's. But if doing empirical research on a topic as controversial and emotional as the intersection of religion and violence is difficult, refusing to do it risks abandoning the field of disagreement to the deadly interplay of force and fear. Ignorance in this context is not bliss; it is the abyss.

ISLAMISM AND INJURY

At the heart of the case for shunning the term *Islamism* lie assertions of agency and outcome: First, that the word, in and of itself, *causes* injury to Muslims; and second, that by not using it, "we"—scholars and other concerned individuals—can *cause* it to disappear from discourse.

On the first score—harming Muslims—Varisco is unequivocal: Islamism is "a term that uniquely *brands* Muslims as terrorists." The word should be abandoned "because it is *harmful* to the ongoing public perception of Muslims." In Varisco's view, "If we who study Islam in academe allow a single word which defines Islam as such to be born again in ideological fervor as a special kind of religious extremism, then we might as well be *hurling sticks and stones* at our Muslim colleagues."

Varisco quotes Feisal Abdul Rauf's opinion that the term "merges the faith of Islam with modern political movements in such a way as to make non-Muslims think that Islam itself is the source of the militancy." Abdul Rauf in his comment reciprocates no less explicitly: "Muslims perceive the term *Islamism*" as "laden with Western negative prejudice toward religion in general and Islam particular. . . . Muslims are sensitive to and detect such negative valuation." Syed Farid Alatas agrees that the term *Islamism* "is offensive to Muslims because it is derived from a God-given term via revelation, that is, Islam, but generally refers to unholy ideas, individuals, and groups." For him, the word "continues to be associated with violence, extremism, and with backward, or at best, conservative ideas."

It may be helpful to compare these statements with the findings of a comprehensive survey of the perceptions of Muslim and non-Muslim university students in the United Kingdom undertaken by the Centre for Social Cohesion (CSC) in London in 2007–2008. Each student was given two statements about Islam and Islamism, and asked to select the one that came closer to his or her own opinion. Of the Muslim respondents, 36 chose "Islam is a religion whilst Islamism is a political ideology"; 15 percent chose "They are both part of the same thing—politics is a big part of Islam"; 22 percent preferred neither statement; and 27 percent were unsure.[7]

The CSC did not ask respondents what the term *Islamism* meant to them, or whether it should be used or not. Notwithstanding the proliferation of survey research on the attitudes of Muslims around the world, neither Muslim nor non-Muslim respondents have, to my knowledge, been asked these questions. But the CSC survey did offer respondents a choice of assertions about Islamism in which the word appeared as if it were a normal part of discourse. If the term were as thoroughly injurious to Muslims as Varisco, Abdul Rauf, and Alatas contend, one might have expected a large majority of the Muslim respondents—not 22 percent—to have rejected both statements for using a derogatory term, *Islamism*, as if it were neutral. As for these experts' view that the word *Islamism* necessarily and invidiously implicates the religion of Islam, the most popular assertion (chosen by 36 percent of the students) *distinguished* the one from the other. Only a small (15 percent) minority seems to have identified Islamism with Islam.[8]

Even if we bend over backward on behalf of the argument that references to *Islamism* are intrinsically offensive to Muslims, and impute that reaction to the other 49 percent of the sample—those could accept neither assertion or were unsure—it remains surprising that merely half of those surveyed would have rebuffed the word as a slur. Also remarkable is the CSC's finding that, by this generous measure, those who had joined "Islamic societies" on campus (and thus may have identified more with Islam) were even less plausibly upset by the term *Islamism* than were their unaffiliated (and thus arguably more secular) fellow students.[9] And even if these interpretations of the survey results are unpersuasive, or the sample is dismissed as unrepresentative, the sheer diversity of the students' responses is hardly congenial to the idea that all, nearly all, or even a large majority of Muslims feel injured by the term.

UNDOING USAGE?

Now consider the second causality in the case against *Islamism*: the ability of academics to affect word usage. My co-authors and I are not so naive as to think that anyone can single-handedly alter what is customary in the English language. What happens to *Islamism* and its derivatives will depend on many conditions and events, including the future nature, scale, and frequency of violence involving Muslims, and how such violence is reported by the media and construed in public speech and writing; the relevant policies of the United States and other governments; the distribution of (in)tolerance toward Muslims and Islam in the minds of hundreds of millions of people; and so on. In this momentous context, the notion that scholars can change usage seems a risible conceit.

Nevertheless, on this score, between Anouar Majid's convinced pessimism and Alatas's cautious optimism, I stand closer to the latter view. Majid is fatalistic: Whatever happens, "Islam will be to blame in the end." Nothing can "withstand the suspense and drama of countdowns to wars against Muslims." Muslims will be misrepresented; "their truth will not be televised." Mere "semantic differentiations through word choice will not, in any way, alter the larger syntax of the West."

"The larger syntax of the West" is a straw person. Obviously a scholar's decision to use or not use the word *Islamism* will not revamp the way "the West" thinks, speaks, and writes. It does not follow, however, that such a large and diverse aggregation as "the West" is doomed to express itself in words that are, and can only be, Islamophobic. Alatas is more careful about the limited difference that experts might be able to make: Just as "Muslim and Western scholars of the last century conspired to stop using 'Muhammadanism,' resulting in the term falling out of use, . . . the same fate may await Islamism if we put ourselves up to it."

Alatas could be right. The comparison with *Muhammadanism* is, however, problematic. The shift from that term to *Islam* occurred at a time when Muslims, their religion, and associated controversies were less prominent in discourse around the world than these matters are today. The media, electronically augmented, are far more pervasive than they were then, and the use of *Islamism* has become widespread. I am less sure than Anouar is that Muslim "truth" (whatever that might be) "will not be televised" at all. But scholars who use nuanced reasoning to oppose the term *Islamism* will be hard put to change the vocabularies favored by videographers on YouTube or by talking if not shouting heads on television. It is also worth recalling that, in competition as a word of choice, *Islam* was advantaged by its brevity over the polysyllabic *Muhammadanism*, just as the currency of *Islamism* benefited from its lexical economy in contrast to the length of *fundamentalism*.

As Varisco notes, *Muhammadanism* as a name for the religion was supplanted by *Islam* in the early-to-mid-twentieth century. The substantive rationale for this shift was impeccable: *Muhammadanism* was neither considerate nor accurate, having offended Muslims by misconstruing their faith. If there is an equivalent to Jesus in Islam it is not Muhammad but the Qur'an.

Compared with this earlier, theological critique of the term *Muhammadanism*, however, the argument against *Islamism* is more problematic. Periodically since the turn of the present century, spectacular events have juxtaposed Muslims, Islam, and mayhem. However unrepresentative of Islamic doctrine and Muslim behavior these episodes may have been, they have made less persuasive the charge that *Islamism* is an invidious and falsely violence-imputing name. One need only recall, among other incidents: the 9/11 attacks in the United States (2001); the bombings in Bali (2002), Casablanca (2003), Madrid (2004), London (2005), Amman (2005), Sharm el-Sheikh (2005), Mumbai (2006), Karachi (2007), and Islamabad (2008); the killing of Theo van Gogh (2005); and the also deadly aftermath of the Danish cartoons mocking Muhammad (2005).

To this envenoming sequence must be added, of course, the far greater death tolls of the ongoing American wars in Afghanistan, in Iraq, incipiently in Pakistan, and in the other Muslim-majority venues of U.S. President George

W. Bush's eight-year "war on terror." The circumstances behind these multiple occasions and locations of violence were, and in the ongoing cases still are, extraordinarily varied. As a matter of accuracy, all this diversely situated and motivated violence cannot be blamed on innately Muslim or Islamic aggression. Such a sweeping verdict makes no empirical sense. Yet the decade's record of violence by even a few Muslims in their faith's name has at least complicated the task of enlisting non-Muslim public opinion on behalf of greater sensitivity toward Muslims and their religion, not to mention the case for censoring oneself in discourse about them. Although some observers will infer from this deadly but selective record the need for consideration toward Muslims and Islam generally, if only to isolate the specifically violent fringe, others will cite these same incidents to declare that conclusion naive.

In noting these limits on the power of scholars to change how people use words, I am of course challenging not only my own hope, but the very premise of this book: that a discussion of terms *can* make a difference in whether or how they are used. I share this expectation, but only in a form that is modest enough to be achievable. A merely scholarly dislike of the word *Islamism* and its variants *Islamist* and *Islamists* will not result in their demise. Less implausibly, however, one could try to encourage the diversity of ways in which these terms are already being used—ways that include commitments that are not militant and actions that are not violent. Advocating the application of different adjectives in different contexts to an existing and already polysemic noun seems more realistic than recommending its disappearance. (That said, I admit that following Varisco's example and deleting *Islamism* from one's own vocabulary is the most realistic—immediately practicable—course of all.)

REVIVALISM? RESURGENCE? RELIGIONISM?

Islamism would be easier to replace if there were a good word to replace it with. Varisco has two in mind: *revivalism* and *resurgence*. Would they fill the bill? One could still speak or write of a "democratic Muslim revivalism" or "the political resurgence of Islam." I doubt, however, that Varisco's terms would help us differentiate across the wide range of beliefs and behaviors encompassed by my understanding of Islamism and Islamists.

"In the battle between Osama bin Laden and the Saudi government," Abdul Rauf asks, "whom would we label Islamist?" My answer is that they are both Islamist, but with significance differences that qualifiers can readily convey. Bin Laden the terrorist, an "insurgent Islamist" with a "revolutionary

Islamist" agenda, can be usefully contrasted and compared with the "incum-
bent Islamist" regime in Riyadh and its "conservative" if not "ultra-conservative
Islamist" agenda.

By comparison, the explicitly retrospective character of *revivalism* and *resurgence* greatly limits their flexibility and scope—that is, their utility. For
example: The European public intellectual Tariq Ramadan is an Islamist by
my definition. He is a Muslim who is committed to public action to implement what he regards as an Islamic agenda. But his agenda is not revivalist.
His aim is not to bring back an Islamic past. Nor does he advocate a resurgence of Islam in the sense of lifting it up to a prominence or dominance that,
in Muslim-majority settings, it may once have enjoyed. Ramadan's notion of a
"European Islam" that can help Europe's Muslim minority adapt and integrate
without losing its identity is meant to create a future not revive the past,[10] and
favors coexistence not resurgence. *Revivalism* and *resurgence* are inadequate
alternatives to *Islamism*—too specialized and too linked to a particular interpretation of history to accommodate the full spectrum of ways in which Muslims have used and are using Islam as a referent in public expression and
activity.[11]

As for erasing *Islamism* without replacing it, doing that would reduce our
ability to make careful factual distinctions precisely at a time when stereotyping, demonization, and paranoia have made them so necessary. Using *Islamist*
frees *Muslim* to specify or at least connote the person, and reserves *Islamic* for
denoting his or her faith in ways that exaggerate neither the importance of
religion to a Muslim nor the importance of politics to Islam.

Is a Muslim democrat (1a) a Muslim who supports democracy at least in
part because he or she believes it is Islamic to do so, or (1b) a Muslim who just
happens to be a democrat? The adjective *Muslim* is helpfully ambiguous as
regards these interpretations; it suspends (or postpones) choosing between
them. Is an Islamic suicide-bomber engaged in that action at least in part because (2a) he or she believes it is Islamic to do so, or (2b) it really is Islamic to
do so, because the religion really does encourage suicidal murder? The adjective *Islamic* is disturbingly prejudicial as regards these interpretations; without quotation marks around "Islamic," the religion is demonized by default.
In contrast, an Islamist democrat is clearly (1a) not (1b); an Islamist suicide-
bomber is clearly (2a) not (2b); and our lexical ability to register and convey
the difference thus contributes to accuracy and consideration at the same
time.[12]

Abdul Rauf prefers *Islamic religionism* to Islamism. But his choice, like Varisco's, curtails the usefully broad scope of the term it would replace. Abdul Rauf defines *Islamic religionist* in a way that apparently excludes from its coverage any Muslim who is committed to hurtful, hateful, or even merely disrespectful actions and agendas toward others. For such a Muslim could hardly "hold that religion does and should be accorded its rightful and respectful place in the public debate on how to build the Good Society." Taking part in a respectful public debate on the Good Society is not what those who kill in the name of religion have in mind.

I oppose the purely invidious use of *Islamism*, by which I mean its restriction to Muslim intolerance and violence alone. But how can we talk about the ways in which Muslims, Islam, and violence do sometimes intersect without having words for these phenomena as well? Quarantining these intersections from the scope of *Islamic religionism* implies that they are unrelated to Islam, which leads to denial: A Muslim believes in Islam; Islam is a nonviolent religion; Osama bin Laden is violent; therefore he must not believe in Islam; therefore he must not be a Muslim. Conversely, incorporating Al Qaeda's behavior within a field of diverse behaviors described not as *Islamic* but as *Islamist* acknowledges that Muslims can and do disagree about what their religion requires, allows, and disallows. The use of *Islamist* thus facilitates contextualization—respect for facts as well as feelings.

Varisco shares Abdul Rauf's complaint that the word *Islamism* uniquely and unfairly singles out Islam and Muslims. "Despite centuries of internal European blood baths in the name of Christ," writes Varisco, "no one has yet to suggest a need for *Christianism*." In fact, the Latin-based word *Christianism* dates from the sixteenth century and has, like *Islamism*, been redefined, and in a broadly comparable way—from naming a religion to identifying an ideology that would advance a particular understanding of that religion in the public and especially the political realm.[13]

HEGEMONY AND HOMOGENEITY

For Varisco, "word choice is inevitably part of a power play." Tell that to a poet trying to express a nuanced feeling or idea. Nadia Yassine describes "the manipulation of terms such as *Islamism*" as "an indispensable tool of aggression." Tell that to a peacemaker engaged in "the manipulation of terms" with intent to persuade warring parties to agree on the text of a truce. Varisco does not say that word choice is inevitably determined by whoever is more powerful.

Yassine does not say that interpretations of Islamism are always tools of aggression. But their comments evoke a "Humpty Dumpty" notion of language as a mere plaything of elites who have sole power to decide and control what a word is believed to mean.[14]

It is not necessary to believe in a fantasy—that language change is always democratic, as if each user had only a single vote in a constant referendum on what to say and how to say it—in order to doubt this Humpty Dumpty view. The ability to promote or demote words and to load them with particular meanings is unevenly distributed across individuals, groups, organizations, and governments. The media do powerfully influence word use. However, in the information-dense environment of today's increasingly wired world, divergent views may be only a click away. We should not underestimate the ability of "ordinary people"—non-elites—to think for themselves and to produce language as well as consume it.

Compared with elite hegemony, semantic homogeneity is a more serious objection to my recommendation to use *Islamism* while construing it broadly. But two thresholds must be cleared if Varisco's narrow reading of the term is to be sustained. *Islamism* must be shown, first, to be a synonym for Islam itself, and second, to denote violence—and thereby to slander Islam as a homogeneously violent religion.

In our opening essays, Varisco and I both criticize Daniel Pipes's association of *Islamism* with violence. But not even in Pipes's highly pejorative rendition is the term equated with Islam. "Islamism is an ideology" are the first words of a 1998 talk by Pipes that Varisco himself cites. Pipes went on to say that "in devising strategy towards Islamism we must very specifically and very repeatedly distinguish between Islam and Islamism." He contrasted "traditional Islam, a religion [with] close to a billion adherents," with "Islamism," which he described as "an effort to turn Islam, a religion and a civilization, into an ideology"—"a total transformation of" and "a huge change from traditional Islam."[15] Clearly, for Pipes, Islamism is not synonymous with Islam.

Pipes does, on the other hand, homogenize Islamism by associating it with extremism, militancy, and violence. When asked in October 2001 whether there could be something about Islam itself "that facilitates this transformation [of faith into ideology]," Pipes replied, "Islam is the most political of religions, the one most oriented toward power. This is a modern evolution of something that was always in Islam but takes it to an ideological extreme." Later in the interview he described Islamism as a "form of militant Islam," and called militant Islam "the enemy." "Islamists," he had written a few weeks before, constituted "perhaps 10 to 15 percent of the population" of Muslims around the world, and many were "peaceable in appearance," yet "all must be considered potential killers."[16] Observers who applied Pipes's statistics and took his advice in the world of 2009 would see, and presumably be terrified by, an otherwise undifferentiated mass of 136–204 million Islamists of potentially murderous intent.[17]

I strongly object to these among other aspects of Pipes's writings on Islamism. But the linkage of Islamism with violence is not so entrenched in common practice as to doom the term. In my opening chapter I listed a lengthy series of writings published in 2000–2006 whose authors used Islamism and derivative terms broadly "to include nonviolence, compromise, and moderation" (see n. 28). To reinforce this point, the list is extended and updated here to include more than thirty additional such publications.[18]

This is not to say that the word *Islamism* and its variants are applied more often to moderate stances and movements than to extremist ones. The core concern that Varisco and I share is precisely the disproportional association of *Islamism* with radical views and actions, including terrorism, in public discourse. Where we differ is in my contention that alongside this clearly and substantially skewed usage, *Islamism* and its derivatives have also come to be used, with appropriate qualifiers, to denote persons, organizations, ideas, and behaviors that are nonviolent, tolerant, democratic, and even liberal in character.[19]

The tilt in usage toward extremism is more noticeable in general discourse than among specialized scholars. In cyberspace, as of May 2009, Web pages containing the phrase *radical Islamists* outnumbered those that mentioned *moderate Islamists* by an estimated ratio of 7.8:1. If Googling is a reliable way of accessing public discourse—a questionable assumption—analysts who use *Islamism* and its cognates diversely must acknowledge this coloration. Other things being equal, the larger this ratio grows, the less plausible in general discourse the notion that there are *moderate Islamists* becomes.[20]

Two comparisons may serve to put this finding in perspective. First, the skew toward *radical* decreased over a period of several years from August 2005 to May 2009: from 11.4:1 (in 2005) to 8.8:1 (in 2008) to 7.8:1 (in 2009). It would be foolish to extrapolate these results and predict increasing diversity in the associations that the term *Islamists* will, in future, call to mind. Much will depend on the behavior of Islamists themselves, what they actually do and refrain from doing in the name of their religion. But to the extent that one can meaningfully compare these three ratios, they suggest that the phrase *moderate Islamists*, however construed, is alive and well and living in the English lexicon.[21]

Second, in May 2009 I also ran for the first time a Google search for these phrases in *books*. That far narrower scan yielded a nearly equal ratio of documents referring to *radical Islamists* compared with those referring to *moderate Islamists*, namely: 1.2:1. It would be naive to portray the authors of books as an open-minded vanguard leading the public toward diversified usage. But authors who construed, employed, and qualified *Islamism* diversely in 2009 at least found themselves in good literary company.[22]

BEYOND POLITICAL ISLAM

Non-Muslim observers of the Muslim world may wish that moderate Muslims would, more vocally and in larger numbers, denounce the attempted hijacking of their religion by terrorists. But those same observers would do well to ask themselves to what extent their own vocabularies enhance or impede an awareness of moderation in that vast and varied Muslim mainstream whose understandings and behaviors need not cause alarm. Adjectival *Islamism* can serve this end. But it cannot do so if the meaning of the noun standing alone, unqualified, is preempted by an indelibly political preconception that makes it harder to acknowledge the full range of these understandings and behaviors—that inhibits contextualization.

Picture five concentric circles: The first and smallest defines *Islamism* as religious carnage. It nests inside a second and somewhat larger definition of *Islamism* as intolerance including violence. That semantic circle is encompassed by a third and still larger definition of *Islamism* as a synonym for *political Islam*. *Political Islam* is included in a fourth and even broader circle in which *Islamism* means support for, and actions on behalf of, subjectively Islamic agendas in the public sphere—my definition. That fourth understanding, in turn, falls within a fifth and final circle that subsumes under *Islamism* everything and anything having to do with Muslims and their religion.

The fifth and clearly vacuous definition is easy to reject. But why prefer "public" in the fourth definition to the narrower "political" criterion required by the third?

Demonizing Islam as a uniquely belligerent religion of war is neither accurate nor considerate. But how accurate and considerate is the essentialization of Islam as a necessarily political religion? Anyone who studies the discourses of Muslims regarding their own religion will sooner or later encounter this assertion in Arabic: *Islam din wa dawla*—Islam is the religion and politics of the state. This highly normative and restrictive statement implies that if you are not political and do not concern yourself especially with the politics of the state, in order to ensure its truly Islamic character, you cannot be a good Muslim. In fact, most Muslims in the world, like most non-Muslims, are not so piously political—or so politically pious. They do not spend their waking hours scheming of ways to establish or improve the Islamic complexion of the state.

Why trade one semantic straitjacket (Islamism as necessarily violent) for an only somewhat larger one (Islamism as necessarily political)? Democratic Islamism is not a contradiction in terms. Why should nonpolitical Islamism be? Rendering Islamism synonymous with political Islam and reducing Islamist agendas to a single item—building and defending an Islamic state—leaves unnamed the zone of expression and activity that is not political in the sense of being focused on the state, but is also not personal in the sense of being private. In a capacious public realm—my fourth circle—that includes the state without being circumscribed by it, Muslims advance ideas and engage in activities that may or may not have political motivations and consequences, and that may concern society at least as much as, if not more than, they affect the state. Muslims for whom Islam is a reason to take part in projects for community development; to staff schools and clinics on behalf of local education and welfare; to organize self-help movements; to support banking practices that avoid (or at any rate rename) interest; to organize cultural events to project interpretations of Islam through lectures, music, and film; to express their religious identities in public or on YouTube; to join evangelical movements; to endorse or oppose women's rights in televised discussions; to participate in open dialogues with adherents of other religions; to write books and blogs about what constitutes an Islamic society—all of these activities and more would qualify as *Islamist* by my inclusive definition.[23]

Political Islamism helpfully distinguishes the faith from its many interpretations. The faith and one such interpretation are fused in *political Islam*. Accuracy and consideration meet in language that differentiates what is relative (multiple existing and even contradictory uses and glosses of the religion) while suspending judgment as to what is absolute (what Islam "really and truly" is and means). *Political Islam* (as opposed to *political Islamism*) can imply that Islam is inherently and permanently political, across time and space.

Or it can imply the decentering and deconstruction of Islam, the replacement of its unity and singularity with multiple different Islams—political, cultural, economic, quietistic, militant, violent, and so on ad infinitum.

The first choice falsely essentializes what is empirically diverse, while the second impiously diversifies what is, for most believing Muslims, one single, monotheistic faith. I am not suggesting that non-Muslims cease using the terms *Islam* and *Islamic*. I am arguing that these terms should be used with care, and that when interacting with Muslims, diversely using *Islamism* can be a good choice: between being inaccurately reductionist about Islam and being inconsiderate toward those who nevertheless believe in *it*.[24]

SPEEDING A TREND?

In this essay I have advocated a diverse understanding of Islamism that is more accurately and considerately inclusive than purely and narrowly political Islam. I am not confident that, in discourses of the future, my version, as opposed to Varisco's aversion, will succeed. Future usage may disappoint us both. Yet if this book stimulates awareness of words, their uses, and their implications, its authors will not have written in vain.

Mohammed Ayoob recently wrote, "If there is a discernible long-term trend in Islamist politics"—note the welcome difference in clarity between that phrasing and *political Islam*—"it points toward moderation and constitutionalism, not violence and extremism."[25] If he is right, as I hope, it is time to refine our words in ways that will accommodate the realities and diversities of Islamism—and thereby, however modestly, speed the trend that Ayoob sees. If he is wrong, however, a critical and self-critical awareness of the issues debated in this book could help make him less mistaken than he might otherwise be.

NOTES

Preface

1. James Davison Hunter, *Culture Wars: The Struggle to Define America* (New York: Basic Books, 1991).

2. The case that this was happening was made most directly the following year by John L. Esposito, *The Islamic Threat: Myth or Reality?* (New York: Oxford University Press, 1992).

3. Martin E. Marty and R. Scott Appleby, *Fundamentalisms Observed* (Chicago: University of Chicago Press, 1991). This was the first of several volumes in the Fundamentalism Project, underwritten by the John D. and Catherine T. MacArthur Foundation.

Introduction: The Debate About Islamism in the Public Sphere

1. Gilles Kepel, *Jihad: The Trail of Political Islam*, trans. Anthony F. Roberts (Cambridge, MA: Belknap Press, 2002), p. 23.

2. Paul Berman, "The Philosopher of Islamic Terror," *New York Times Magazine*, March 23, 2003. Also see Berman, *Terror and Liberalism* (New York: W. W. Norton, 2003); Qutb, *Milestones* (Burr Ridge, IL: American Trust Publications, 1991).

3. John L. Esposito, "Political Islam: Beyond the Green Menace," *Current History*, Vol. 93, Iss. 579, 19–25. Also see Elaine Sciolino, "Seeing Green: The Red Menace Is Gone. But Here's Islam," *New York Times,* January 21, 1996.

4. See for example the results of Washington Post-ABC News Poll: Views of Islam released on April 5, 2009 where 48% of respondents said they had an unfavorable view of Islam (up from 39% in October, 2001) and 29% said that they believed mainstream Islam encouraged violence (up from 14% in January, 2002), http://abcnews.go.com/images/PollingUnit/1088a5ViewsofIslam.pdf (accessed April 21, 2009).

5. Gregory Crouch, "Dutch Film Against Islam Is Released on Internet," *New York Times*, March 28, 2008. For the film see: www.themoviefitna.com (accessed October 1, 2008).

6. "Islamization"—the social and cultural processes of become or making "Islamic," is also confusingly a term for Islamism. However, it usually denotes "becoming Islamic or Islamized," as when societies to which Islam spread and eventually governed took on Islamic cultural characteristics, even among non-Muslim subgroups, such as the Christians and Jews of medieval Baghdad. The Late Marshall Hodgson referred to these as "Islamicate" societies.

7. IslamistWatch.org, www.islamistwatch.org (accessed July 1, 2008). There is also a competing site with a similar name: islamist-watch.org, which is a project of the Middle East Forum.

8. Ibid.

9. These networks of institutions, while monitoring "Islamist" activity, often also take aim at American institutions that allegedly serve as "apologists for Islamism." David Horowitz's "Discover the Network" project, for example, argues that groups such as the Carter Center, the American Civil Liberties Union, and Human Rights Watch "lend considerable support to Islamo-fascists and their 'fellow-travelers' by running interference on their behalf and helping them achieve their more immediate objectives." Such political activity is testimony to the way in which the debate about Islamism—regardless of its efficacy, accuracy, or utility—has become a routine part of American political discourse. David Horowitz Freedom Center, www.discoverthe networks.org/viewSubCategory.asp?id=772 (accessed July 26, 2008).

10. For example see the work of Gary Bunt generally, but especially his *Islam in the Digital Age: E-jihad, Online Fatwas and Cyber Islamic Environments* (London: Pluto Press, 2003).

11. For example see John Kelly and Bruce Etling, "Mapping Iran's Online Public: Politics and Culture in the Persian Blogosphere" (Cambridge, MA: The Berkman Center for Internet and Society at the Harvard Law School, Research Publication 2008-1). http://cyber.law.harvard.edu/publications/2008/Mapping_Irans_Online_Public (accessed October 1, 2008).

12. The Center for Islamic Thought, www.islamicthought.org/icit-doc.html (accessed August 2, 2008).

13. Islamophobia Watch, www.islamophobia-watch.com/about-us/ (accessed August 2, 2008).

14. See Mahmoud Mamdani, *Good Muslim, Bad Muslim: America, the Cold War, and the Roots of Terror* (New York: Pantheon, 2004); Richard C. Martin, "September 11: Clash of Civilizations or Islamic Revolution?" in *Roads to Reconciliation: Approaches to Conflict in the Twenty-First Century*, ed. Amy B. Brown and Karen M. Poremski (Armonk, NY: M. E. Sharpe, 2004).

15. www.whitehouse.gove/infocus/ramadan/islam.html.

16. David E. Kaplan, "Hearts, Minds, and Dollars: In an Unseen Front in the War on Terrorism, America Is Spending Millions . . . To Change the Very Face of Islam," *U.S. News and World Report*, April 17, 2005. We were led to this and the following reference by Saba Mahmood, "Secularism, Hermenuetics, and Empire: The Politics of Islamic Reform," *Public Culture* 18, no. 2 (2006): 323–47.

17. In an ironic twist, Al-Hurra came under scrutiny in 2007 when it was realized that it had allotted air-time in some of its programming to avowed terrorists. See Joel Mowbray, "Television Takeover: U.S.-Financed Al-Hurra Is Becoming a Platform for Terrorists," *Wall Street Journal*, March 18, 2007.

18. Ibid.

19. Five Pillars: Bearing witness to God and His Messenger, Muhammad; the five daily prayers; caring for those less fortunate through charity; fasting during the month of Ramadan; and making the annual pilgrimage (*hajj*) to Mecca. Six Articles of Faith: Belief in God, His prophets, angels, scriptures sent down by God, the Day of Judgment and Resurrection, and predestination.

20. See James Piscatori, *Islam, Islamists, and the Electoral Principle in the Middle East* (Leiden, Netherlands: ISIM, 2000). www.isim.nl/files/paper_piscatori.pdf (accessed August 18, 2008).

21. See "The Useful Diversity of Islamism," p. [000].

22. Graham E. Fuller, *The Future of Political Islam* (New York: Palgrave Macmillan, 2003), p xi.

23. On the development and implications of the common quranic phrase in Islamic religious and legal thought, see Michael Cook, *Forbidding Wrong in Islam: An Introduction* (New York: Cambridge University Press, 2003).

24. Oliver Roy and Antoine Sfeir, *The Columbia World Dictionary of Islamism*, trans. and ed. John King (New York: Columbia University Press, 2007).

25. See "Between Etymology and Realpolitik," p. [000].

26. Quoted from Varisco in Part III, "Mititgating Misrepresentation," p. [000].

Inclusive Islamism: The Utility of Diversity

Editor's note: Here and in this author's chapter in Part III, key terms such as *Islamism*, *Islamist*, and *Islamists* appear in italics when his focus is on the words themselves. When they are not italicized, his focus is on the phenomena to which they refer.

1. "Ninety-Nine Names of Allah," a poster made by Sultan and Sulaiman Universal Products, Indianapolis, IN.

2. Quoted in Craig S. Smith, "In Mourning Slain Filmmaker, Dutch Confront Limitations of Their Tolerance," *New York Times*, A9, November 10, 2004, national edition.

3. Quoted in "The Future of Europe," *Playboy* 52, no. 1 (November 2005): p. 46.

4. Also known as "the Global War on Terrorism," or "GWOT," as in Andrew Harvey, Ian Sullivan, and Ralph Groves, "A Clash of Systems: An Analytical Framework to Demystify the Radical Islamist Threat," *Parameters: US Army War College Quarterly* 35, no. 3 (Autumn 2005): 80–81, www.carlisle.army.mil/USAWC/parameters/05autumn/harvey.pdf (accessed April 24, 2009).

5. George Lakoff, *Don't Think of an Elephant! Know Your Values and Frame the Debate—The Essential Guide for Progressives* (White River Junction, VT: Chelsea Green Publishing, 2004), pp. 113, 119.

6. "We understand [that] this crusade, this war on terrorism, is going to take a while." U.S. President George W. Bush, September 16, 2001, as quoted in Jonathan Rabin, "September 11: The View from the West," *The New York Review of Books* 52, no. 14 (September 22, 2005): 4.

7. Huntington, "The Clash of Civilizations?" *Foreign Affairs* 72, no. 3 (Summer 1993): 22–49.

8. Craig S. Smith, "Dutch Charge 7 Muslim Men in Killing of Critic of Islam," *New York Times*, A7, November 11, 2004, national edition. The sites of Muslim-linked violence (and the number of items concerning that site) were: Iraq (6), Palestine (2), Netherlands (1), Iran (1), and Ivory Coast (1). Follow-up coding of the *Times* arbitrarily on the sixth of each month yielded comparable results. On September 6, 2005, for instance, of twenty "International" news items in the *Times*, thirteen mentioned violence (real or feared). Eleven of these thirteen, or 84.6 percent, implicated Muslims— as actors in two items, as both actors and victims in nine. Three of these eleven reports were about Iraq; the others concerned Afghanistan (1), Kashmir (1), Kosovo (1), Lebanon (1), Netherlands (1), Pakistan (1), Palestine (1), and Somalia (1).

9. The poll was sponsored by the Council on American-Islamic Relations (CAIR). According to CAIR, the survey was conducted in June–July 2004 by "an independent research firm," Genesis Research Associates (GRA); comprised one thousand telephone interviews with "a gender-balanced random sample of respondents across the continental United States"; and yielded results within an error margin of +/−3.1 percent with 95 percent confidence. "Poll: 1-in-4 Americans Holds Anti-Muslim Views," ISLAM-INFONET, October 4, 2004, distributed to the listserve islam-infonet@cair.biglist.com and accessible through islam-infonet-help@cair.biglist.com. A replication of the survey by CAIR-GRA in 2005 found declines in neutral and negative comments to 57 and 26 percent, respectively, and a rise in positive remarks to 6 percent. However, the same proportions as before—about one-fourth—agreed that Islam "teaches violence and hatred" and that Muslims "teach their children to hate" and "value life less than other people." (Asked to respond to the first of these statements, 27 percent agreed, 43 percent disagreed, and 30 percent had no opinion.) See www.cair.com/Portals/0/pdf/american_public_opinion_on_muslims_islam_2006.pdf (accessed April 25, 2009).

10. I leave aside anti-empirical "scholarship" that rejects the very notion of factuality and pugnacious "diplomacy" that relies on threats to extract concessions.

11. Mahmood Mamdani, *Good Muslim, Bad Muslim: America, the Cold War, and the Roots of Terror* (New York: Pantheon Books, 2004), pp. 253–54.

12. For example, "'Islam Is Peace,' Says President," Office of the Press Secretary, White House, Washington, DC, September 17, 2001, www.whitehouse.gov/news/releases/2001/09/20010917-11.html (accessed November 2008) and www.submission.org/George_W_Bush/islam.html (accessed April 25, 2009). Compare Jonathan Tobin, "Prudence, Not Prejudice," *Jewish World Review*, February 13, 2003.

13. Metin Kaplan is a Turk who was known as "the Caliph of Cologne" when he lived in that city. In December 2004, in a courtroom in Istanbul, he defended himself against the charge of having unsuccessfully plotted to crash an airplane into Kemal Ataturk's mausoleum on Turkey's independence day in 1998. "I am a Muslim, and a Muslim cannot be a terrorist," said Kaplan in testimony replete with Qur'anic quotes. As cited by Susan Sachs, "Turkey: 'Cologne Caliph' Denies Plot," *New York Times*, A6, December 21, 2004, national edition. For a later instance of denial, see Michael Slackman, "Many in Jordan See Old Enemy in Attack: Israel," *New York Times*, A1, A6, November 12, 2005, national edition.

14. The distinction between "lesser" and "greater" jihad—*al-jihad al-asghar* and *al-jihad al-akbar* in Arabic—does not appear in the Qur'an. Nor is there strong evidence that the Prophet actually made such a remark. See, for example, G. F. Haddad, "Documentation of 'Greater Jihad' Hadith," Living ISLAM—Islamic Tradition, www.abc.se/~m9783/n/dgjh_e.html (accessed April 26, 2009).

15. Can one sidestep the polemic between denial and stigmatization by asserting that "Islam is a religion of *just* war"? That statement should not offend the many Muslims for whom fighting the unjust enemies of Islam is warranted by the Qur'an and by what Muslims have already suffered at their hands. But what is a just war? What kind of justice is involved? For the benefit of whom? The same polarity between denial and stigmatization is likely to recur on the altered terrain. Avowals that jihad is always and necessarily *just* may collide with no less sweeping disavowals. Again the remedy lies in contextualizing justice along a spectrum of actual examples and conditions. Introspection will be necessary on the part of deniers and stigmatizers alike if their rival simplifications are to be broken down. Deniers will need to realize that some wars fought by believing Muslims have been unjust by some standard. Stigmatizers will need to entertain the reverse conclusion. For this to happen, both parties must be enabled—educated—to distinguish normative from empirical truth, faith from fact. And if that smacks of relativism and even secularization, so be it.

16. I do not mean to suggest that all non-Muslims are frictionless two-way-streeters when their own religions are involved. A careful comparison of relevant texts and actual practices would reveal degrees of resistance to exit. Such resistance would, however, be

substantially lower in non-Muslim world religions today than in Islam. One should also keep in mind that all comparisons of present-day Islam among Muslims with present-day Christianity among Christians may be considered historically misleading insofar as Christianity has had some six centuries longer to evolve. Lastly, many contingencies will affect—strengthen or weaken—the behavioral, on-the-ground antipathy of Muslims to apostasy. These contingencies include changes in the popularity and credibility of Muslim scholars and jurists who denounce renouncing Islam.

17. It is striking in this context that Professor Lakoff (*Don't Think*), "one of the world's best-known linguists," a man steeped in "the scientific study of the nature of thought and its expression in language" (p. 123), could refer unselfconsciously to "radical Islamic terrorism" (p. 59). This phrase implies that terrorism is Islamic—prescribed by, and inherent in, the religion itself. As for the leading adjective "radical," it is either (1) redundant (how could terrorism not be radical?); (2) reinforcing (Islamic terrorism as even more extreme than non-Islamic varieties of the phenomenon); or (3) bizarre (as if "radical Islamic terrorism" were being distinguished from something called "moderate Islamic terrorism").

18. For example: Edward Said, "There Are Many Islams," *CounterPunch* [Petrolia, CA], September 16, 2001, www.counterpunch.org/saidattacks.html (accessed April 27, 2009); Aziz al-Azmeh, *Islams and Modernities,* 2nd ed. (London: Verso, 1996); Abdul Hamid el-Zein "Beyond Ideology and Theology: The Search for an Anthropology of Islam," *Annual Review of Anthropology,* 6 (1977): 227–54.

19. In the radically anti-homogenist view of Al-Azmeh (*Islams*, p. 2), "there are as many Islams as there are situations that sustain it." One wonders how many such situations he has in mind. Dozens? Hundreds? Thousands? The higher the number, the more substantively meaningless his already ungrammatical "it" becomes.

20. James Piscatori, *Islam, Islamists, and the Electoral Principle in the Middle East* (Leiden, Netherlands: ISIM, 2000), p. 2.

21. A caveat: In the eyes of some Muslims, the suicide bombing of noncombatant Israelis is not heinous terrorism; it is praiseworthy martyrdom in self-defense. The more widespread and influential such a view, the less "tiny" this sliver of Islamist commitment is likely to be.

22. Replacing "political" with "public" dovetails with Charles Hirschkind's acknowledgment that the "vast majority" of Muslim movements are not trying to "capture the state" as such but are engaged in missionary work, building mosques, and generally fostering "community action" to realize "public virtue." These activities are indirectly political inasmuch as they may require doing business with the state (e.g., to obtain licenses) and may fulfill functions (e.g., providing welfare) that may be associated with the state. See Hirschkind, "What Is Political Islam?" *Middle East Report,* 205 (October–December 1997), www.merip.org/mer/mer205/hirschk.htm (accessed April 26, 2009). One could, of course, enlarge the meaning of "political" to include this

indirectly political agenda. But doing so risks implying that these community-based activities are not undertaken in their own right, as socioreligious assistance, but are a mere façade to conceal the only possible agenda that a Muslim activist can have: building an Islamic state. Subsuming both denotatively and connotatively "political" activities under the more general rubric of "public action" avoids this risk while leaving the analyst free to distinguish, case by case, the various ways in which they may— or may not—be "political."

23. As quoted by Elisabeth Bumiller, "Cheney Sees 'Shameless' Revisionism on War," *New York Times*, A1, A12, November 22, 2005, national edition. See also Bumiller, "White House Letter: 21st-Century Warnings of a Threat Rooted in the 7th," *New York Times*, A21, December 12, 2005, national edition. See also National Intelligence Council, *Mapping the Global Future: Report of the National Intelligence Council's 2020 Project* (Washington, DC: Government Printing Office, 2004), pp. 13, 16, 83–91, 93, www.foia.cia .gov/2020/2020.pdf (accessed April 26, 2009).

24. As does, among others, David Thaler, "The Middle East: The Cradle of the Muslim World," in Angel M. Rabasa, Cheryl Benard, Peter Chalk, C. Christine Fair, Theodore Karasik, Rollie Lal, Ian Lesser, and David Thaler, *The Muslim World after 9/11* (Santa Monica, CA: RAND Corporation, 2004), p. 70.

25. Daniel Pipes, "Protecting Muslims While Rooting Out Islamists," *The Daily Telegraph* [London], September 14, 2001, www.danielpipes.org/article/66 (accessed April 26, 2009).

26. Among alternative words, *fundamentalism* comes quickly to mind. But in discourse specifically about Muslims, *Islamism* is by far the more malleable noun. *The American Heritage Dictionary*, 4th ed. (New York: Bantam Dell, 2004 [copyright Houghton Mifflin, 2001]), for instance, fixes the meanings of *fundamentalism* as "a Protestant movement holding the Bible to be the sole authority" and "a movement marked by rigid adherence to basic principles." Advantageously from my standpoint, the same source does not define *Islamism* at all. A "moderate fundamentalist Muslim" is a walking oxymoron. A "moderate Islamist" is not. Compared with *fundamentalism*, the term *Islamism* is not a blank slate, but there is more room for writing on it, witness the debate in this book. See also Martin Kramer, ed., *The Islamism Debate* (Tel Aviv: Moshe Dayan Center for Middle Eastern and African Studies, 1997). On fundamentalism as a common feature of particular movements in different religions, see Martin E. Marty and Scott Appleby, eds., *Fundamentalisms Observed* (Chicago: University of Chicago Press, 1991); Marty and Appleby, eds., *Fundamentalisms Comprehended* (Chicago: University of Chicago Press, 1995).

27. This usage would enable one to differentiate among *Islamisms*, a term without the heretical import of *Islams*.

28. For example: Anthony Bubalo and Greg Fealy, *Between the Global and the Local: Islamism, the Middle East, and Indonesia*, Analysis Paper No. 9 (Washington,

DC: The Brookings Institution Saban Center for Middle East Policy, 2005), pp. 1–6, 15–16; Daniel Byman, "How to Fight Terror," *The National Interest*, 79 (Spring 2005): 129; Larry Diamond, "Universal Democracy?" *Policy Review*, 119 (June–July 2003): 24; Saad Eddin Ibrahim, "A Helsinki Accord for the Arab World," *New Perspectives Quarterly*, 22, no. 3 (Summer 2005): 63; Amr Hamzawy, *Policy Brief—The Key to Arab Reform: Moderate Islamists* (Washington, DC: Carnegie Endowment for International Peace, 2005); Henri Lauzière, "Post-Islamism and the Religious Discourse of 'Abd al-Salam Yasin," *International Journal of Middle East Studies*, 37 (2005): 252; Abdeslam Maghraoui, *What Do Islamists Really Want? An Insider's Discussion with Islamist Leaders*, USIPeace Briefing (Washington, DC: United States Institute of Peace, May 2006); Alix Philippon, "Bridging Sufism and Islamism," *ISIM Review* [Leiden, Netherlands], 17 (Spring 2006): 16–17, and "Sufislamism: The Paradoxical Invention of a New Political Modernity in Islam? The Pakistani Case Study of Minhaj-ul-Qur'an," MA thesis, Institut d'Études Politiques d'Aix en Provence, France, 2004; Piscatori, *Islam, Islamists* (2000); Max Rodenbeck, "The Truth about Jihad," *The New York Review of Books* 52 no. 13 (August 11, 2005): 55; Azzam S. Tamimi, *Rachid Ghannouchi: A Democrat within Islamism* (Oxford: Oxford University Press, 2001); Bryan S. Turner, "Class, Generation and Islamism: Towards a Global Sociology of Political Islam," *British Journal of Sociology* 54, no. 1 (March 2003): 142; "Should the West Always Be Worried If Islamists Win Elections?" *The Economist* (April 30, 2005): 41–42; *The United States and the Muslim World: Critical Issues and Opportunities for Change*, Policy Bulletin, The Stanley Foundation, Muscatine, IA, 2005, p. 2. References to "moderate political Islam" may also be found in both scholarly and media discourse—e.g., Dexter Filkins, "Boys of Baghdad College Vie for Prime Minister," *New York Times*, A8, December 12, 2005, national edition.

29. Omitted from this listing is an early draft of this chapter, given at the 2004 MESA convention as a paper with "Islamism" in its title. Figures for the 2005 MESA convention were comparable: Of eight paper titles, three implied a possible compatibility of Islamism with democracy and none linked Islamism to violence.

Inventing Islamism: The Violence of Rhetoric

1. In Montesquieu's *Le lettres persanes* (Paris, 1721), letter 131, Usbek refers to monarchy as *un état violent qui dégénère toujours en despotisme* (a violent state that always degenerates into terrorism). www.site-magister.com/persanes.htm (accessed April 5, 2009).

2. Quoted in Dorothee Metlitzki, *The Matter of Araby in Medieval England* (New Haven, CT: Yale University Press, 1977), p. 14. For more information on Bede's view of Saracens, see John V. Tolan, *Saracens: Islam in the Medieval European Imagination* (New York: Columbia University Press, 2002), pp. 72–77.

3. Dante Alighieri, *The Inferno*, trans. John Ciardi (New York: New American Library, 1954), p. 236. The most offensive lines (Canto 28:28–30) read: "Between his legs all of his red guts hung with the heart, the lungs, the liver, the gall bladder, and the shrivelled sac that passes shit to the bung."

4. Imam Feisal Abdul Rauf, *What's Right with Islam: A New Vision for Muslims and the West* (San Francisco: Harper Collins, 2004), p. 116.

5. As of April 2009, the Google return for "Islamism" netted 2,230,000 hits, highlighting the uncritical Wikipedia entry first and placing a Daniel Pipes article fourth.

6. Daniel Pipes, "Distinguishing Between Islam and Islamism," Center for Strategic and International Studies, 1988, www.danielpipes.org/article/954 (accessed September 2004). Slightly earlier Pipes used the same description for Islamic fundamentalism, even though this was in an edited volume on Islamism. Pipes, "The Western Mind of Radical Islam," in *The Islamism Debate*, ed. Martin Kramer (Tel Aviv: Moshe Dayan Center for Middle Eastern and African Studies, 1997), p. 60. For critiques of Pipes, see Edward Said, *Covering Islam*, 2nd ed. (London: Routledge, 1997), pp. xviii–xix, and John Trumpbour, "The Clash of Civilizations: Samuel P. Huntington, Bernard Lewis, and the Remaking of Post-Cold War World Order," in *The New Crusades: Constructing the Muslim Enemy*, ed. Emran Qureshi and Michael A. Sells (New York: Columbia University Press, 2003), pp. 96–99.

7. Equating Islamism with Oriental totalitarianism is quite commonly found these days. See, for example, Mehdi Mozaffari, "Is It Possible to Combat Radical Islamism without Combating Islam?" History News Network, 2003, http://hnn.us/articles/1805.html (accessed October 2004).

8. The Web page URL is www.danielpipes.org/blog/300. The quote is from Frank J. Gaffney, "The Islamist Challenge to American Security," The Middle East Forum, MEF Wires, 2004, www.meforum.org/article/639 (accessed November 2004).

9. *American Heritage Dictionary of the English Language*, 4th ed., 2000, www .bartleby.com/61/79/I0247900.html (accessed January 2005).

10. Webster defines Islamism as "The true faith, according to the Mohammedans; Mohammedanism." He further notes that the word is derived from Arabic *salama*, "to be free, safe or devoted to God." This usage for Islam as such was also true in French, where it survived longer than in academic English. Noah Webster, *An American Dictionary of the English Language*, vol. 1 (New York: S. Converse, 1828), p. 114.

11. Lesley Brown, *The New Shorter Oxford English Dictionary*, vol. 1 (Oxford: Clarendon Press, 1993), p. 1422.

12. Hadji Erinn, "Regarding Islamism," *The Path* 8 (1893): 112–15. One of the last academic usages of the term *Islamism* as a synonym of Islam was a lecture by David Margoliouth in 1908 for the Christian Knowledge Society.

13. For a recent account of medieval European perceptions of Muhammad, see Tolan, *Saracens*, 2002. The older work of Norman Daniel, *Islam and the West* (Edinburgh: Edinburgh University Press, 1960) is still of great value in covering the sources.

14. H. A. R. Gibb, *Mohammedanism,* 2nd ed. (Oxford: Oxford University Press, 1962), p. 2.

15. Fazlur Rahman, "Islam and Social Justice," *Pakistan Forum* 1, no.1 (1970): 4–5, 9. The contrast between *Islamisme* (in the sense of traditional Islam) and *socialisme* is found earlier in French writing, for example, Mouhssine Barazi, *Islamisme et socialisme* (Paris: Geuthner, 1929). John Ruedy, "Introduction," *Islamism and Secularism in North Africa* (New York: St. Martin's Press, 1994), p. xv, observes that the English usage of Islamism for political Islam appears to have filtered recently into English from French academic writing.

16. William E. Shepard makes this point, noting that a charismatic figure like al-Mawdudi represents "radical Islamism." Shepard, "Islam and Ideology: Towards a Typology," *International Journal of Middle East Studies* 19, no. 3 (1987): 308.

17. Graham Fuller, *The Future of Political Islam* (New York: Palgrave, 2003), p. xi. Jytte Klausen takes this a step further in defining Islamism as "a political movement that seeks to curtail the spread of Western secularism." Klausen, *The Islamic Challenge: Politics and Religion in Western Europe* (Oxford: Oxford University Press, 2005), p. 160. But is the rejection of modern secular values not the original rationale for the coining of Christian fundamentalism?

18. Bruce Lawrence, *Shattering the Myth: Islam beyond Violence* (Princeton: Princeton University Press, 1998), p. 40.

19. Salman Rushdie, *Imaginary Homelands: Essays and Criticism 1981–1991* (London: Granta Books, 1991), p. 382. Well-read American readers will not fail to recognize that red-blooded, at least figuratively, Americans branded Russian and Chinese Communists as the red tide. The "yellow" peril referred first to World War II Japan and then, by extension, to China (e.g., Hal Lindsay, *The Late Great Planet Earth* [New York: Bantam, 1973], p. 70), which makes the latter doubly colored in the rhetoric of conservatives.

20. I choose *spokesmen* not out of political incorrectness, but to stress the point that virtually all prominent Christian fundamentalist voices are male. A year after the 9/11 tragedy, evangelical media star Rev. Pat Robertson labeled Muhammad "an absolute wild-eyed fanatic." And Rev. Jerry Vines, past president of the Southern Baptist Convention, defamed the Prophet Muhammad as a "demon-possessed pedophile."

21. A prime example of this association is in the writing and drawing of cartoon evangelist Jack Chick. See Chick, *The Prophet*, Alberto Series Part Six (Chino, CA: Chick Publications, 1988). I analyze Chick's Islamophobia in Varisco, "The Tragedy of a Comic: Fundamentalists Crusading against Fundamentalists," *Contemporary Islam* 1, no. 3 (2007): 207–30.

22. There are many nuances in the use of fundamentalist for certain Protestant Christians in America. See Susan Harding, *The Book of Jerry Falwell: Fundamentalist Language and Politics* (Princeton, NJ: Princeton University Press, 2000), pp. xv–xvi. Related, at times quite loosely, terms include *Bible-believers, born-again Christians, conservative Christians,* the *Christian Right* and *evangelicals*.

23. For a succinct account of this text's creation and reception, see Ernest R. Sandeen, *The Roots of Fundamentalism: British and American Millenarianism, 1800-1930* (Chicago: University of Chicago Press, 1970), pp. 188–207. That one of the project backers, Lyman Stewart, was also the head of an oil company may be of interest to conspiracy theorists.

24. Bulliet argues: "The past and future of the West cannot be fully comprehended without appreciation of the twinned relationship it has had with Islam over some fourteen centuries. The same is true of the Islamic world." Bulliet, *The Case for Islamo-Christian Civilization* (New York: Columbia University Press, 2004), p. 45.

25. We English speakers have *evangelicalism*, but so far no *evangelicalists*. The term *fundamentalist* is loosely applied for Christians. One of the more egregious examples is referring to "fundamentalist activity" of the National Conference of Catholic Bishops. Mary Hegland, introduction to *Religious Resurgence: Contemporary Cases in Islam, Christianity, and Judaism*, ed. R. Antoun and M. Hegland (Syracuse, NY: Syracuse University Press, 1987), p. 1.

26. Morroe Berger, *The Arab World Today* (Garden City, NY: Anchor Books, 1964), p. 416.

27. R. Stephen Humphreys, "Islam and Political Values in Saudi Arabia, Egypt and Syria," in *Religion and Politics in the Middle East*, ed. Michael Curtis (Boulder: Westview Press, 1981), p. 290. According to Humphreys, "We may define Fundamentalism as the reaffirmation, in a radically changed environment, of traditional modes of understanding and behavior" (ibid., 289). He borrows three terms from the American vocabulary: *fundamentalism, modernism, secularism*. In a later work, he defends use of "Islamic fundamentalism," but laments that it is indiscriminately applied in the media. Humphreys, *Between Memory and Desire: The Middle East in a Troubled Age* (Berkeley: University of California Press, 1999), p. xvi.

28. Lawrence, *Shattering*, 40, associates its first consistent application with the Iranian hostage crisis in 1979. It is noteworthy that the term *fundamentalism* is not mentioned by Edward Said (*Covering Islam*, 1997) in the first edition narrative of his scathing critique of academized media coverage of Islam in the wake of the hostage crisis, although he rejects the term in his introduction to the second edition. Nor does it appear in Richard C. Martin's survey of approaches to Islam in religious studies. See Martin, "Islam and Religious Studies: An Introductory Essay," in *Approaches to Islam in Religious Studies*, ed. R. C. Martin (Tucson: University of Arizona

Press, 1985), pp. 1–21. In searching the catalog of the Library of Congress for titles with "Islamic fundamentalist" or its variants, the earliest I found was Emmanuel Sivan, *Islamic fundamentalism and anti-Semitism* (Jerusalem: Hebrew University of Jerusalem, 1985), also published in Hebrew, which is a polemical work comparing it with anti-Semitism. In 1988 Watt published *Islamic Fundamentalism and Modernity* (London: Routledge). In all I can document no more than a dozen books on Islam that contain the term in a title before 1990, after which there is a surge of such labeling.

29. George M. Marsden, *Fundamentalism and American Culture* (Oxford: Oxford University Press, 1980), p. 227.

30. Martin E. Marty and R. Scott Appleby, "The Fundamentalism Project: A User's Guide," in *Fundamentalisms Observed*, ed. M. E. Marty and R. S. Appleby (Chicago: University of Chicago Press, 1991), p. ix. For critiques of the coverage of Islam in this set of volumes, see Ian Lustick, "Fundamentalism, Politicized Religion & Pietism," *MESA Bulletin* 30 (1996): 26–32; Saba Mahmood, "Review: Islamism and Fundamentalism," *MERIP* 191 (1994): 29–30; and Jane I. Smith, "The Fundamentalism Project Observed: Views of Islam," *MESA Bulletin* 28 (1994): 169–72.

31. Marty and Appleby, "The Fundamentalism Project," p. viii.

32. Lawrence Davidson, *Islamic Fundamentalism* (London: Greenwood Press, 1998), p. 17. For a more balanced view of Islamic "reformers," see John L. Esposito, *Islam: The Straight Path*, rev. 3rd ed. (Oxford: Oxford University Press, 2005). The pan-Islamist (in the old sense) scholar al-Afghani is the subject of an important analysis by Nikki Keddie. See Keddie, *An Islamic Response to Imperialism: Political and Religious Writings of Sayyid Jamâl al-Dîn "al-Afghânî"* (Berkeley: University of California Press, 1968).

33. Barbara Metcalf, "'Remaking Ourselves': Islamic Self-Fashioning in a Global Movement of Spiritual Renewal," in *Accounting for Fundamentalisms*, ed. M. E. Marty and R. S. Appleby (Chicago: University of Chicago Press, 1994), p. 706. C.A.O. Van Nieuwenhuijze, "Islamism—a Defiant Utopianism," *Die Welt des Islams* 35, no. 1 (1995) similarly rejects application of fundamentalism to Islam in favor of Islamism. Roy Mottahedeh suggests that "lavish, ignorant, and sensationalizing uses of words like *fundamentalism* have blinded us to their [Muslim] humanity and diversity." Mottahedeh, "The Clash of Civilizations: An Islamicist's Critique," in *The New Crusades: Constructing the Muslim Enemy*, ed. Emran Qureshi and Michael A. Sells (New York: Columbia University Press), p. 141. Even Prince Charles ("Islam and the West," *Islam and Christian Muslim Relations* 5, no. 1 [1994]: 70), in a speech to the Oxford Centre for Islamic Studies, cautions against use of "that emotive label, 'fundamentalism'."

34. Bruce Lawrence, *Defenders of God: The Fundamentalist Revolt Against the Modern World* (Columbia: University of South Carolina Press, 1995), p. 190.

35. Michael Williams, *Rethinking "Gnosticism:" An Argument for Dismantling a Dubious Category* (Princeton, NJ: Princeton University Press, 1996), p. 3. Elizabeth Brown, "The Tyranny of a Construct: Feudalism and Historians of Medieval Europe," *American Historical Review* 79 (1974):1063–88 made a similar call for abandoning the overwrought term *feudalism* in medieval studies.

36. Bulliet, *The Case for Islamo-Christian Civilization*, p. 1.

37. Fadwa El Guindi, *Veil: Modesty, Privacy and Resistance* (Oxford: Berg, 1999), p. xiv. She writes as an anthropologist, a Muslim, a feminist, and a filmmaker.

38. Akbar Ahmed, *Islam Today: A Short Introduction to the Muslim World* (London: I. B. Taurus, 1999), p. 9. I do not read this as an apologetically circular argument that anyone who does not believe the pillars can not be a "true" Muslim. Note that the Christian "fundamentals" are entirely doctrinal and at the time had been subjected to a liberal dose of demythologizing within mainstream Christian theology, whereas the Islamic "pillars" are primarily concerned with ritual; nor does belief in one deity and a human prophet require as great a leap of faith from Enlightenment rationality. If all Christians had to do was believe in one God and that Jesus is God's messenger, almost all Christian sects would have to be labeled fundamentalist.

39. Ironically, Said (*Orientalism* [New York: Pantheon, 1979]) tolled the death knell for *Orientalism* just as fundamentalism began to be applied to Muslims. For an analysis of the impact of Said's Orientalism thesis, see Varisco, *Reading Orientalism: Said and the Unsaid* (Seattle: University of Washington Press, 2007).

40. H. M. Hopfl, "Isms," *British Journal of Political Science* 13, no. 1 (1983):13.

41. Michael R. Dressman, "The Suffix 'Ist,'" *American Speech* 60, no. 3 (1985): 238. Most of the details in this paragraph are taken from this informative source.

42. One wonders why it took so long for individuals to recognize the terror inherent in capitalism.

43. Adrienne Lehrer, "A Note on the Semantics of 'Ist and 'Ism," *American Speech* 63, no. 2 (1988): 183, argues that this shift started with *racism*, extended to *sexism* and finally to the sense of -ism as such. Hopfl ("Isms," p. 4) argues that from the very start in the sixteenth century "-isms have tended to shed any determinant referent, and to become vague and derogatory synonyms for heresy and for pernicious doctrines and practices in general."

44. The use of -ism is also decidedly Whiggish in the historical sense defined by Herbert Butterfield (*The Whig Interpretation of History* [London: G. Bell and Sons, 1931]). Referring to concepts such as feudalism, Richard Southern warned that such *-ism* terms "belong to a recent period of history, and their use injects into the past the ideas of a later age." Southern, *Medieval Humanism* (New York: Harper and Row, 1970), p. 29.

45. The *OED* notes that the Arabic meaning has also been generalized to include "a campaign or crusade in some cause." Turning Jihadists and *mujahadeen* into Jihadis, as Mary Habeck (*Knowing the Enemy: Jihadist Ideology and the War on Terror*

[New Haven, CT: Yale University Press, 2006]) inconsistently does, only compounds the problem with an impossible Arabic construction.

46. The blast map site was at www.nuclearterrorism.org/blastmaps.html.

47. Free World Academy, www.freeworldacademy.com/globalleader/newwarcontent.htm. One must wonder about a site that thinks the Muslim holy book is the "Khoran," as the site read in 2004.

48. For a critique of American support of the Afghan jihad before taking out the Taliban, see Abid Ullah Jan, "Distinguishing between Jihad and Jihadism," The Independent Centre for Strategic Studies and Analysis, 2004, http://icssa.org/Jihadism.htm (accessed November 2004).

49. Monte Palmer and Princess Palmer, At the Heart of Terror: Islam, Jihadists, and America's War on Terror (Lanham, MD: Rowman & Littlefield, 2004).

50. Quoted in Dwight Lee, "The Origins of Pan-Islamism." The American Historical Review 47, no. 2 (1942): 280.

51. See Esposito, Islam, pp. 165–66 for a succinct summary of the ideological framework of Islamic revivalism. Esposito (What Everyone Needs to Know about Islam [Oxford: Oxford University Press, 2002], p. 44) rejects the term fundamentalism because it has been applied to a broad spectrum of idealists and reformers, noting a difference between those who wage jihad and those who advocate ijtihad (reinterpretation).

52. Richard Antoun and Mary Hegland, eds., Religious Resurgence: Contemporary Cases in Islam, Christianity, and Judaism (Syracuse, NY: Syracuse University Press, 1987), p. 258.

53. Ernest Renan, The Poetry of the Celtic Races, and Other Studies, trans. William G. Hutchinson (London: Walter Scott, 1896), p. 85. The translated title of the lecture is "Islamism and Science."

54. Ibid., p. 97.

55. Abdul Hamid el-Zein, "Beyond Ideology and Theology: The Search for the Anthropology of Islam," Annual Review of Anthropology 6 (1977): 252. I discuss the implications of el-Zein's thesis in Varisco, Islam Obscured: The Rhetoric of Anthropological Representation (New York: Palgrave, 2005), pp. 146–50.

56. As Fawaz A. Gerges shows, President Ronald Reagan was so concerned with Soviet Communism that he "often reiterated his support for the Islamically oriented mujaheden 'freedom fighters' because they resisted the Soviets." Gerges, America and Political Islam: Clash of Cultures or Clash of Interests? (Cambridge: Cambridge University Press, 1999), p. 71.

Terminological Problems for Muslim Lives

1. I appreciate the thoughtful contributions by Donald Emmerson and Daniel Varisco that frame this volume. At the outset, let me state that I find myself in

agreement with Varisco's position. In the interests of full disclosure let me also state that although I have never met and do not know Emmerson, I have spent long hours into the night in conversation with Varisco, who I consider to be as much a friend as a colleague. I hope that this does not mean that I read Emmerson uncharitably.

2. Neil Postman and Steve Powers, *How to Watch TV News*, rev. edn. (New York: Penguin, 2008).

3. Joe Sacco, *Palestine: The Special Edition* (Seattle: Fantagraphics Books, 2007).

4. Derek Evans, *Before the War* (Kelowna, BC: Wood Lake Books, 2004).

5. *Ibid.*, pp. 87–113.

6. James Clifford and George E. Marcus, eds., *Writing Culture: The Poetics and Politics of Ethnography* (Berkeley: University of California Press, 1986); Benedict Anderson, *Imagined Communities: Reflections on the Origin and Spread of Nationalism*, rev. edn. (New York: Verso, 1999); Rosaldo Renato, *Culture and Truth: The Remaking of Social Analysis* (Boston: Beacon Press, 1993).

7. For information on this work, see Islam by Choice. "Apostasy and Islam," http://apostasyandislam.blogspot.com (accessed April 10, 2009).

Between Etymology and Realpolitik

1. Jul, *La croisade s'amuse*, ed. Albin Michel (Paris: n.p., 2006), p. 1.

Academic Word Games

1. For more on this document, see Nathan Brown and Amr Hamzawy, "The Draft Party Platform of the Egyptian Muslim Brotherhood: Foray Into Political Integration or Retreat Into Old Positions?" (Washington DC: Carnegie Endowment for International Peace, 2008). See www.carnegieendowment.org/publications/index.cfm?fa=view&id=19835&prog=zgp&proj=zme (accessed May 6, 2009).

Islamism: *ism* or *wasm*?

1. Adjectives can be overused. The Kavkaz Center Internet News Agency (www.kavkazcenter.com), when reporting on Taliban efforts in Afghanistan, regularly refers to their opponents, sometimes twice in the same sentence, as "American Christian kafir terrorist occupation military." See, for example, Anon, "Mujahideen Fight Invaders and Occupying Troops," April 12, 2007, http://old.kavkazcenter.com/eng/content/2007/04/12/8013.shtml (accessed April 13 2009).

2. See, for example, James Barr, *Fundamenalism* (London: SCM Press, 1977).

3. Lionel Caplan, ed., *Studies in Religious Fundamentalism* (London: MacMillan, 1987).

4. For nationalist fundamentalism, see Richard Tapper and Nancy Tapper, " 'Thank God We're Secular!' Aspects of Fundamentalism in a Turkish Town," in Caplan, *Studies in Religious Fundamentalism*, pp. 51–78.

5. We have told the story of this rethinking of *Islamism* in Ziba Mir-Hosseini and Richard Tapper, *Islam and Democracy in Iran: Eshkevari and the Quest for Reform* (London: I B Tauris, 2006).

6. See Olivier Roy, *l'Echec de l'Islam Politique* (Paris: Le Seuil, 1992); Asef Bayat, "The Coming of a Post-Islamist Society," *Critique: Critical Middle East Studies* 9 (Fall 1996): 43–52; Gilles Kepel, *Jihad: Expansion et Déclin de l'islamisme* (Paris: Gallimard, 2000).

Rejecting Islamism and the Need for Concepts from Within the Islamic Tradition

1. Martin Kramer, "Coming to Terms: Fundamentalism or Islamists," *Middle East Quarterly* (Spring 2003): 65–77. www.geocities.com/martinkramerorg/Terms.htm (accessed February 10, 2005).

2. Ibid., p. 2.

3. Ibid.

4. Ibid., p. 7.

5. Gilles Kepel, *Le prophéte et pharaon: Les mouvements islamistes dans l'Egypt contemporaine* (Paris: La Decouverte, 1984).

6. Robert H. Pelletreau Jr., Speech to Council on Foreign Relations, May 8 1996, http://dosfan.lib.uic.edu/ERC/bureaus/nea/960508PelletreauMuslim.html (accessed February 13, 2005).

7. Karl Mannheim, *Ideology and Utopia: An Introduction to the Sociology of Knowledge* (London: Routledge and Kegan Paul, 1936), pp. 36–37.

8. Ibid.

9. Both orientations were heavily criticised by the mainstream schools of the early Islamic period. *Ghuluw* was used to refer to extremist Shiites on account of their attribution of divinity to the imams. See ibn Khaldun, *Muqaddimat Ibn Khaldun (The Prolegomenon of Ibn Khaldun)* (Beirut: Dar al-Qalam, 1981), p. 198. The *hashwiyyah* are the anthropomorhists and strict textual literalists. See al-Hujwiri, *Kashf al-Majhub (Unveiling of the Veiled)*, Vol. 2 (Cairo: Al-Ahram, 1985), p. 484.

10. Alatas, Syed Farid, "Understanding the Relationship Between Islam and Reform: A Khaldunian Perspective," in Ahmad Murad Merican, Ahmad Suhaimi Ismail, R. Jeevaratnam, Rahmat Mohamad, Rozita Hajar, Umminajah Salleh, and Zaini Abdullah, eds., *Proceedings of the International Conference—The Ummah at the Crossroads: The Role of the OIC* (Shah Alam: Institute of Knowledge Advancement [InKA] & Kuala Lumpur: Institute of Diplomacy and Foreign Relations Malaysia [IDFR], 2005), pp. 11–21.

11. Bernard Lewis, *The Political Language of Islam* (Chicago: University of Chicago Press, 1988), p. 117, n3.

12. Nazih N. M. Ayubi, *Political Islam: Religion and Politics in the Arab World* (London: Routledge, 1991), p. 256, cited in Kramer (see note 1).

13. Sadik J. Al-Azm, "Islamic Fundamentalism Reconsidered: A Critical Outline of Problems, Ideas and Approaches," *South Asia Bulletin* (1993): 1–2.

Islam at Risk: The Discourse on Islam and Violence

1. Henry Munson, Jr., "Western Academic and Islamic Fundamentalism," in *Contention* 5, no. 3 (Spring 1996): 96–117. Both Beth Baron and Mark Juergensmeyer wrote rejoinders, the latter perceptively noting that the huger battle of stereotypes re Islam lay just ahead due to the publication of Samuel Huntington's blinkered essay, "The Clash of Civilizations?" in *Foreign Affairs* 72 (Summer 1993).

2. Defined by Piscatori and cited in Emmerson's chapter above: "Islamists are Muslims who are committed to political action to implement what they regard as an Islamic agenda, Islamism is a commitment to and the content of that agenda."

3. See Abdullahi An-Na'im, *Islam and the Secular State: Negotiating the Future of Shari'a* (Cambridge, MA: Harvard University Press, 2008), p. 260. He invoked this phrase in discussing the relationship between Islam, the state, and society in contemporary Indonesia, but it also applies to the dyadic categories under review in this essay.

4. The argument I am advancing here evokes in summary form the distinction elaborated by Bruce Lincoln in *Holy Terrors: Thinking About Religion After September 11* (Chicago: University of Chicago Press, 2003), pp. 6–7. There Lincoln demurs from Geertz, Talal Asad, and others in offering his own "polythetic and flexible" definition of religion, to wit, that it "comprises discourse, practices, community and institutions." I prefer to use but three tangents and terms to discuss religion, namely, *language*, *values*, and *institutions*, though my crucial agreement with Lincoln, and indebtedness to him, is to accent the critical role of institutions in any assessment of what is meant by religion and how it functions cross-culturally.

5. An-Na'im, *Islam and the Secular State*, p. 261.

6. Jacques Waardenberg, "Muslim States, Islamic Norms and Secular Realities," (unpublished article, ca. June 1990). Waardenberg goes on to distinguish between two kinds of Islamists, the more reflective being "fundamentalists," the more political "activists." However, in my view, one of the defining characteristics of fundamentalists is their insistence on implementing religious ideals in the political sphere; fundamentalists are invariably political rather than reflective. It is on this crucial point, and also on the essentialist tone of his arguments about the concept of Islam, that my approach differs from another of Waardenberg's wide-ranging essays: "Islam as a Vehicle

of Protest," in Ernest Gellner, ed., *Islamic Dilemma: Reformers, Nationalists and In-dustrialization: The Southern Shore of the Mediterranean* (The Hague: Mouton, 1985), pp. 22–48.

7. Nasr Hamid Abu Zayd, *Reformation of Islamic Thought—A Critical Historical Analysis* (Amsterdam: Amsterdam University Press, 2006), p. 11.

8. Ibid., p. 46.

9. Ibid., p. 89.

10. India is arguably a Muslim minority polity with implications for the nature of Muslim minorities throughout Africa and Asia, as Marshall Hodgson observed over fifty years ago.

11. An-Na'im, *Islam and the Secular State*, p. 296.

12. Lincoln, *Holy Terrors*, p. 111n14.

13. Peter Mandaville, *Global Political Islam* (London: Routledge, 2007), p. 58.

14. Olivier Roy, *The Failure of Political Islam* (Cambridge, MA: Harvard University Press, 1994).

15. Asaf Bayat, "What Is Post-Islamism?" *ISIM Review* 16 (2005): 5, but also see his earlier and more substantive essay, "The Coming of a Post-Islamist Society," *Critique* (Fall 1996): 43–52.

16. Ibid.

17. Roy, *Failure of Political Islam*, p. 202.

Naming Terror

1. George Weigel, "The War Against Jihadism: Why Can't We Call the Enemy by Its Name? We're Going to Have to In Order to Win," *Newsweek*, Feburary 5, 2008; Weigel, *Faith, Reason, and the War Against Jihadism: A Call to Action* (New York: Doubleday, 2007).

2. See Gilles Kepel, *Fitna: Guerre au Coeur de l'islam* (Paris: Gallimard, 2004).

Political Islam, Liberalism, and the Diagnosis of a Problem

1. Zuhdi Jasser, "Americanism vs. Islamism: A Personal Perspective," Foreign Policy Research Institute, January 2008, www.fpri.org/enotes/200801.jasseramerican-ismislamism.html (accessed May 21, 2008).

2. Ibid.

3. M. Sa'id al-Ashmawy, *Against Islamic Extremism* (Gainesville: University Press of Florida, 1998).

4. Said Qutb, *Milestones (Ma'alim fi al-Tariq)* (Cairo: Kazi Publications, 1964). See also, Hassan Al-Banna, *Our Message* (attribution, non-commercial), www.scribd.com/doc/2386566/Our-Message-by-Imam-Hassan-Al-Banna.

5. Oliver Roy, *Globalized Islam: The Search for the New Ummah* (New York: Columbia University Press, 2004).

6. Zuhdi Jasser, "The Synergy of Libertarianism and Islam," *Vital Speeches of the Day* 72, no.14 (July 19, 2006): 454–57.

7. The Official Website of the Amman Message, *The Amman Message*, November 9, 2004, www.ammanmessage.com/ (accessed May 21, 2008).

8. Zuhdi Jasser, "Exposing the Flying Imams," *Middle East Quarterly* 15, no. 1 (Winter 2008): 3–11.

Ideology, Not Religion

1. Norman Cohn, *The Pursuit of the Millennium* (Oxford: Oxford University Press, 1970).

2. There is no equivalent of the all-encompassing Sharia law in the Western European tradition. Even at the height of papal power from the eleventh to the thirteenth centuries, the legal codes of Western European states were based on Roman civil law or common law, not on religious sources. Medieval as well as modern Europeans acknowledged the boundaries between the secular and ecclesiastical spheres, although the boundaries between the two spheres were often contested. Western medieval and early modern history is replete with conflicts between the secular and religious authorities.

3. The Abbasid caliphate came to an end in 1258, when Hulagu sacked Baghdad. In 1261 the Mamluk sultan of Egypt, wishing to legitimize his rule, installed a scion of the Abbasids in Cairo as figurehead caliph. This arrangement continued until the Ottoman conquest of Egypt in 1517. Some scholars have disputed the validity of the transference of the caliphate to the Ottomans. See Cyril Glassé, ed., *The New Encyclopedia of Islam* (Walnut Creek, CA: AltaMira Press, 2002), p. 530.

4. Juan Cole, *Sacred Space and Holy War: The Politics, Culture and History of Shi'ite Islam* (London: I.B. Tauris, 2002).

5. Youssef M. Choueiri, *Islamic Fundamentalism* (Boston: Twayne Publishers, 1990), pp. 36–38.

6. Hasan al-Banna observed that "the civilization of the West, which was brilliant by virtue of its scientific perfection for a long time, and which subjugated the whole world with the products of this science to its states and nations, is now bankrupt and in decline." in Richard P. Mitchell, *The Society of the Muslim Brothers* (Oxford: Oxford University Press, 1993).

7. Islamists reject the separation of religion (*din*) and state (*dawla*) because Islam is not just din but a way of life that includes political, economic, and social behavior. Therefore, din is not distinct from dawla. Both are expressions of Islam. Richard P. Mitchell, *The Society of the Muslim Brothers*, p. 243.

8. Of course, Wahhabis consider the term pejorative and prefer to call themselves *al-Muwahhidun* or *Ahl al-Tawhid*, "the people [who uphold] the unity of God," but *Wahhabi* is the commonly used term.

9. One example of abrogation is the following: Qur'an 2.109 states, "Many of the followers of the Book wish that they could turn you back into unbelievers after your faith, out of envy from themselves, (even) after the truth has become manifest to them; but pardon and forgive, so that Allah should bring about His command; surely Allah has power over all things." It is abrogated by Qur'an 9.29: "Fight those who do not believe in Allah, nor in the latter day, nor do they prohibit what Allah and His Apostle have prohibited, nor follow the religion of truth, out of those who have been given the Book, until they pay the tax in acknowledgment of superiority and they are in a state of subjection." Joseph N. Kickasola, "The Clash of Civilizations Within Islam: The Struggle Over the Qu'ran Between Muslim Democrats and Theocrats," paper delivered at "Mr. Jefferson Goes to the Middle East: Democracy's Prospects in the Arab World," conference sponsored by The Center for Vision & Values, Grove City College, Grove City, PA, April 6, 2006.

10. Mahmoud Mohamed Taha, *The Second Message of Islam*, trans. Abdullahi An-Na'im (Syracuse: Syracuse University Press, 1996).

11. Shmuel Bar, discussion with author, Washington, DC, November 2006.

12. Mitchell, *The Society of the Muslim Brothers*, p. 207; originally in 'Abd al-Mun'im Ahmad Ta'lib, *Al-Bay'a: Sharh Risalat al-Ta'alim* (Cairo: n.p. 1952), p.56. *Jahiliyya* refers to the "age of ignorance" before Muhammad's revelation.

13. For the current posture of the Egyptian Muslim Brotherhood, see Israel Elad-Altman, "Democracy, Elections and the Egyptian Muslim Brotherhood," in *Current Trends in Islamist Ideology*, vol. 3, ed. Hillel Fradkin, Hussain Huqqani, and Eric Brown (Washington, DC: Hudson Institute, 2006).

Why Islamism Should Be Renamed

The ideas of this essay are expanded from my book *What's Right with Islam Is What's Right with America* (San Francisco: Harper San Francisco, 2005), from which Professor Varisco quotes my antipathy to the use of the term *Islamism*.

1. As Varisco points out, because the word *Negro* had at one time a negative valuation, especially its derogatory version, *nigger*, it was stricken from usage. The argument that it is an intellectually accurate description of an ethnic race became trumped by the derogatory implications of the term, and a momentum built to make it politically incorrect.

2. This nomenclature would therefore suggest *Christian religionism, Jewish religionism, Hindu religionism, Buddhist religionism*, and so forth, making our nomenclature more coherent and less susceptible to the problematic nomenclature of the

term *fundamentalism*, with its roots in the history of early twentieth-century American Protestantism.

3. Michael Novak, "The Most Religious Century," *New York Times*, May 24, 1998.

4. See Madeleine K. Albright, *The Mighty and the Almighty: Reflections on God, America, and World Affairs* (New York: HarperCollins, 2006), in which she discusses the importance of factoring in the role of religion in foreign policy; Marc Gopin, "Counter Religious Extremism with Religious Compassion," *Christian Science Monitor*, September 7, 2006; Jim Wallis, *Living God's Politics: A Guide to Putting Your Faith Into Action*, (San Francisco: Harper San Francisco, 2006); and Richard Land, *Imagine! A God-Blessed America: How It Could Happen and What It Would Look Like* (Nashville, TN: B&H Publishing Group, 2005).

5. The three Abrahamic religions—Judaism, Christianity, and Islam—share the two greatest commandments: (1) To love God with all our heart, mind, soul, and strength, and (2) To love our neighbors—that is, our fellow human beings, regardless of race, religion, and ethnic or cultural background—as we love ourselves.

Mitigating Misrepresentation

1. Richard Bulliet, *The Case for Islamo-Christian Civilization* (New York: Columbia University Press, 2004), p. 70.

Broadening Representation

For helpful conversations and correspondence, I am grateful to Syed Farid Alatas, Ahmed Alwishah, Jackie Armijo, Khalil Barhoum, Hicham Benabdallah, John Bowen, Susan Chira, David Giovacchini, Shadi Hamid, Robert Hefner, Erik Jensen, Gilles Kepel, Farhad Khosrokhavar, Rami G. Khouri, Damien Kingsbury, R. William Liddle, Abdeslam Mahgraoui, Richard C. Martin, Angel Rabasa, Olivier Roy, Daniel M. Varisco, and Charles U. Zenzie, who are in no way responsible for what survives their information, opinions, and advice.

1. Samuel P. Huntington, "The Clash of Civilizations?" *Foreign Affairs* 72, no. 3 (Summer 1993), www.foreignaffairs.com/articles/48950/samuel-p-huntington/the-clash-of-civilizations?page=5 (accessed April 28, 2009); *The Clash of Civilizations and the Remaking of World Order* (New York: Simon & Schuster, 1996), p. 258.

2. I do believe that Huntington's words injured Muslim self-respect. But the plausibility of even that assertion could benefit from evidence. Such evidence is likely to show variation in the extent to which the self-respect of human beings who consider themselves Muslims is, in fact, endangered by negative evaluations of Islam. We should be at least willing to entertain the possibility that a Muslim could disagree with Huntington

without feeling personally victimized by him. Imputing to all Muslims a monolithically personal insecurity linked to criticism of their religion makes it easier to conclude that Huntington's comments must be inaccurate simply and solely because they are inconsiderate. Without separating the premise (insult) from the inference (falsity), we cannot replace mere personal distaste ("Huntington is mean") with solid contrary evidence ("Huntington is wrong").

3. Huntington, *Clash*, p. 258.

4. Monty Marshall, comp., "Major Episodes of Political Violence 1946–2006," Center for Systemic Peace (CSP), as updated through September 18, 2007. A research professor at George Mason University, where he heads the CSP, Marshall has collaborated with University of Maryland professor emeritus Ted Robert Gurr on a variety of surveys of armed conflicts. In using this evidence, I relied on the actual data, which were later updated to the end of 2008, when 27 conflicts were ongoing. For the latest list, see www.systemicpeace.org/warlist.htm (accessed April 29, 2009).

5. The most often cited estimates of the proportion of the world's population who profess Islam vary in a narrow band between 21 and 19 percent. Compare the 21, 20, and 19 percent figures in, respectively, Central Intelligence Agency, *The World Factbook*, www.cia.gov/library/publications/the-world-factbook/geos/xx.html #People; Ohio Consultants on Religious Tolerance, "Religions of the World," www .religioustolerance.org/worldrel.htm; and the Vatican yearbook's estimate for 2008 as reported in Reuters UK, "Muslims More Numerous than Catholics: Vatican," March 30, 2008, http://uk.reuters.com/article/UKNews1/idUKL3068682420080330. (These sites were accessed April 29, 2009.)

6. For more on the value of qualitative research, see my "Southeast Asia in Political Science: Terms of Enlistment," in Erik Martinez Kuhonta, Dan Slater, and Tuong Vu, eds., *Southeast Asia in Political Science: Theory, Region, and Qualitative Analysis* (Stanford, CA: Stanford University Press, 2008), pp. 302–24. For a soft copy of the chapter, see The Walter H. Shorenstein Asia-Pacific Research Center, http://aparc.stanford .edu/publications/southeast_asia_in_political_science_terms_of_enlistment/ (accessed April 29, 2009).

7. John Thorne and Hannah Stuart, *Islam on Campus: A Survey of UK Students* (London: The Centre for Social Cohesion, 2008), p. 35; italics mine. More than six hundred Muslim and over eight hundred non-Muslim students were surveyed.

8. Someone opposed to the term *Islamist* might reply that although a plurality (36 percent) of the Muslim students were not fooled by the hijacking of Islam by Islamism— the appropriation and contamination of religion by ideology—it is the non-Muslim students who would have mistakenly and prejudicially confused the two as "part of the same thing." On the contrary, a plurality (41 percent) of non-Muslim respondents also chose to distinguish Islam from Islamism. Thorne and Stuart, *Islam on Campus*,

p. 100. Obviously these data are far from representative of Muslims or non-Muslims in general, but they do at least suggest that both types of university students in the United Kingdom are more able to separate religion from ideology than opponents of "Islam-as-Islamism" might allow.

9. Among the Muslim respondents, only 30 percent of those belonging to "Islamic societies" declined to choose either of the two statements, compared with 50 percent of the non-members who did so. Thorne and Stuart, *Islam on Campus*, p. 90.

10. Illustrating this point is the reference to the future in the title of Ramadan's book, *Western Muslims and the Future of Islam* (New York: Oxford University Press, 2004).

11. Other critiques of revivalism and resurgence as leitmotivs include Eric Davis, "The Concept of Revival and the Study of Islam and Politics," in Barbara Freyer Stowasser, ed., *The Islamic Impulse* (London: Croom Helm, 1987), pp. 37–58; Salwa Ismail, *Rethinking Islamist Politics: Culture, the State and Islamism* (London: I. B. Tauris, 2003), pp. 7–10, 16.

12. I realize how difficult it is for outsiders to know which of these motivations applies. Pending better evidence, however, the circumstances of the case and the self-reporting of the actors involved should be taken at face value: Examples of democratic Islamism could include Muslims whose support for democracy is self-justified with reference to Islam, or practiced through membership in a group identified with Islam. Examples of Islamist terrorism could include comparable evidence of self-expression and group membership, including the invocation of Islam prior to or during the act of violence itself. Muslims should *not* be assumed to have religious motivations for everything they say and do.

13. As of April 2009, Wikipedia's entry for *Christianism* defined it as "the belief that Christianity is superior to all other religions"; enmity, based on that belief, against non-Christian persons or religions; and "the quest" for Christian dominance throughout society and around the world, http://en.wikipedia.org/wiki/Christianism (accessed April 30, 2009). For Andrew Sullivan ("My Problem with Christianism," *Time*, May 7, 2006),

> Christianism is an ideology, politics, an ism. The distinction between Christian and Christianist echoes the distinction we make between Muslim and Islamist. Muslims are those who follow Islam. Islamists are those who want to wield Islam as a political force and conflate state and mosque. Not all Islamists are violent. Only a tiny few are terrorists. And I should underline that the term Christianist is in no way designed to label people on the religious right as favoring any violence at all. I mean merely by the term Christianist the view that religious faith is so important that it must also have a precise political agenda. It is the belief that religion

dictates politics and that politics should dictate the laws for everyone, Christian and non-Christian alike.

The coinage and currency of *Christianism* is helpful to my case for *Islamism*, and Sullivan rightly contextualizes terrorism by Muslims as the activity of a "tiny few." But his exclusion of violence from Christianist repertoires is hard to reconcile with the massacre of Palestinian refugees by Christian Phalange militias in the Sabra and Shatila camps in Lebanon in 1982, or with the killing of Protestants by Catholics and vice versa in Northern Ireland, or with other instances of arguably Christianist violence dating back through the Crusades. Using a double standard compounds the fallacy of denial. I accessed Sullivan's essay at www.time.com/time/magazine/article/ 0,9171,1191826,00.html on April 30, 2009.

14. Said Humpty Dumpty to Alice, "When *I* use a word, it means just what I choose it to mean—neither more nor less." When Alice doubted "whether you can make words mean so many different things," Humpty replied, "The question is which is to be master—that's all." Lewis Carroll, *Through the Looking Glass and What Alice Found There* (New York: Bloomsbury / St. Martin's Press, 2001 [1871]), ch. 6, www .literature.org/authors/carroll-lewis/through-the-looking-glass/chapter-06.html (accessed on April 30, 2009). If Humpty, by saying he could use words as he wished, meant that anyone could and should do so, he might be welcomed as a humanist warning against propaganda. But not if he meant that the meanings of words are wholly and only determined by whoever is master, that is, by the outcome of a struggle for power over language. In the latter, conventional version of Humpty's position, subjectivity and domination are inextricably linked and given causal supremacy over meaning. Such a caricature turns ordinary language-users into passive consumers of elite ideology, and reduces consensus to a mere facade for elite hegemony. Given the actual openness, dynamism, and complexity of languages and how they evolve, radical Humptyism in this sense is empirically grotesque. Especially when it comes to words— their interpretation, alteration, innovation—people have long proven themselves more than blotters and sheep.

15. Daniel Pipes, "Distinguishing Between Islam and Islamism," Center for Strategic and International Studies, Washington, DC, June 30, 1998, www.danielpipes.org/ 954/distinguishing-between-islam-and-islamism (accessed May 3, 2009). See also Pipes, "Daniel Pipes Explains 'Islamism,'" *The Minaret*, September 2000, www.danielpipes .org/351/daniel-pipes-explains-islamism (accessed May 3, 2009).

16. Daniel Pipes, "Protecting Muslims while Rooting Out Islamists," *Daily Telegraph* [London], September 14, 2001, www.danielpipes.org/66/protecting-muslims-while -rooting-out-islamists (accessed May 3, 2009).

17. In updating the absolute number of presumed "potential killers," of course, I am assuming that "perhaps 10 to 15 percent" of all Muslims hypothetically still fit that

category. Were Pipes himself updating his estimate eight years after he made it, he might lower—or raise—his original 10 to 15 percent range. My calculation relies on *The World Factbook*'s figure for the world's population in mid-2009 (6.8 billion) and the previously cited estimate that Muslims account for 20 percent of this number; see endnote 5 above.

18. The following publications illustrate inclusive usages of *Islamism*; chapter and page numbers between brackets, when given, pinpoint such usages. All of these URLs were accessed on May 1, 2009. Khalil Al-Anani, "Changing Islamist Politics in the Middle East," June 4, 2008, Saban Center, Brookings Institution, summarized in www.brookings.edu/events/2008/0604_arab_world.aspx; Madeleine Albright et al., *Changing Course: A New Direction for U.S. Relations with the Muslim World* (Washington, DC: U.S.-Muslim Engagement Project, September 2008), pp. 54, 63, 97, www.sfcg.org/programmes/us/pdf/Changing%20Course.pdf; Yusuf al-Qaradawi, as quoted in Tarek Masoud, "Islamist Parties and Democracy: Participation Without Power," *Journal of Democracy* 19, no. 3 (July 2008): 31–36 [34–35]; Mohammed Ayoob, *The Many Faces of Political Islam: Religion and Politics in the Muslim World* (Ann Arbor: The University of Michigan Press, 2008), pp. 88, 94; Raymond William Baker, *Islam Without Fear: Egypt and the New Islamists* (Cambridge, MA: Harvard University Press, 2003); Greg Barton, *Jemaah Islamiyah: Radical Islamism in Indonesia* (Singapore: Ridge Books, 2005), p. 28; Peter Beinart, "The Rehabilitation of the Cold-War Liberal," *The New York Times Magazine*, April 30, 2006, pp. 40–45 [45]; François Burgat, as quoted in Arthur L. Lowrie, "The Campaign against Islam and American Foreign Policy," *Middle East Policy* 4, nos. 1–2 (September 1995): 210-19 [215]; R. Hrair Dekmejian, *Islam in Revolution: Fundamentalism in the Arab World*, 2nd ed. (Syracuse, NY: Syracuse University Press, 1995 [1985]), ch. 5 and pp. 156, 161, 175–76, 211, 213, and 216, cf. 4–5; *The Economist*, "How to Win the War Within Islam," July 17, 2008, www.economist.com/opinion/displaystory.cfm?story_id=11750386; Moataz A. Fattah, *Democratic Values in the Muslim World* (Boulder, CO: Lynne Rienner, 2006), pp. 138–39; Noah Feldman, *The Fall and Rise of the Islamic State* (Princeton, NJ: Princeton University Press, 2008), pp. 155–56; Robert W. Hefner, "Introduction: Islamism and U.S. Policy in South and Southeast Asia," *NBR Analysis* 19, no. 4 (August 2008): 3–12 [4, 11]; Khaled Helmy, "Disaggregating Islam from Social Science Analysis: The Internal Dynamics of Parliamentary Islamism in Comparative Perspective," *Items & Issues* 3, nos. 3–4 (Summer–Fall 2002): 25–28, http://publications.ssrc.org/items/Items3.3_4.pdf; International Crisis Group, "Islamism, Violence and Reform," updated July 2008, www.crisisgroup.org/home/index.cfm?id=2969; International Crisis Group, "Understanding Islamism," March 2, 2005, www.crisisgroup.org/home/index.cfm?id=3301; Salwa Ismail, "Islamism, Re-Islamization and the Fashioning of Muslim Selves: Refiguring the Public Sphere," *Muslim World Journal of Human Rights* 4, no. 1 (2007): Article 3,

pp. 1–21 [2], www.bepress.com/mwjhr/vol4/iss1/art3/; Randal K. James, "The Isla-mist Challenge in the Middle East and North Africa," research report, Air War Col-lege, Maxwell Air Force Base, Alabama, April 1996, p. iv, www.au.af.mil/au/awc/ awcgate/awc/james_rk.pdf; Gilles Kepel, *Jihad: The Trail of Political Islam*, trans. Anthony F. Roberts (Cambridge, MA: The Belknap Press of Harvard University Press, 2002), pp. 13–14, 368–69; Rami G. Khouri, "Understanding Islamism," *Agence Global*, March 15, 2006, www.tompaine.com/articles/2006/03/15/understanding _islamism.php; Hans Küng, *Islam: Past, Present, Future*, trans. John Bowden (Oxford: Oneworld, 2007), pp. 548–50; Robert S. Leiken and Steven Brooke, "The Moderate Muslim Brotherhood," *Foreign Affairs* 86, no. 2 (March–April 2007), www .nixoncenter.org/publications/LeikenBrookeMB.pdf; Marc Lynch, "Islamist Views of Reform," Saban Center, Brookings Institution, February 2008, www.thedohafo-rum.org/assets/taskforce/lynch.pdf; Abdeslam Maghraoui, "What Do Islamists Re-ally Want? An Insider's Discussion with Islamist Leaders," United States Institute of Peace, Washington, DC, May 2006, www.usip.org/pubs/usipeace_briefings/2006/ 0522_islamists.html; Peter Mandaville, *Global Political Islam* (London: Routledge, 2007), ch. 4, esp. p. 101ff.; Pankaj Mishra, "Where Alaa Al Aswany Is Writing From," *The NewYork Times Magazine*, April 27, 2008, pp. 42–47 [44]; Robert H. Pelletreau, "Dealing with the Muslim Politics of the Middle East: Algeria, Hamas, Iran," Coun-cil on Foreign Relations, May 8,1996, http://dosfan.lib.uic.edu/ERC/bureaus/nea/ 960508PelletreauMuslim.html; Ahmad Shboul, "Mapping Spheres of Influence— Globalisation and the 'Islamic Factor' in the Arab World," *The Muslim Reader* [Sin-gapore] 23, no. 2 (May–August 2005): 3–6 [4]; Tamara Wittes, "Islamist Parties and Democracy: Three Kinds of Movements," *Journal of Democracy* 19, no. 3 (July 2008): 7–12; Robin Wright, "Two Visions of Reformation," *Journal of Democracy* 7, no. 2 (1996): 64-75 [64–65]; David Wright-Neville, "Dangerous Dynamics: Activists, Mili-tants and Terrorists in Southeast Asia," *The Pacific Review* 17, no. 1 (March 2004): 27–46 [42]; Malika Zeghal, "Islamist Parties and Democracy: Participation Without Power," *Journal of Democracy* 19, no. 3 (July 2008): 31–36 [34–35].

19. On liberal Islamism and liberal Islamists, see, e.g., Sean Brooks as para-phrased by Sherif Mansour, "The Challenge of Democracy in the Muslim World," *Muslim Democrat* 8, no. 1 (October 2006): 4–8 [7] (www.csidonline.org/images/ stories//muslim_democrat_oct_06_small[1].pdf); Shenaz Bunglawala's review of Gilles Kepel, *Jihad: The Trail of Political Islam* (2002), in *Ethics & International Af-fairs* 16, no. 2 (September 2002): 155–57 [156]; Marc Lynch as interviewed by Brad-ford Plummer, "Voices of the New Arab Public," *Mother Jones*, January 12, 2006, www.motherjones.com/interview/2006/01/marc_lynch.html; Laith Kubba, "Rec-ognizing Pluralism," *Journal of Democracy* 7, no. 2 (1996): 86–89 [88–89]; K. Sub-rahmanyam, "Engage Liberal Islamists," *Times of India*, December 3, 2002, http://

meaindia.nic.in/opinion/2002/12/03002.htm; Dennis Walker, "Recent Malay Religious Magazines as Approaches to Islamic High Culture," presented to the Joint Centre for Malaysian Studies and the Centre of Southeast Asian Studies, Monash University, Clayton, Victoria, Australia, October 26, 2006, summarized in http://arts.monash.edu.au/mai/cms/seminars/seminars06.php. For a contrasting argument that liberal Islamists are wolves in sheep's clothing, see Mohamed Imran Mohamed Taib, "The 'Liberal Islamists': A Preliminary Observation," The Reading Group [Singapore], www.thereadinggroup.sg/Articles/The%20Liberal%20Islamists.pdf. Bracketed page numbers pinpoint relevant usages. (All of these URLs were accessed on May 2, 2009.)

20. Googled data must be treated with caution: They ignore material that may exist in hard copy, on listserves, or in emails, but is not on the Web; the number of Web pages yielded by a search are approximations; and the same document can be counted under different URLs. In this particular comparison, Web pages containing at least one mention of "radical Islamists" and those with at least one reference to "moderate Islamists" numbered 209,000 and 26,900, respectively. Although these two sets of documents were not mutually exclusive, the overlap between them was quite small: Only some 2,310 Web pages contained at least one "radical Islamists" *and* at least one "moderate Islamists." By this measure, the discourse on Islamists appeared to be polarized. The search was done on May 2, 2009.

21. Again, proportionally very few of these Web pages included references to both "radical Islamists" and "moderate Islamists," suggesting again that users of normatively opposed terms related to Islamism *may* be more inclined to prefer one valence over another and not to contrast them in the context of the fuller spectrum that I have in mind. Alternatively, of course, all three datasets may have underestimated this overlap. (On this point, see the next endnote.) The earlier scans were done on August 1, 2005, and October 21, 2008.

22. Books that referred to "radical Islamists" at least once numbered 790, compared with 639 in which "moderate Islamists" occurred. In addition to the caveats above regarding the Web-page searches, one must note that in 2009 many books were still not in Google's database; nor was it clear how thoroughgoing the search of each book might have been. Google's limitations were especially evident when I searched for the overlap within these 1,429 instances of usage. Although Google counted only 157 books that used both phrases, their engine only identified books in which both phrases occurred *on the same page*. In contrast, when searching the typically unpaginated Web for cases of double usage, Google registered occurrences of one and the other wording regardless of their proximity in a given document. What this suggests to me is that the usage of these two phrases by book authors is less polarized than it is on the Web—or to simplify the point, that compared with

blogs, books are more likely to acknowledge the diversity of Islamism. Then again, of course, being longer than Web items, books afford more room for complexity and nuance.

23. Social anthropologist Robert Hefner's notion of "civil Islam" applies to these instances of "Islamism-in-society"—instances that, I am arguing, an equation of Islamism with merely political Islam omits. He understood, of course, that civic associations could hardly thrive without being protected by a state committed to the rule of law. See Robert W. Hefner, *Civil Islam: Muslims and Democratization in Indonesia* (Princeton, NJ: Princeton University Press, 2000). Regrettably if understandably, political scientists have been less willing to acknowledge the nonpolitical uses of Islam. The one difficulty with the notion of *civil Islam* is that it may be mistaken to imply what Hefner did not intend—that Islam itself, as a religion, is entirely civil, as if there were no such thing as *uncivil Islam*, as if in his account accuracy had succumbed to consideration. Anyone who reads *Civil Islam* will not make this error. But on the circuits of our wired world, buzzwords outpace books. A notion of *social Islamisms* that construe Islam in ways that may either support or subvert the construction of a civil society is convenient and realistic, and it distances the religion—Islam—from its many and contested interpretations.

24. For these reasons, although I disagree with Syed Farid Alatas that we ought not use *Islamism* at all, I agree with him that it is problematic when used synonymously with *political Islam*. For the same reasons, I question the implication of the title and subtitle of our book: that the debate about *Islamism* is a debate about *political Islam*, as if they denoted the same thing. They do not.

Many of the scholars and specialists who are content to use the phrase *political Islam* do, of course, understand that the religion of Islam is not innately or exclusively political, and acknowledge, to varying extents, the case for its underlying unity and singularity at least in the eyes of its believers. The phrase *political Islam* is, in any event, too popular to dislodge from general usage. As with the previous comparison of references to *radical* versus *moderate Islamists*, however, *political Islamism* is proportionally far more common in books than it is in the congeries of documents available on the Web. A Google search of the Web on May 3, 2009, identified 429,000 documents using *political Islam* and only 7,960 using *political Islamism*, whereas the comparable figures for usage in books were 1,618 and a proportionally substantial 617.

After finishing this chapter I randomly sampled one of these 617 titles: Alan Richards and John Waterbury, *A Political Economy of the Middle East*, 3rd ed. (Boulder, CO: Westview Press, 1997). On pp. 362–63 these knowledgeable authors interpret Islamism diversely, argue against using *political Islam*, and define and use *political Islamism* for reasons consonant with my own. Similarity is hardly vindication, but the company is welcome.

25. Mohammed Ayoob, *The Many Faces of Political Islam: Religion and Politics in the Muslim World* (Ann Arbor: The University of Michigan Press, 2008), p. 88. Notwithstanding my preference for *political Islamism*, I admire Ayoob's effort to diversify what *political Islam* means and to distinguish religion from politics in his analysis—in ways that parallel my own attempt to acknowledge varieties of *Islamism* while distinguishing that term from Islam.

SUGGESTIONS FOR FURTHER READING

Islam: General References and History

Crone, Patricia. *God's Rule; God and Government: Six Centuries of Islamic Political Thought*. New York: Columbia University Press, 2005.

Denny, Frederick. *An Introduction to Islam*. Upper Saddle River, NJ: Pearson Prentice Hall, 2005.

Esposito, John L., ed. *Oxford Encyclopedia of the Modern Muslim World*. 4 vols. Oxford: Oxford University Press, 1995.

Hodgson, Marshal. *The Venture of Islam: Conscience and History in a World Civilization*. 3 vols. Chicago: University of Chicago Press, 1974.

Lapidus, Ira M. *A History of Islamic Societies*. Second Edition. Cambridge: Cambridge University Press, 2002.

Martin, Richard C. *Islamic Studies: A History of Religions Approach*. Upper Saddle River, NJ: Prentice Hall, 1996.

Martin, Richard C., ed. *Encyclopedia of Islam and the Muslim World*. 2 vols. New York: Macmillan Reference U.S.A., Thomson/Gale, 2004.

Rabasa, Angel M.; Benard, Cheryl; Chalk, C. Peter; Fair, Christine; Karasik, Theodore; Lal, Rollie; Lesser, Ian; and Thaler, David. *The Muslim World after 9/11*. Santa Monica, CA: RAND Corporation, 2004.

Islam and the West

Asad, Talal. *Formations of the Secular: Christianity, Islam, Modernity*. Stanford, CA: Stanford University Press, 2003.

Bowen, John R. *Why the French Don't Like Headscarves: Islam, the State, and Public Space*. Princeton, NJ: Princeton University Press, 2007.

Bulliet, Richard. *The Case of Islamo-Christian Civilization*. New York: Columbia University Press, 2006.

Buruma, Ian, and Avishai Margalit. *Occidentalism: The West in the Eyes of Its Enemies*. New York: Penguin Press, 2004.

Crooke, Alastaire. *Resistance: The Essence of the Islamist Revolution*. London; New York: Pluto Press, 2009.

Devji, Faisal. *Landscapes of the Jihad: Militancy, Morality, Modernity*. Ithaca, NY: Cornell University Press, 2005.

Hirschkind, Charles, and David Scott, eds. *Powers of the Secular Modern: Talal Asad and His Interlocutors*. Stanford, CA: Stanford University Press, 2005.

Huntington, Samuel. *The Clash of Civilizations and the Remaking of World Order*. New York: Simon and Schuster, 1996.

Ismail, Salwa. *Rethinking Islamist Politics: Culture, the State, and Islamism*. London and New York: I.B. Taurus, 2003.

Kepel, Gilles. *The War for Muslim Minds: Islam and the West*. Translated by Pascale Ghazaleh. Cambridge, MA: Harvard University Press, 2004.

———. *Jihad: The Trail of Political Islam*. London: I. B. Tauris, 2006.

Lewis, Bernard. *What Went Wrong: Western Impact and Middle Eastern Response*. Oxford and New York: Oxford University Press, 2002.

Lincoln, Bruce. *Holy Terrors: Thinking about Religion After September 11*. Chicago: University of Chicago Press, 2003.

Majid, Anouar. *A Call for Heresy: Why Dissent Is Vital to Islam and America*. Minneapolis: University of Minnesota Press, September 2007.

Mamdani, Mahmoud. *Good Muslim, Bad Muslim: America, the Cold War, and the Roots of Terror*. New York: Pantheon Books, 2004.

Mandaville, Peter. *Global Political Islam*. London: Routledge 2007.

Roy, Olivier. *Globalized Islam: The Search for a New Ummah*. New York: Columbia University Press, 2004.

Said, Edward. *Orientalism*. New York: Vintage Books, 1979.

Varisco, Daniel. *Islam Obscured: The Rhetoric of Anthropological Representation*. New York: Palgrave MacMillan, 2005.

Movement and Country Case Studies

Abrahamian, Ervand. *Iran Between Two Revolutions*. Princeton, NJ: Princeton University Press, 1982.

Baker, Raymond William. *Islam Without Fear: Egypt and the New Islamists*. Cambridge, MA: Harvard University Press, 2003.

Deeb, Lara. *An Enchanted Modern: Gender and Public Piety in Shi'i Lebanon*. Princeton, NJ: Princeton University Press, 2006.

Emmerson, Donald. "One Nation Under God? History, Faith, and Identity in Indonesia." In *Religion and Religiosity in the Philippines and Indonesia: Essays on State, Society, and Public Creeds* edited by Theodore Friend. Washington D.C.: Paul H. Nitze School of Advanced International Studies, John's Hopkins University Press, 2005.

Fuller, Graham. *The Future of Political Islam*. New York: Palgrave MacMillan, 2003.

Ghomari-Tabrizi, Behrooz. *Islam and Dissent: Abdolkarim Soroush, Religious Politics, and Democratic Reform*. New York: I.B. Tauris, 2008.

Hourani, Hani, ed. *Islamic Movements in Jordan*. Amman, Jordan: Al-Urdun Al-Jadid Research Center, 1997.

Husain, Ed. *The Islamist: Why I Joined Radical Islam in Britain, What I saw Inside and Why I Left*. London; New York: Penguin, 2007.

Jackson, Sherman A. *Islam and the Blackamerican: Looking Toward the Third Resurrection*. New York: Oxford University Press, 2005.

Kurzman, Charles. *The Unthinkable Revolution in Iran*. Cambridge, MA: Harvard University Press, 2004.

Lawrence, Bruce B. *Defenders of God: The Fundamentalist Revolt against the Modern Age*. San Francisco: Harper & Row, 1989.

Mir-Hosseini, Ziba. *Islam and Gender: The Religious Debate in Contemporary Iran*. Princeton, NJ: Princeton University Press, 1999.

Nasr, Vali R. *The Vanguard of the Islamic Revolution: The Jama'at-i Islami of Pakistan*. Berkeley: University of California Press, 1994.

——. *The Shia Revival: How Conflicts Within Islam Will Shape the Future*. W. W. Norton, 2007.

Navaro-Yashin, Yael. *Faces of the State: Secularism and Public Life in Turkey*. Princeton, NJ: Princeton University Press, 2002.

Norton, Augustus Richard. *Hezbollah: A Short History*. Princeton, NJ: Princeton University Press, 2007.

Pape, Robert. *Dying to Win: The Strategic Logic of Suicide Terrorism*. New York: Random House, 2005.

Rana, Muhammad Amir. *A to Z of Jehadi Organizations in Pakistan*. Lahore, Pakistan: Mashal, 2004.

Rashid, Ahmed. *Taliban: Militant Islam, Oil, and Fundamentalism in Central Asia*. New Haven, CT: Yale University Press, 2000.

Sageman, Marc. *Understanding Terror Networks*. Philadelphia: University of Pennsylvania Press, 2004.

White, Jenny B. *Islamist Mobilization in Turkey: A Study in Vernacular Politics*. Seattle: University of Washington Press, 2002.

Wickham, Carrie Rosefsky. *Mobilizing Islam: Religion, Activism, and Political Change in Egypt*. New York: Columbia University Press, 2002.

Wiktorowicz, Quintan. *The Management of Islamic Activism: Salafis, the Muslim Brotherhood, and State Power in Jordan.* Albany: State University of New York Press, 2001.

——. *Radical Islam Rising: Muslim Extremism in the West.* Lanham, MD: Rowman & Littlefield, 2005.

Yavuz, M. Hakan. *Islamic Political Identity in Turkey.* New York: Oxford University Press, 2003.

Zaman, Muhammad Qasim. *The 'Ulama in Contemporary Islam: Custodians of Change.* Princeton, NJ: Princeton University Press, 2002.

Primary Sources

Abdul Rauf, Imam Feisal. *What's Right with Islam: A New Vision for Muslims and the West.* San Francisco: Harper San Francisco, 2004.

Al-e Ahmad, Jalal. *Occidentosis: A Plague from the West.* Translated by Robert Cambell and Hamid Algar. Berkely, CA: Mizan Press, 1984.

An-Na'im, Abdullahi. *Islam and the Secular State: Negotiating the Future of Shari'a.* Cambridge, MA: Harvard University Press, 2008.

Cornell, Vincent J., ed. *Voices of Islam.* 5 vols. Westport, CT:Praeger Publishers, 2005.

Esposito, John, and John Donohue, eds. *Islam in Transition: Muslim Perspectives.* Oxford: Oxford University Press, 2006.

Ibrahim, Raymond, ed. *The Al-Qaeda Reader.* New York: Double Day, 2007.

Khomeini, Ruhollah. *Islam and Revolution: The Writings and Declarations of Imam Khomeini.* Translated and edited by Hamid Algar. London: Routledge and Kegan Paul, 2002.

Lawrence, Bruce, ed. *Messages to the World: The Statements of Osama Bin Laden.* Translated by James Howarth. London and New York: Verso, 2005.

Noe, Nicholas, ed. *Voice of Hezbollah: The Statements of Sayad Hassan Nasrallah.* London and New York: Verso, 2007.

Qutb, Sayyid. *Social Justice in Islam.* Translated by John B. Hardie with revised translation by Hamid Algar. Oneonta, NY: Islamic Publications International, 2000.

Ramadan, Tariq. *Western Muslims and the Future of Islam.* New York: Oxford University Press, 2004.

CONTRIBUTORS

Syed Farid Alatas is head of the Department of Malay Studies and associate professor of sociology, National University of Singapore (http://www.fas.nus.edu.sg/soc). His areas of research and teaching include the historical sociology of Muslim societies, Muslim reform ideologies, inter-religious dialogue, and the philosophy and history of the social sciences. His recent publications include *Alternative Discourses in Asian Social Science: Responses to Eurocentrism* (2006) and "From *Jāmi' ah* to University: Multiculturalism and Christian–Muslim Dialogue," *Current Sociology* (2006).

Abbas Barzegar is a Ph.D. candidate in the Graduate Division of Religion at Emory University. In addition to work on contemporary Muslim political movements, his research focuses on Muslim historical writing in the context of Sunni-Shii polemics during the 'Abbasid period. He has also conducted extensive fieldwork on Muslim communities in the United States.

Donald K. Emmerson is professor of political science at Stanford University where he is affiliated with the Abbasi Program in Islamic Studies and directs the Southeast Asia Forum. His interests include Islam and democracy, especially in Southeast Asia. Relevant essays include "One Nation under God? History, Faith, and Identity in Indonesia" in *Religion and Religiosity in the Philippines and Indonesia* (2005) and "Presumptive Universals and the Cult of Local Knowledge" (2004).

Hillel Fradkin, Ph.D., is currently senior fellow at the Hudson Institute where he is the director of its Center on Islam, Democracy and the Future of the Muslim World. Fradkin received his degree in Islamic Studies from the University of Chicago for work done under the direction of the late Pakistani scholar and theologian Fazlur Rahman. He is co-editor with Husain Haqqani and Eric Brown of the journal *Current Trends in Islamist Ideology*. His recent publications include "The History and Unwritten Future of Salafism" (2008) and "Recent Statements of Islamist Ideology: Bin Laden and Zarqawi Speak" (2005).

Graham E. Fuller is adjunct professor of history at Simon Fraser University in Vancouver, BC. He worked and lived overseas for seventeen years, mostly in the Middle East. He is a former vice-chair of the National Intelligence Council at the CIA, responsible for strategic forecasting. Mr. Fuller was a senior political scientist at the RAND Corporation for twelve years. He has written many books and articles relating to the Middle East, global geopolitics, democracy in the Muslim world, and Islamic politics. Among others, his books include *A Sense of Siege: The Geopolitics of Islam and the West* (1995), *The Arab Shi'a: The Forgotten Muslims* (1999), and *The Future of Political Islam* (2003).

Hassan Hanafi is professor of philosophy at Cairo University in Egypt. His many books and articles are well known for his interpretations of Islamic thought for Western scholars and his application of Continental philosophy, especially hermeneutic theory, to Muslim texts. He studied at the Sorbonne in Paris and wrote two dissertations in French, and he later studied the works of Edmund Husserl in German. Among his many works are *From Creed to Revolution* (1988, in Arabic) and *Introduction to the Study of Occidentalism* (1991, in Arabic). Dr. Hanafi has lectured and taught in the Middle East, Asia, Europe, and the United States.

Amir Hussain is associate professor in the Department of Theological Studies at Loyola Marymount University in Los Angeles. He specializes in contemporary Muslim communities in North America but is also interested in comparative religion as well as religion in popular culture. He is the author of *Oil and Water: Two Faiths, One God* (2006) and *Muslims: Islam in the West in the 21st Century* (forthcoming).

M. Zuhdi Jasser is a physician in private practice in Phoenix, Arizona, specializing in internal medicine and nuclear cardiology. He served as the president of the Arizona Medical Association (ArMA) until June 2007 and chairs the bioethics committee for Good Samaritan Regional Medical Center. He co-founded the Children of Abraham, a local Jewish-Muslim dialogue group in 2000 and is on the board of the Arizona Interfaith Movement. Dr. Jasser has also been an advisor on Islamic affairs to the U.S. Embassy in the Netherlands.

Bruce Lawrence is the Nancy and Jeffrey Marcus Humanities Professor of Religion at Duke University. He lectures on Islam widely in the United States and in the Muslim world. Among his many published articles and books are *Messages to the World: The Statements of Osama bin Ladin* (2005), *New Faiths, Old Fears: Muslims and Other Asian Immigrants in American Religious Life* (2004), *Shattering the Myth* (1998) and *Defenders of God: The Fundamentalist Revolt Against the Modern Age* (1995).

Anouar Majid is professor and founding chair of the Department of English at the University of New England in Maine. He is the author of *Unveiling Traditions: Postcolonial Islam in a Polycentric World* (2000), *Freedom and Orthodoxy: Islam and Difference in the Post-Andalusian Age* (2004), and *A Call for Heresy: Why Dissent Is Vital to Islam and America* (2009). He also published a novel titled *Si Yussef* (2005) and edits *Tingis*, a Moroccan-American magazine he co-founded in 2003. His new book about Moors and minorities in the modern West will be published in 2009.

Richard C. Martin is professor of Islamic Studies and History of Religions at Emory University and president of the American Research Center in Egypt. He writes and lectures on Islamic religious thought; religion, social conflict, and violence; and Islam and secularism. With Mark R. Woodward and Dwi Atmaja, he is the author of *Defenders of Reason in Islam: Mu'tazilism from Medieval School to Modern Symbol* (1997). He is editor-in-chief of *The Encyclopedia of Islam and the Muslim World*.

Ziba Mir-Hosseini holds a Ph.D. in social anthropology from the University of Cambridge and lectures at the London University School of Oriental and African Studies. She is an educator, writer, and filmmaker whose research focuses particularly on feminist and development issues. Her books include *Feminism and the Islamic Republic: Dialogues with the Ulema* (1999) and, with Richard Tapper, *Islam and Democracy in Iran: Eshkevari and the Quest for Reform* (2006). With Kim Longinotto she produced the documentary films *Divorce Iranian Style* (1998) and *Runaway* (2001).

Angel Rabasa, Ph.D. is a senior political scientist at the RAND Corporation. He has written extensively about religious and political trends in the Muslim world and in Southeast Asia in particular. He was the lead author of the RAND studies *The Muslim World After 9/11, Beyond al-Qaeda (Parts 1 and 2)* (2005), and *Building Moderate Muslim Networks* (2008). He has contributed to the International Institute for Strategic Studies (IISS) Adelphi Paper series and the Hudson Institute's *Current Trends in Islamist Ideology,* among other publications.

Feisal Abdul Rauf is founder and CEO of the American Society for Muslim Advancement (ASMA Society) and Imam of Masjid Al-Farah, a mosque in lower Manhattan. Imam Feisal is also the architect of the Cordoba Initiative, an inter-religious blueprint for improving relations between the Muslim world and the West. He is the author of several works, including *What's Right with Islam: A New Vision for Muslims and the West* (2004). He appears frequently on CNN, BBC, and other international media.

Richard Tapper is professor emeritus of anthropology in the University of London. He has conducted extensive field research in Iran, Afghanistan, and Turkey. His interests include cultural and historical aspects of pastoral nomadism; tribal and ethnic minorities and the state; ethnographic film; and anthropological approaches to Islam. His most recent books are *The New Iranian Cinema: Politics, Representation and Identity* (edited, 2002) and, with Ziba Mir-Hosseini, *Islam and Democracy in Iran: Eshkevari and the Quest for Reform* (2006).

Daniel M. Varisco is professor and chair of the Department of Anthropology at Hofstra University and former president of the Middle East Section of the American Anthropological Association. He has conducted ethnographic and historical research in Yemen, Egypt, and Qatar. He is the author of *Reading Orientalism: Said and the Unsaid* (2007) and *Islam Obscured: The Rhetoric of Anthropological Representation* (2005). He serves as editor of the online journal *CyberOrient* (www.cyberorient.net), co-editor of *Contemporary Islam*, and webshaykh of the blog Tabsir (www.tabsir.net).

Nadia Yassine is founder and head of the feminist branch of the Moroccan Islamist movement, Al Adl Wa Al Ihssane (Justice and Spirituality). She is the daughter of Cheikh Abdesslam Yassine, popular founder and spiritual leader of the organization. She has written and lectured widely on the need for Islamic reforms in Morocco and elsewhere in the Muslim world and is author of *Toutes voules dehors* (*Full Sails Ahead*, 2003). http://nadiayassine.net/en/service/whoishe/htm.